FOUR RIVERS,

DEEP MAPS

FOUR RIVERS, DEEP MAPS

Edited by Jo Jones
with Neil Curtis

UWA PUBLISHING

First published in 2022 by
UWA Publishing
Crawley, Western Australia 6009
www.uwap.uwa.edu.au

UWAP is an imprint of UWA Publishing
a division of The University of Western Australia

This book is copyright. Apart from any fair dealing for the purpose of private study, research, criticism or review, as permitted under the *Copyright Act 1968*, no part may be reproduced by any process without written permission. Enquiries should be made to the publisher.

Copyright © collection Jo Jones 2022
The copyright to each individual essay remains with its author.

The moral right of the authors has been asserted.

ISBN: 978-1-76080-218-9

 A catalogue record for this book is available from the National Library of Australia

Cover image: Susanna Castleden
Cover design by Anna Maley-Fadgyas, Book Designs
Typeset in 12 point Bembo Book
Printed by Lightning Source

 uwapublishing

Contents

Contents	v
List of Illustrations	vii
Acknowledgements	vii
A Note on Spellings of Indigenous Words	ix
Prelude by Jo Jones	xi
Jo Jones – Introduction: Deep Maps	1
Neil Curtis and Jo Jones – Introduction: The Dee and the Don	9
Gerald Rochford – Dee Estuary 1; Dee Estuary 2	25
Meredi Ortega – The Lower Dee: Swimming Upstream/Nowhere	27
David Wheatley – River Don Office	47
Ian Grosz – The Don: A Sacred River	51
Ashleigh Angus – The Cucking of a Scold: River Dee, Aberdeen, Scotland	73
Adam Kealley – The Dark, the Light, the River	85
Paolo Gruppuso and Simona Trozzi – *An Imaginative Map of Water in Seaton Park*	97
Sheena Blackhall – The River Dee; Oh Gently, Gently Rins the Dee; Dee Journey	101
Jo Jones – The Derbarl Yarrigan (Swan River) and Dyarlgarro Beeliar (Canning River)	105
Chris Fremantle – *The Diaries of Fremantle (an Ancestor) Burnt into Map*	121

CONTENTS

Samantha Owen – A Tale of Black Beaks: *Naturaliste* Explorers Encounter the Derbarl Yerrigan — 129

Nandi Chinna – Stirling's Garden; Rivière des Cygnes (Swan River); Derbarl Yerrigan (Swan River); Rocky Bay (Kairp Ngungar); Writing on Water; Swan River Canyon; The Eye — 147

Cass Lynch – Haiku — 159

Carol Millner – Directions; Your directions; Weather Words; The way I go; CHOGM week; Derbarl Yerrigan — 161

Maureen Gibbons – this land speaks — 169

Daniel Juckes – The Wonder Book — 171

Qassim Saad – Exile, Rivers and Design: A Designer's Journey across Rivers — 189

Susanna Castleden – *A Single Day's Riding* — 215

Tom Wilson – Moving Bodies along the Swan River — 221

Susan Midalia – Watching — 237

James Quinton – Dolphins; Cyclist; The Seer — 239

John Kinsella – *Inferno* Canto 3 Liszt's River Dante Opening Form to Antiphony [D minor] — 245

Claire Jones – Tidal Tensions and Littoral Potential: Coming of Age and the Derbal Yerrigan — 249

David Whish-Wilson – The Gill Net — 259

Anna Haebich – LOSS: Dyarlgarro Beeliar/Canning River — 269

Vanessa Corunna – *Eagle Warrior* — 289

Notes — 291

List of Contributors — 307

Acknowledgements

As I outline in the introduction, this book came together through shared resonances and interests from the academic and artistic communities of Perth, Australia, and Aberdeen, Scotland. From my early visits to the University of Aberdeen (enabled through the Curtin–Aberdeen mobility scheme) I enjoyed not only the kindness and geniality of university staff but was met with positive and energised responses to the idea of collecting material about the rivers and, in particular, framing and interpreting a collection of responses through the key tenets of deep mapping. Friendships and productive dialogue worked freely and easily across disciplines. Some of these warm and productive connections are represented in the book, in particular the University of Aberdeen's head of museums, Neil Curtis; the Perth writer located abroad, Meredi Ortega; and the poet Sheena Blackhall, Makar for Aberdeen, who so generously shared her time of knowledge of the rivers and their rich folkloric history. Other artists, curators, academics and writers contributed to the incubation and development of this project, including Wayne Price and Ally Lumsden, Elizabeth Curtis, Tom McKean and Pete Stollery. I never met the poet Gerard Rochford in person and, sadly, he died before the completion of the book, but his family have kept in close contact.

At Curtin University I am grateful for the support of the Curtin–Aberdeen mobility program and my fellow staff in the School of Media, Creative Arts and Social Inquiry, many of whom have contributed material to this volume. I also give thanks to family and close friends who have given feedback on early drafts and offered many valuable suggestions – Claire Jones, Lucy Dougan and Matteo Pantalone. I also extend thanks to my fellow members of the Connecting to Rivers research group at Curtin University.

My thanks and appreciation also go to the staff of UWA Publishing including, early in the process, Terri-ann White and, later, Kate Pickard, who has been endlessly supportive and patient while I collected and curated this material during a challenging time.

When the pandemic struck in 2020 I had already collected many of the contributions for this volume. Some authors have been in touch since to make alterations to their work, although most contributions are what we would now call 'pre-COVID' pieces. Looking back to my last trip to Scotland this volume stands a tribute to the beauty and uniqueness of the north east and my appreciation of its people. Now, more than ever, I thank the rivers here, at home in Perth, and elsewhere, for the psychic and bodily solace and succour they provide now that the world has changed.

A Note on Spellings of Indigenous Words

You may notice some variation in spellings of Indigenous place names and words amongst contributors. Authors have conscious preferences for different renderings of Indigenous words for cultural and scholarly reasons. These preferences are represented in this volume.

Prelude[1]

Jo Jones

Creek Dreams

Did serpents make the lands of Britain?/do they wonder/where their people went?

Wagyl warn moonboorli-wardan-boodja unna?/baalap kaadatj/windji baalabang moort koorl?

Creator Serpents make beyond-ocean-country yeah?/them know/where their family go?

Cass Lynch[2]

We all spend the first eternal dreamtime of our lives in the same eternal mother ocean.
Roger Deakin[3]

They say that people locate themselves in the world according to their proximity to water.[4] This works in big and small ways. Are you north or south of a river? East or west? Past that sharp bend in the river, that place beyond such-and-such a bridge? Where you live and work will be defined, to some extent, by the gradient of the land, the ways that water runs at certain times of the year. Of course, much of this process is hidden now under grates and buried stormwater drains, and the routes we take overlay the trails which water takes so that we negotiate rivers at every turn even if the lines of our lives are asphalt now.

Living in Perth, my life retraces many paths. The early incursions of British explorer–settlers were shaped by the inwards and upwards movement of the Swan River (named two centuries ago by the Frenchman Nicolas Baudin). They reached as far as the rare pockets of fertile land to the east and then came back again, some of their seaward journey aided by the river's downstream flow. The Wadjuk people traversed the paths and crossings of this river system too, without the intervention of roads and bridges, and their songlines have knitted human and country together for over 40,000 years.[5] Countless generations of babies were born on specified birthing sites at the river's edge, the subject of a local community arts project *Babies of the Swan*. The Swan, however, no longer flows downstream in the way it did. The large sandbar at the river's mouth was removed, a fierce change made to an isolated British outpost, one among many acts of desperate modernisation. Without the sandbar the river became an estuary, and, to this day, its water is salty until you reach 120 kilometres inland.

My house is on a large outer suburban block bordering a nature reserve which follows the course of a creek. The creek begins on the high ground of the Darling Scarp (a plateau). The scarp consists of subtly undulating folds of land that mark an interstitial zone between two distinct regions: the sandy coastal plain known as the Swan Basin and, inland, a massive flat expanse of arable earth that covers part of the oldest mass of rock on the planet, the Yilgarn Craton. The creek is just one tiny rivulet in a watershed, or catchment area, of over 400 square kilometres. Throughout my lifetime (I was nine years old when my parents moved here) it has nearly always been dry in summer, but, with the rains in spring, the flow can swell to four or five metres across.

I have always dreamt of the creek, this little river that snakes across country in its soft silt bed, edging through culverts and exposed drains, under the Perth airport and on its way to the river. Each dream varies, yet there are patterns and repetitions, and the creek is always wider, deeper and bigger than its real-life equivalent. The British writer Olivia Laing talks about the experience of water being, at times, vestigial. Layers of modern acculturation may make for a profound dulling of human receptors to water's 'dark frequencies', yet there is an urge or signal we are drawn to like the tug of a diviner's rod.[6] The word 'vestige' is derived from the Latin *vestigium*: a footprint, a trace of something that is leaving or has left. There is no question that, for me, the presence of this same creek, behind the house, down in a gully, contains the vestigial in a psychic sense. The creek dreams I have are undoubtedly connected to past states, particularly of childhood. For instance, my ten-year-old self used to escape to the creek when robbers (a word my mother was fond of) attempted to enter the house. Now, I often dream that children swim in the water, although, in reality, it is rarely deep or wide enough for that. And when my mother died, just over a year ago, I dreamt the creek was a ravine; at its base, instead of the diminutive, intermittently flowing stream, there was a vast still pool.

When the mid-twentieth century theorist Gaston Bachelard claimed that dreams and water coalesce as both elemental and creative forces, he invoked the vestigial presence of our collective – or, we might say now, our species – memory. My own water dreams are certainly to do with intuited, reshaped memory and experience, most likely associations of water and vitality such as cleansing and curing through rituals like baptism, the Jewish marriage ritual of mikveh and the many contemporary forms of what we now call hydrotherapy. Water stories can be about death, danger and uncontrollable extremes of emotion, as with Shakespeare's Ophelia and the types of historical trauma intimated by books like Charles Kingsley's *The Water Babies*. As is widely recognised, we are also reliant on water for so many linguistic figurations[7]: we are flooded with emotion, immersed in grief, bathed in happiness. A powerful belief in Indigenous culture is that a child jumps up from the river into the mother's womb and is sent by ancestors – the past, gestation and futurity are thus one and the same. I find this a deeply comforting idea. The experimental Scottish poet MacGillivray redirects the modern reader to the near drowning visions of Highland pagan prophets during uprisings, who would lie under falling water, half-drowned, full of 'dream-traiked crystal' revelations, the 'rustic mirror shades water-scryed intent'.[8] The sibylline half-corpse prefigures the darkly sublime dimensions of British genocides over the coming centuries and further afield.

My lived relationship to Perth's waters – to state a sharply manifest fact – is different from Noongar women of my age and at this particular chronographic juncture: it is only ever a series of soft-edged refractions of the intensity of *koolark* and *boodja*. This is because the water stories of my childhood are European, and more specifically British, such as that of Kenneth Grahame's riverbank. I was entranced, too, by the nineteenth-century literary landscape of the British Lakes and by the curious but complementary paired texts of William Wordsworth's shorter poems and the stories of Beatrix Potter. My mother's family, a century and a half back, are from Sussex. They perhaps even knew the Ouse before it wound its way into the writing of Virginia Woolf and, then, into the place-essaying of Olivia Laing.

Wadjuk Noongar women travelled up, down, across and back over Perth's rivers, through different places and paths, depending on seasons and clan groupings. They knew specific locations to birth children, to mourn, places where ancestor-creators dwell and places where one knows not to go, or swim, or to send children to swim.[9] While I'm both anxious and suspicious about the complex shapes of my own settler imaginings, the river remains a space of longing for me. But I can't claim to know it. All I have really, with any degree of intimacy, is a little stretch of sweet water – a creek that is both here and there, at the base of the plateau on the Swan coastal plain and inflected with a palimpsest of British river texts and the fractured, displaced traces of family memory.

The presence of the creek was doubtless part of my decision to move into my mother's house after her sudden death. Now, I believe the water contained my mourning for a long time, in relative terms, before my mother died. Like the time-slip novels of the 1970s and 1980s I devoured as a child, events follow inexplicable paths and portals. Mourning itself requires a past-in-present-in-pastness that bleeds outside conventional chronology, as if that initial exit from my mother's womb was a weirdly pre-emptive echo of a world minus its originary maternal form: as if we move incrementally away from a state of being at once held and weightless. Perhaps the vestige of the little river is a quantum-bound container of the beginning and the end. After all, the Noongar term for 'water', *bilya* or *beeliar*, is also the word for umbilical cord. In a similar way, maybe the hours I spent in an old pink bath a decade ago, after the birth of my second child, are inseparable from my own watery entry into the world, from the vast and varied feelings that accompany the arrival of children and even from my own eventual death and dissolution.

During the last thirty years theorists have argued that water is a repository of planetary memory which signals enmeshment with other species and geographical entities.[10] Not only does the watery body and brain (made up of four-fifths water) contain individual and genetic memories of relatively recent times, it also keeps some of the movement, patterning and change of the chronological time of history, which descends in turn into the deep-time cycles of ancestors. Stories have always told us something similar. The rivers Styx and Jordan are transitory entities between life and death – although, often, the endpoint turns out to be less than final. Toni Morrison's famous ghost of a murdered infant – her titular 'Beloved' – crawls backwards through the dank river silt of the Ohio River, then further back still, into the physical-psychic trauma of the middle passage, dark fathoms down in the Atlantic Ocean. When that ghost emerges from the river more than a decade later, the river itself gives the lie to the discreteness of life and death. In Perth, and soon, rains will come. Water will edge down the hillside and vein through the garden in the same way it has every year during my living memory. Here the rain is warm and the gullies and channels which appear with the wet are somehow just the right size for this place – and for me – as they take their small and separate courses to the creek, all glistening and pulsing as they go. It may be, in the future, that these aqueous particles join the river – that sinuous, muscular serpent which runs, arches, watches, sleeps and gathers our separate selves with all the nutrients of life's blood.

Introduction: Deep Maps

Jo Jones

This project is a volume that collects, in two sections, responses to places: more specifically, two places and four rivers. Each of the cities – Perth, Australia, and Aberdeen, Scotland – has received relatively little attention as specific geographical–cultural locales. Often perceived as industrial, isolated and lacking romantic association, they nevertheless have rich historical, narrative and creative traditions that characterise interactions between humans and place, particularly along the length of the four rivers. The regions are geographically and culturally distinctive but, also, notably similar: provincial, isolated, poised between industry and distinctive environs. Anyone who heard the cities Perth and Aberdeen mentioned in the same sentence would likely assume the subject was fossil fuel mining and refining[1], or perhaps to do with migration and the ongoing nature of Scottish diaspora, with many Scots (old migrants and new) communities found in Perth suburbs. But there are other connections worth looking into. Using a deep time geographical approach one may look deeper for other patterns. Millions of years after the gas seam or oil deposit was formed it continues to shape the ways we reside and our relationship to the land and water. In contemporary times our cities are shaped by workers who leave home for weeks at a time, living on rigs or in temporary towns. The regular flight from the urban centre to isolated operations at the edges of things is commonplace in an often-dizzying pattern of human movement across space. This points to a central paradox. These geologically stable regions and the mineral riches their stability affords, have given rise, firstly, to unceasing and often alienating human mobility and dislocation and, secondly, to irreversible planetary change apparent in the process of mining itself, and have contributed to the effects of centuries of carbon emissions, generated around the globe wherever our gas, oil, coal, ore have been shipped and processed. But as is sometimes the way of things, an embodied connection to place, especially out-of-the-way ones, gives rise to lively subcultures that resist the capitalist and expansionist imperatives that seem to define the history of a location. This volume rose out of this kind of different cross-pollination or counter current – intellectual and aesthetic – and is bound together by shared interests and themes in arts and humanities communities.

The contributions of this book are woven together through strands of deep mapping and connected and compatible ideas of place, history and inhabitation. In some ways our countercultures seem to 'come back' to specific place knowledge that predates industrialisation, whether in the traditional shapes of the Noongar knowledge of the Derbarl Yarrigan (Swan River) and Dyarlgarro Beeliar (Canning River) or the traditions and ancient patterns of Aberdeenshire: we come back to these profound knowledge systems that, in fact, never went away.

Deep mapping is an inherently multidisciplinary approach to place that conveys a vitally different experience of location – an approach that diverges profoundly to many modern modes of inhabitation. To deep map is to focus *in depth* on specific sites and regions. As Pearson and Shanks aptly put express it 'pays attention to the patina of place'[2]. It, at once, invokes the 'ambiguous, the haptic, the opaque, the embodied, the in-between'[3]. The deep mapper is in search of the crucial connection between lived experience of specific environments to cultural practice and histories in moving, sinuous strands. It seeks what Tim Ingold calls the *meshwork*[4] that binds place and inhabitation, the flow of space-time between material phenomena and vestigial and often amorphous traces of human and nonhuman habitation. It links past and present as a palimpsest or embedded state, interpreting 'the historical and the contemporary, the political and poetic, the factual and fictional, the discursive and the sensual'.[5]

In 2010 the British visual artist and academic Iain Biggs described his current practice as being in the process of 'metamorphising into a variant of deep mapping'. Further, he explains it as 'interweaving many disparate, tensioned strands of experience, genres of writing, knowledge positions and narrative perspectives so as to produce a richer, more resonant patterning of meaning while retaining the pleasures of discrete threads within the larger whole'.[6]

Some 30 years after *PrairyErth*, William Least Heat-Moon's seminal incursion to the place and people of Flint County on the Kansas prairie, deep map exploration into complex and melded backdrops of both human and geographical space and time has taken so many other shapes. Many deep mapping–themed projects in Aberdeen have emerged since the beginning of work on this volume and reveal how the category has developed and expanded. Local distinctiveness has been central to early definition and theorisations of deep mapping, so it is little surprise that the term is now embraced by those curating exhibitions, community projects or indeed editorial work such as the collected entries that appear in this volume.

Biggs' 2021 discussion of deep mapping can be directly applied to my own approach in collecting and curating the many and varied works in this volume. The idea for an edited volume rose from my own work as an educator and academic in Perth, Australia and as a visiting scholar in Aberdeen, Scotland. While at the University of Aberdeen the strong and similar currents of work-in-place – both creative and traditional researched-based projects – were noticeable and the urge to bring them together was impossible to resist.

Anyone who works 'away' for a time in any place finds connections and patterns between 'home' and 'away' – creative and intellectual synergies are often found. But the energy surrounding deep mapping, and the related outward and inward journeys of place, seemed worthy of investigation for the following reasons. Firstly, deep mapping and regional scholarship have long and distinguished histories in both Western Australia and the north east of Scotland. The comparison between places – connections and differences – looked, from the start, to yield productive and extraordinary discussion. Secondly, a project that connected works about deep time in singular locales had strong connections to the emerging variants and adaptations of earlier forms of deep mapping. Branching out from single-volume studies and embracing the notions of deep mapping as multidisciplinary and with many practitioners prompted me to consider editing and curation as a further form or 'variant' of deep mapping. In this volume there are, as Biggs puts it, many 'discrete threads' and their grouping here, with editorial framing and interactions, aims to enhance the resonance between them, working towards an act of curation. When one considers the Latin etymology of 'curate' – to care or cure – the editorial work in this volume seeks to frame each separate strand in relation to the work as a collective whole in sympathetic interrelation.

Rivers and movement
The interesting thing about water is the way it is everywhere. Thinking about rivers in geographical terms inevitably involves the consideration of the volume, course, current flow, but also catchment, riparian zones of banks, groundwater and rain cycles – all of the ways water comes to the river through other places: seeping up from deep earth, oozing through mud, falling from the air and running off and through rocks. This study is not the first to note how water – planetary repository of life – is the element in which connections of the human and non-human world, the living and non-living are so intricately bound (Chen et al; Neimanis;

Strang 2014, 2015, 2020a, 2020b).[7] Water is a repository of memory that spans well beyond decades of a human life. It is the water that constitutes more than two thirds of body, now as past, through countless living and non-living entities for what seems like an impossibly immense span of time. It is memory, not the memory of waking life, or chronological narrative, but memory so much deeper, more slippery. In the last thirty years theorists have argued that water is a repository of planetary memory that most deeply signals enmeshment with other species and geographical entities. Not only does the watery body and brain (four-fifths water) contain individual and genetic memory of relatively recent time, but the movement and patterning and change of the chronological time of history and the deep time cycles of ancestor and eons. Placing the journeys of water in geological scales – both sobering and exciting – reminds us of the precepts of actor-network theory and relationality[8] and that the environmental elements aren't waiting to be shaped by living entities but, rather, the conditions of existence are a lively exchange of relations, events and places as co-constituted by many entities or 'actors' of human and non-human agency.

Drawing on anthropological theories of water and rivers, this volume explores the similarity between the relative openness of deep mapping as practice and its theory to the fluidity and action of rivers. Rivers are simultaneously in place and moving, where materiality and metaphor are inseparable, where physical experience is profoundly altered by destabilising immersion.[9] Rivers are at the foundation of human narrative in varied human cultures and myth through time and space. Like the limbic system deep within the spiralling layers of a human brain, rivers collect experience through linking and recollection to sense response (the hippocampus), home to a remembered moving flow of emotion (the amygdala), experience and response between living and non-living things, and a repository of deep truths and eons of genetic information.

This project brings a different dimension of materiality to deep mapping and its configurations. It is an investigation into the ways the rivers and water are viable conduits for relationality. It explores the intrinsic connectedness between the human and non-human world and the way creative and narrative texts have been drawn into the flow of rivers since the earliest examples of human imaginative expression, from the sacred river of the goddess Ganges to the classical Styx, Dante's Acheron or the biblical Jordan.[10]

Another key way this volume differs from the recent proliferation of deep maps and their theorisation is in the notion of deep-mapping a river. An aspect of deep mapping that has, perhaps, not received due emphasis is that dwelling in place, or deeply engaging any particular space, which is often action defined by movement, whether in the day to day movement of any most human lives, as in Rhett Bloom and Nuno Sacramento's works about a daily Aberdeen commute in *Deep Mapping*, or in a detailed and theorised study of time and space such as Paul Carter's study of the Australian Mallee region, *Ground Truthing*. The texts collected in this volume attest to the ways in which one can be at once in place, and even at home, and moving. Movement up, down and through rivers is an intrinsic pattern of human mobility on small and large scales, whether the river is travelled *on* (in a vessel) or beside, as a food and water source or navigational marker. When comparing the river texts of the Don and Dee in Scotland's north east or the Swan and Canning Rivers of Australia's Swan coastal plain, thematic patterns become immediately apparent. The course of rivers becomes the focus of the passage of time, whether it's a span of a human life or the observations of environmental cycles. Rivers are the locale of both inner and outer journeys, from formational and coming-of-age narratives to the observed cyclical journeys of non-human species such as shrimp, salmon, swans, and cormorants. Rivers are a liminal site for the experience of profound emotional and existentially challenging states, including the impact of industry on water and the persistence of life in altered forms and the ultimate 'other' of material life forms – the movement from life to death.

Concepts of relationality – simply put, how human and non-human entities relate and connect to each other – have become a vital element of many fields of environmental humanities. In this discussion of existence of movement within the process of deep mapping, this state of fluid interconnectivity connects the length of rivers, and their catchment systems. Further, all rivers invite intraplanetary attention to both environmental and cultural relations. John Wylie in his famous essay 'A Single Day's Walking', drawing on Deleuze and Guattari, draws the affective responses prompted by the material environment while explaining that the exterior and interior of the self are never discrete. Whereas the human self appears conceptually presented as contained and separate, our interaction with the non-human enacts a profound 'fold'.

> Just is there is no question of confining all sense meaning and passion to the interior of the self, so there is no *a priori* and fixed exterior matter determining perception. Instead the upsurge of affect and precepts is precisely the *relation*, the primary capacity of affecting and being affected (Massumi 2002), from which these two horizons, inside and outside, self and landscape, precipitate and fold.[11]

The fold itself isn't a singular act but an exponential process of connecting with and relating to the world that is continuous and transformative. This folding of the human self with place and non-human others remains the inspiration for this volume and sets the pattern for the editorial discussion about the works, linking and connecting each piece with its region, and in a wider sense, inviting comparison between the rivers and regions themselves, drawing attention to the geological, environmental and cultural connections that run through them.

This book contains writing and visual art that explores the connections between Scotland's north east and the sandy Swan coastal plain. The contributions reveal a wealth of productive creative connections. These include the way 'reading' a river, when one moves from one place to another, can often mean superimposing shapes or templates built elsewhere, an example being the way that early European explorers navigated the Swan River with an eye to forming a colony – looking for habitable places with freshwater and access to food and to a newly industrialised sense of transportation, settlement and expansion. The customs, folklore and beliefs of one place fit strangely into another. Entities, often a form of genius loci such as gods, spirits, monsters, shadows, are clearly not the same, but traditions make interesting patterns in terms of affective, pre-modern frames of connection and experience. As in John Kinsella's formulation of polysituatedness, the displaced modern subject sees many places when they see one – the sight of one river summons cultural and genetic memories of others. Whether of the kelpie (mythical water horse) or Wagyl (Noongar creator-serpent), the river is a repository of unseen energies such as the subconscious, and the altered conscious, the repressed and dark terrains that are to do with death or in a strangely connected way the space before life. When the movement runs from south to north, east to west, the 'antipodean' in the 'old world' sees other patterns and differences, rivers with endless water and unseen depth in comparison to the often walkable passage across the Swan and Canning. Perth-based folk may see in Scotland a watercourse neatly contained rather than swampily sprawled and spread up and down dune systems. Some traditional Noongar people may see rivers oddly straight and bounded rather than formed by the mighty coils of a creator snake whose path takes it both over and underground, creating water not only in rivers but in limestone aquifers and interconnected swamps systems that run both north and south.

The following two sections of these book about the Don and Dee (Scotland's north east) and Derbarl Yerrigan/Swan and Dyarlgarro/Canning (south-western Australia) make no claims to be an exhaustive historical, geographical or hydrological study, but they do invite you, the reader, to make many *folds* and investigate the relation between rivers, places, regions and space; art and language; human and non-human patterns of habitation; all the meanings and association that rivers contain and the histories of their interpretation.

Introduction: The Dee and the Don

Neil Curtis and Jo Jones

For the most appalling quality of water is its strength. I love its flash and gleam, its music, its pliancy and grace, its slap against my body; but I fear its strength. I fear it as my ancestors must have feared the natural forces that they worshipped. All the mysteries are in its movement. It slips out of holes in the earth like the ancient snake. I have seen its birth; and the more I gaze at that sure and unremitting surge of water at the very top of the mountain, the more I am baffled. We make it all so easy, any child in school can understand it – water rises in the hills, it flows and finds its own level, and man can't live without it. Bud I don't understand it. I cannot fathom its power.

Nan Shepherd[1]

[...]
Except now and then, on a big black tide
when the stream bulked like a black back,
we'd catch a salty breath that said sun and moon were pulling together.
Stretching
The invisible membrane, interface,
Where salt and sweet met skin to skin,
They lay against each other, reaching

A mile of more in from the sea; two
Cold waters flowing in two directions,
Different, separate, each unbroken,
And the mass of the river piling.

Harry Smart[2]

The modest title of Rob Petit's cinematic meditation on the upper reaches of the Dee, *Upstream* (2020), conceals extraordinary acuteness of creative vision and is a useful example of both deep mapping and the poetics of rivers. If the process of deep mapping is defined by an internalised intention toward verticality rather than horizontality,[3] *Upstream*'s midwinter journey of air, water, earth and granite, towards the Dee's high-altitude source, certainly qualifies. Like many examples of deep mapping in Scotland's north east, and many of the entries that appear in this volume, this evocative film is different to the earlier, seminal version of deep mapping in the last century. As deep mapping relies on local particularities, marked variation in the form and tone of space–place vernaculars are inevitable.

There are complexities in deep mapping a river – a shifting amorphous entity – and the creative vision of *Upstream* invokes the specificities one would expect from a deep map and, also, the existential complexities associated with rivers. In an early planning discussion, film maker Rob Petit and writer Robert Macfarlane agreed that the moving, downward-directed image recorded by a drone-mounted camera contained a dream-like quality. Bachelard's

The mouths of the Don (north) and Dee (south) Aberdeen.[4]

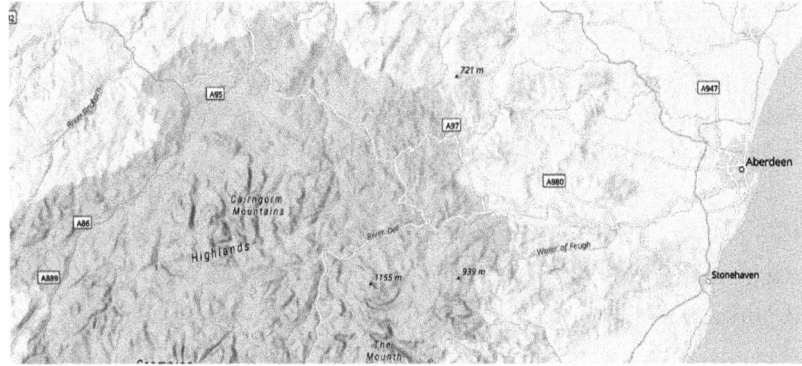

Scotland's north east, terrain of the Don and Dee.[5]

explanation of the connection between the material work and the human explains how water brings us into oneiric power, that dream states induce innate connections with and through elements. He writes that 'dreams mime the life of matter'.[6] Petit's film combines human creative vision with an elemental connection that resembles a sounding line, connecting the varied and moving surfaces of water to the separate tumbled rocks of the lower, wider river beds, to the dramatic striation of white quartz in granite, to black pools in the ice. Sometimes there are traces of habitation – the rough-hewn foundation shapes that once were bothies and stone walls – sometimes a vast white expanse. The film creates a patterned reflection of imagination and depicts the interconnectedness of living and non-living things, which is deeply particular.

The palimpsest nature of deep mapping is present in the film but, compared to the deep maps of the last century, it is perhaps strangely made and more haunted, maybe in response to both the mood of eco-crisis and pandemic. The sound design melds with the vertical range of the moving image and the shifting between upper and lower cello registers working as both upward flight and cavernous depth. The interlacing of Robert Macfarlane's sometimes-rhymed verses addressed to the river are indebted – as with all of his writing – to the Deeside writer Nan Shepherd. Uttered by male and female voices in English and Gaelic, sometimes inaudibly murmured, the effect is something immeasurably strange and, somehow, only half grasped by the listener. One might approach the source of a river to find an impossible place – unreachable – and perhaps the closest one can come to knowing it is to glimpse a black, reflectionless eye. Like Petit's journeys, human expeditions, occurring through millennia, are nano-fragments in time–space vastness.

Coming back downstream from the mountains, either down the valleys of the Dee or Don (that begins only fifteen miles from the Dee) the specific bends of rivers, burns and the echoes of wells provoke the same questions as the river at altitude. What is the relationship between humanity and the world we inhabit, and what are the limits to our understanding of these connections?

Place and people: on the edge

When one speaks to the people of Aberdeenshire it becomes quickly apparent that the Don and Dee have distinct identities. They are distinct characters within the landscape, with layered narratives, historical and cultural. The mouth of these rivers are an easily walkable 4 kilometres apart from the tiny and beloved Victorian fishing village of Fittie up to Old Town, home of University of Aberdeen and St Machar's Cathedral. People also tend to have a favourite – the beautiful ancient Dee, edged by picture-perfect stone villages and even a royal estate, or the narrower, perhaps wilder towns of the historically poorer districts in which the Don flows.

At the mouth of the Dee, Aberdeen is a hub. A port. A little city. The stern granite-faced Victorian city suits the seriousness of wealthy merchant–trader – the more respectable cousin of Glasgow. The glint of mica, however, hints at the presence some kind of secret – perhaps an ancient disco held on the old Green – now buried under layers of stone, or perhaps the fey ancestry of a waterway whose name has meant 'goddess' since the Iron Age at least. The scurry of human movement plays out with a slow bass rhythm of cargo ships and ferries bound for the islands, Scandinavia and the Baltic, and forms a somewhat majestic backdrop, particularly as the graceful NorthLink ferries – all at least 100 metres long – display a horned Wagnerian Viking on the side of each vessel.

Flints from the Mesolithic, perhaps 10,000 years old, have been found beneath the old Green, testimony to this long and rich habitation. The Green is now a hip and bustling cobbled square in the heart of downtown Aberdeen. In current times, the heaviness of modern industry has re-shaped the port, the town centre and the peripheral streetscapes, the wealth of international trade endeavours evidenced in the Victorian facades of houses and civic buildings. After the straight edge of the port, past the post-war estate of Torry on the south bank, the Dee winds through parks, leafy suburbs, the university. The river widens further east through Nan Shepherd's home ground of Cults and further upstream to lively stretches around many villages, including Banchory and Ballater, where folklore abounds with tales of haunted castles and water horses. Royal forests and large estates set the scene for the romantic Scottish narratives of Victorian times, in which, as is well-known, Queen Victoria's emotional ties to Scotland were so deeply founded. That the valley is now called 'Royal Deeside' arouses varied and complex responses among the population.

The mouth of the Don is deeply connected to the vein of Christian–Gaelic culture that redefined cultural and religious practice and belief from the late 400s onwards. St Machar's Cathedral and Aberdeen university are a short distance from the river – the layout of the surrounding streets preserves the medieval burgh. St Machar, reputedly a disciple of St Columba of Iona, is said to have chosen the Don as a holy site due to the river being shaped like shepherd's crook towards its confluence with the sea. A nearby Bronze Age burial site and the name of the river hint at a longer tradition of sanctity at this spot. The university, founded in 1495, remains an important Scottish centre of learning. Once out of town, the River Don winds through industrial estates and out to green fields, the water a slowly moving ribbon through agricultural terrain, from the higher grounds of the source. It is a different narrative to the Dee, but equally embedded in the people and place.

The Rivers Dee and Don (142 and 142 kilometres long respectively), traverse much of the space between the Cairngorm mountains and the coast. Today the landscape of the north east of Scotland varies, from conditions that resemble Arctic tundra to the green rolling farmlands of Buchan and the plain of Moray. Janus-like, the north east has one face firmly fixed on this fertile hinterland, while the other gazes outwards to the lands and seas beyond – simultaneously surveying the source and confluence of these rivers. Since the end of the last ice age all but the highest slopes have been shaped and reshaped by the process of human habitation, an intimate connection between land and people that is evidenced by a rich cultural and poetic tradition that runs within embeddedness of people within specific regions as well as the movement of peoples, from those who followed the retreat of the ice 15,000 years ago to Picts, Romans and Celtic missionaries. This cultural and geographical flow also included the movement of folk between the eastern and southern Highlands and islands, much of which occurred during times of war and forced displacement, to the recent waves of economic migration from Eastern Europe.

On the edge: an inhabited borderland
While the human eye often identifies a certain primeval drama in the landscape of the north east, partly due to breathtaking geographical formation of the highlands, human inhabitation is relatively new. About 15,000 years ago, the ice sheet which had covered Scotland for the preceding 15,000 years started to melt, eventually revealing a new landscape. The deeply ice-scoured glens and corries of Upper Deeside, the ice-deposited hummocky landscape of much of Aberdeenshire and the steep-sided gullies of the Mearns coastline, eroded by water from the wasting ice, bear many signs of the impact of the ice sheet. As the climate improved, the new land was occupied by plants and animals which arrived from warmer areas to the south, and from the lands to the east which now lie drowned by the North Sea. By 8,000 years ago, much of the lower ground was covered by a patchwork of forests and clearings inhabited by a range of animals including deer, boar and people.

With major natural frontiers of the sea lying to the east and the mountains in the west, the area's main land links have always been north along the Moray Firth and south to Angus and the Mearns. The Mounth forms a natural boundary to the south and is crossed by a number of passes which have been used by people for millennia. The most easterly of these has been the most important: today it is the route taken by the railway and dual carriageway, while it was the route taken by both the Roman army in the early 80s AD and the English army under Edward I. The ditches and banks of one of the Roman camps, built to accommodate the army for a few nights before it crossed the Mounth, can still be seen at Raedykes near Stonehaven. Farther to the west, the Cairn O' Mount dominates the summit beside the Fettercairn to Banchory Road as it has done for almost 4,000 years. Marking both a boundary and a route-way, the cairn was later joined by an early Christian cross slab with similar patterns to those in the ninth century *Book of Deer*. This route also links Huntly, Alford, Kildrummy and Lumphanan to the south – an important strategic route ultimately taken by the eighteenth-century military road. The rich history of invasion, migration and adaptation defines a culture that, like so many borderlands, has grown full and rich through the stimulus of cross-pollination.

The rolling hills around Huntly and Keith, and the low-lying land of the Laich of Moray, are a much more open frontier. The lands around the inner Moray Firth were probably the northern Pictish heartland of Fortriu, marked in Easter Ross by the fine Pictish stones of Rosemarkie, Hilton of Cadboll and Shandwick, the monastery at Portmahomack, and the Pictish fortress of Burghead in Moray, with its nearby ecclesiastical site at Kinneddar. Links between this area and the rest of the north east can be traced back at least 4,000 years when the people who built the Clava Cairns of the inner Moray Firth and the builders of the recumbent stone circles of Aberdeenshire both aligned their monuments on the south west. In more recent centuries, however, this northern focus has gradually lost out to the south. More than any other single event, the death of Macbeth at Lumphanan in 1057 can be seen as marking the end of Moray's dominance, though it was not until 1187 that William the Lion destroyed the independence of Moray.

The seemingly impenetrable Cairngorms conceal strong links with western Scotland. As placenames like Inverbervie and Aquhorthies show, in the early Middle Ages Gaelic was spoken over much of the north east, even to the farthest north-east headland of Kinnaird Head, and survived well into the twentieth century in Upper Deeside. However, the Battle of Harlaw near Inverurie in 1411 between Donald, Lord of the Isles and the Earl of Mar supported by the burgesses of Aberdeen, shows that relationships between the north east and the western Highlands were complex and not always cordial. Later, like the Campbells of Argyll, the role of the Gordons as agents of the Lowland crown in controlling the Highlands again reveals the north east's role as frontier territory.

As a borderland, the north east has been contested with moving geographical borders defined and redefined, as the populace moves, changes, and re-forms in cycles. This region is rich ground for the discussion of new developments in deep mapping. Like the rivers themselves, culture, identity and story are defined through flux and movement that have come to work, somewhat paradoxically, through a strong sense of region and locality.

The land and rivers

While traces left by the early inhabitants are rarely recognised in the modern landscape, some of the few that survive, such as the 5,000-year-old long cairn at Capo by the North Esk and at Balnagowan near Tarland, are monuments erected by people concerned with the productivity of the land and the importance of the previous generations who had tended it. Surrounding the Blue Cairn of Balnagowan are dozens of heaps of stones created 2,000 years later by farmers who cleared the land to improve its fertility, while other patches of hillside which have escaped modern agriculture are marked by the traces of rigs and furrows of medieval and later agriculture. The immense effort over millennia which transformed the damp stony land of Aberdeenshire into the fertile land of today is also seen in the dykes that tie together the modern landscape, connecting past layers of inhabitation to the spaces and patterns of present-day dwelling. The most impressive of these, lying beside the modern housing estates of Kingswells, is over 10 metres wide and two metres high with a paved path running along the top for almost 500 metres. The efforts by landowners to 'improve' the landscape in the eighteenth and nineteenth centuries are also seen in the planned settlements of Laurencekirk, Ballater, Cullen, Archiestown and the abandoned settlements and fields of Upper Deeside. It is the lives of the people whose labours created this landscape that are commemorated in the folklore and customs of the area.

From the earliest flints found on Deeside near Milltimber to the use of the valley of the Don by the Aberdeenshire Canal, the Aberdeen–Inverness railway line and the A96 dual carriageway, the rivers Dee, Don, Ythan and Spey have always linked the coast with the hinterland. Indeed, the names of some of the rivers probably have their origins in prehistory. W. F. H. Nicolaisen has also pointed out that a river was not just something 'in which people might fish, on which they might travel by boat, which might provide water for fishing and other household purposes, and so on, but at one and the same time a divine being which demanded some form of worship and adoration'.[7] Thus the origins of the names of both the Dee and the Don imply divine qualities. He has also noted that a significant number of place names beginning with 'Aber' (meaning 'confluence' or 'river mouth') became parish names, presumably indicating a continuity of sanctity from pre-Christian times. Most notable of these is Aberdeen, the present-day fulcrum between land and sea, where St Machar's Cathedral lies at the mouth of the divine Don. The sources of each river are still relatively close – but much less walkable amid the mountain peaks of the Cairngorms, impassable in winter and only slightly less passable in warmer months. Asking an Aberdonian to describe the difference between each rivers results in, at first, one royal river and one wild one, a richer river, a poorer one; yet beyond initial comparisons details emerged, and qualities in entanglements of affection and awe.

The sea and beyond

From 'Willy the Merchant', who built Craigievar Castle in the seventeenth century from the proceeds of his Baltic trade, to the wealth of local landowners a century later deriving from owning enslaved people in the Caribbean, or to the jet and amber beads found in the burial at Greenbrae near Cruden from 4,000 years earlier, individual people have taken advantage of the way in which the north east juts into the North Sea. Much more distant contacts are primarily a feature of more recent times, but even as far back as 5,000 years ago a handful of highly polished axe heads originating in the Alps reached the area, showing the long-term significance of the east coast route from the Rhine. A millennium later the first metalworkers who established in the north east as one of the main areas of early metalworking in Britain followed the same route. It was also used by Bishop William Elphinstone when travelling to and from the continent and by medieval traders who brought pottery, wine, spices, books and weapons from eastern England and the Low Countries. Finds of pottery from the eastern Mediterranean at the Pictish site at Rhynie and even fragments of silk and elephant ivory on archaeological excavations of medieval Aberdeen hint at even more far flung contacts. Ranging from the unique stone circles of more than 4,000 years ago to the contemporary strength of the Doric language, the north east has a long-lasting sense of its own identity, but one which has taken full advantage of its position as a borderland to face outwards in many directions.

This deep map: a collage

Local distinctiveness is at the core of the notion of deep mapping and the work included in this volume reflects, in a collective entangled way, the sense of a region – the north-east – as well as individual meditations or speculations on place, rivers and history. Varied ways of knowing rivers – from repeated ventures into wild places, to the tenderness of local 'lived-in' details – are reflected in the work below.

When considering the two poems cited at the beginning of this section, the extract from Nan Shepherd's *The Living Mountain* demonstrates her well-known local-romantic vision of the mountain as a poetic testimony to the slippage between the self and other – the human and the non-human walk the mountain to know themselves, yet in doing so, encounter the ineffable, a sublime and somehow truthful incoherence that comes from the intimate knowledge of place and water.

The other extract from 'The Don' by Harry Smart shows a different kind of intimacy to do with place and time and relies on seasonal knowledge that may seem archaic, even arcane, to many – where one bears witness to a moment of shifting water within the tender phrasing of lovers. Salt sweeps over sweet water in the opposition forces of river and tide – the human-formed piling (wooden posts) form a spine in the centre of these liquid layers – water and human interaction forming the expanse of nocturnal intimacies. Different journeys into places, together, immerge as a collage of particularities – a deep map.

This section of the book begins and ends with the work of well-known and loved Aberdonian poets that connect the stages of human lives with the stretches, bends and still or lively courses of the rivers. The exacting lyricism of Gerald Rochford, Aberdeen-based poet, immerses the reader in meditative dialogue with the estuary of the Dee. In 'Dee Estuary 1' the poet intimates the dimension of mortality through the tender merging between the human and non-human journeys, from source to sea. The 'first taste of salt' are 'last rites into the dark fathom'. 'Dee Estuary 2' evokes a sombre yet peaceful immersion into the final stage of life, remembering the force of youth and the Dee upstream forms a later stage in the human–river journey. The river mouth, now 'mouth anointed with salt' is 'forever drowning,/river, river is drowning'. The Dee Estuary poems are even more affecting in the knowledge that Rochford was nearing the end of his life. These final reflections seek the river as a vital space in-between life and death and all profound transformation between states as an unending force of the human consciousness and the elemental interaction of rock, tides, salt and water.

Meredi Ortega, like a number of writers in this volume, writes with deep knowledge of Aberdeen, particularly the Dee, and the Perth region, and imbeds the complex association of migration and new places, memories, patterns and echoes that traverse the globe. Formally original, the work weaves poems into prose, working through personal experiences and referencing writers of rivers including Nan Shepherd and Alice Oswald, anthropologist Veronica

Strang and philosopher William James. After years of living in the town of Fremantle in Western Australia, the port town of Perth at the mouth of the Swan River, Ortega's deep mapping journey into place reflects the strange reversals of an Australian in Europe. Her old associations are of the black swans of the New World, to the new white Swan of the old on the banks of the Dee. Like many works of deep mapping, Ortega's writing is at once memoir, travelogue and local historical and geographical scholarship, with a deep immersion into non-human life. Through water Ortega seeks a transformative inwards journey into place 'allowing old thoughts to kaleidoscope into something else' and into the strangeness of water, space of life and death, the unruliness of the Dee in spate, the solid form of the frozen Dee and the elastic unpredictability of time on the Dee where nothing is exactly how or where it seems, from the precarious 'Shakkin' Briggie' (shaking bridge) or deep winter when 'Earth and river blurred together into a whiteout of language'.

Like Ortega, Ian Grosz takes the reader on a journey, often on foot, to the half-hidden spiritual locales of the Don. Replete with historical and archaeological resonance, his journey through road, trail, stream and field is an elemental dance of often elusive elements. Spiritual faith as a palimpsest of earth, rock, water and culture remains a central theme as he leads as through histories of Gaelic saints, Pictish stones, cairns and distinctive Aberdeenshire stone circles, with their distinctive recumbent stone, perhaps aligned with the rising and setting of the moon in eighteen year cycles. It is a 'ghost pathwork of eerie synchronicity', 'a landscape neck-deep in remanence: in the residual memory of people stretching further back that you are able to see or imagine'. In one striking episode Grosz searches for an eighteenth century holy well from relatively modern folklore. A monk finds three salmon in the well and hence, he and the village abated a famine until further help could be found. As Grosz remarks, pagan belief – including salmon as symbol of wisdom – is housed within Christian mythology in a looping and recursive movement. Just as vitally, holy wells, stone circles, burials mounds, places of transformation and spirituality are never far from the divine river. The ancient goddess endures in a looping and recursive movement that exists differently from linear formulations of time and space.

The whimsical movement of David Wheatley's 'dreamscape' cogitates on a road sign that points, somewhat oddly, to the River Don Office. Falling into sleep next to his infant son the piece enters into the absurdity of a river having an office (charmingly imagined as a bucket of water at a desk). A dream sojourn takes them down and up the Dee in a softly pulsing imagined boat, part Alice in Wonderland, Peter Pan and Puff the Magic Dragon. It is a quiet journey through sweet softness inspired by a sleeping infant but, as the boat bumps on the rocky shoals of the upper reaches of the Dee, childhood is a dream inspired by the adult self, one from which the dreamer inevitably wakes.

Side by side in this collection are two Australian writers who connect with the Dee, significantly, and things take a darker turn. Many Anglo–Celtic Australians, many with Scots ancestry, trace traumatic patterns of exile and the backwards movement to the old world and into the weirdness of history. In these writings the river is simultaneously a frightening and sinister force, and a strange comfort, with a volition of its own. Ashleigh Angus, who is of Scottish ancestry, offers an unsettling vignette of scolds, witches and cucking, which jolts the reader into the fishbowl of seventeenth century village life. The Dee here is both violent accomplice, as the protagonist finds herself thrust beneath its surface, and peaceful escape when the vision of drowning is a restful alternative to the vitriol of village life. The cucking stool – an unsettling bird-like figure – becomes a complex symbol of the pain and promise of immersion. The protagonist imagines that final union with the river is preferable to a life of degradations: 'finally freed from endless sitting; stretching out as the river carried me down and polished my bones as they rattled along the rocks'. Partly indebted to folklore research, partly to 1960s and 1970s British folk horror such as Michel Reeves' 1968 *Witchfinder General,* Angus evokes the claustrophobia of often-gendered violence in ways that reveal the layered private and public acts that continue to linger in the shapes of modernity, despite the impending changes of the Enlightenment.

The extract of a longer story from Perth writer and teacher Adam Kealley weaves tales of Scottish–Australian convict trauma around constantly changing watery locales – from uplands Dee, and Aberdeen amid the grimy blackness of nineteenth-century industrialisation, to the heaving Indian Ocean and the sun-drenched agora of the Swan River settlement. Through the complex patterning of uncanny echoes, rivers tie old and New World together – the protagonists' folkloric understandings of the Dee upstream waters of the fuath (malevolent water spirit) that took his family, endow him with the seed of water understandings elsewhere. The boy protagonist, now at the edge of the Swan River, 'hears a gentle voice behind him, from across the water. It whispers his name. His real name, not the one he gave to the magistrate that cold day in Aberdeen. He does not know if it be the fuathan, the Ghillie Dhu or his dear dead maw. But it calls to him, singing softly of shadows and shelter.'

Paolo Gruppuso and Simona Trozzi's 2017 print design of Seaton Park wetlands (connected to the mouth of the River Don) attempts to restore the role of imagination and dream in cartography. 'An Imaginative Map of Water in Seaton Park' crosses the line between land and water, real and imaginary, inside and outside, the whole and its parts. Merging personal experience, folklore, and mapping with calligraphy, drawing and printing, these series of handcrafted artefacts incorporate 'embodied experiences as instruments of knowing.' This rich linguistic and visual text blends human and non-human worlds. As the artists put it, 'salmon, aquatic birds, otters, squirrels and deer join the river flow where things are fuzzy, unfolding, and not yet given'.

The final writer to be represented in this section is well-known Aberdeen literary figure Sheena Blackhall, one of the most prolific and knowledgeable poets of the region. Like so many other poets Blackhall's work details the compelling entanglements between human lives and the rhythms and movements of the Dee. Blackhall's father managed a local bus company, which contributed to Blackhall's knowledge of the river. She was an expert from a young age on the villages, bridges, pools and stories of the river. Here, three of her poems reveal an aesthetic defined by remarkable fluidity of idiom. She is an expert in the northern dialect of the Scots language – the 'Doric' (or 'rustic') – and also a teacher and singer. 'The River Dee' explores the moods of the water and its resonance with the stages of life with beguiling musicality. 'Oh Gently, Gently Rins the Dee' reaches into Blackhall's rich knowledge of north-east balladry, the sweetest of love songs to a gentle stretch beside the clachan (village) of Aboyne. 'Dee Journey' sings the Dee as an epic heroine, staunch through hellish tempest, down stony falls and dark waters. The road of Kelpies, the river runs a magical journey until the dissolution of confluence.

Blackhall co-edits a treasury of north-east Scottish folklore and the Doric language called the Elphinstone Kist (chest) that collects poetry, fiction, drama, song lyric and memoir. It includes long texts and small fragments, representing centuries and days in the north east. It is in places like this, collections like this, where deep mapping and the curating and collection of texts overlap in significant and productive ways.

Gerald Rochford

Dee Estuary 1

I'd like a word with the maw of this river,
put some questions to the banks of her ears,
before she loses freshness in the tides
which swallow and regurgitate our secrets.

Do you remember the beginning,
bursting through the hair of heather,
then seeing the peaks
nippled with snow?

And do you remember the journey,
those reckless falls of youth,
the penetrations of salmon,
the delicate feet of mirrored deer?

Were you afraid at the first taste of salt,
your last rites into the dark fathom?
And are you now rejoicing,
born again of water and utterly changed?

Dee Estuary 2

Where sky lays hands upon the earth,
a river pauses for final benediction.

In infancy
this river burst through the rock,
grew to uproot boulders, tear out trees,
seduce salmon, promise gold,
nurture and murder cattle.

Now it seems peaceful,
spending a day by the sea.

But river is losing her grip,
holding on to shifty banks
and seeped with sand;
her mouth is anointed with salt.

The river is drowning,
forever drowning,
river, river is drowning.

The Lower Dee:
Swimming Upstream/Nowhere

Meredi Ortega

Transcendence comes from mountains, can only
hope for submergence here,
      downstream and down-valley.

On my daily walks beside the lower Dee, everything is caught between where-now and where-before. The river here, at West Cults on the outskirts of Aberdeen, is a long way from its source. So am I, having moved here from Fremantle in 2012. Following in the footsteps of the writer Nan Shepherd (who lived in West Cults for most of her life), I visit and receive the river as she did the mountain, seeking only to immerse myself. Shepherd's hours of walking 'the flesh transparent' in the Cairngorms enabled her to leave her body and enter the mountain.[1] Down in the lower Dee, submergence will be more a call to concerted non-effort: a dip, a saunter, a sit. Simply loafing beside the river brings about something akin to a transitional state, allowing old thoughts to kaleidoscope into something *else*. A daydream almost, 'until the facts forget themselves gradually like a contrail'.[2] Whatever next, I ask myself, as I sit on the bank of this small stretch of near-flung river.

Where-before
In the riparian margins of my mind, my mother is always sailing a plywood moth on the Swan River. She's the only woman out there sailing a moth and its name is *Wildchild*. Age five, I'm waiting for her, probing wet sand and pacing like an overgrown wader. Children are launching brown jellyfish onto the shore. I'm following in their wake, frantically heaving the spill of jellied bodies back into the water. The parents of these children are watching and smiling fondly; possibly recalling when they, too, were children batting and impaling these gelatinous others, these mere projectiles. To imagine being a jellyfish is not easy and not everyone can do it.

Pampas grass. In my child's-eye memory of the Canning River, these otherworldly feather fountains have arrived from another planet, perhaps in the flying saucer-shaped Futuro house (then encamped nearby on the corner of Leach Highway and Karel Avenue). Are they birds or plants? They can't seem to decide. Their grassy tussocks spread with ease, each flowering plume containing a multitude of seeds. When I move into my house, here in Scotland, part of my yard is over-brimming with pampas as though the past has seeped into the present.

Where-now: Once upon a time
The perfect wife, the Roman satirist Juvenal wrote, was 'a rare bird on this earth, exactly like a black swan'.[3] This came to mean a rare or a non-existent thing, and more recently, 'black swan' has become a catchphrase for an unexpected financial event (perhaps financiers still inhabit a Eurocentric pre-1636 world, and so for them, black swans do not exist). But in the where-before, swans are black. Everyone knows this. Whereas white swans are as fabled as unicorns, only seen in the picture books I read as a child.

All at once they have peeled off the pages and are flying overhead or are floating past me on the river. I tell a birder (you shall know them by their binoculars), as we cross paths beside the river. To look at me jabbing the air with my ball thrower, he might guess that an osprey or a kingfisher is in the offing. But instead I'm singing out, 'There are two white swans down there!' The fast flow and lack of aquatic plants makes the Dee a less than ideal nesting place for mute swans; the first record of them breeding here wasn't until 1995.[4] Another time, I ask him about whooper swans on the reservoir, and learn that the 'w' in 'whooper' is silent. He tells me he once saw a hen harrier above the deer field in winter, which is almost a black–white swan experience.

In early July, a neighbour tells me that five cygnets belonging to the mute swan pair were killed by a fox on the golf course. The next day, I see the unlucky pair on the river, in the shallows, dishevelled and preening themselves in what I imagine to be a listless fashion. A week later I see them again on the river, this time on Facebook. A friend has posted a photo of them from her morning walk with a note about the fox and the five dead cygnets. Several weeks go by and I see a mute pair in the same spot on the river with five large brown-grey cygnets. I tell myself there must be more than one breeding pair hereabouts. This is not the unlucky pair and these are not their resurrected offspring. Or are they? Months later, almost a year, there is a new version of events. The five cygnets were not killed by a fox at all but were trapped in a culvert on the golf course. They were rescued and checked over before being returned to their parents. And they all lived happily ever after.

Three whooper swans had a different ending in 2019, with no good luck or wishful thinking to preserve them. Their bodies were found in plastic bags in the Dee. Two were a short way downriver from Shakkin' Briggie, and one was further down, near Robert Gordon University. Two of the three had been shot and two had flesh removed. Whooper swans typically arrive in autumn from Iceland, where they return in spring. Swan news travels far and wide and this story was reported by various news outlets. One article in the *Evening Express* is accompanied by a highly pixelated photo with a graphic image warning. Using the slider provided, the photo's pink and maroon squares can be drawn to one side like a curtain, revealing the swan's bloodied body, a bone (I'm not sure which), and a dark gaping hole.[5] As I go on to read comments which accuse 'foreign nationals' from Eastern Europe of eating the swans, it is as though we ourselves have been eviscerated, our cruelty and xenophobia laid bare.

Crossings

Before 1837, people on this side of the river had to catch a parish boat to attend Sunday service on the other side. The other side really did mean the other side, as many parishioners from this side were also buried in the Banchory–Devenick kirkyard, on the south side of the Dee. These early crossings for the purpose of worship were fraught with difficulties.

> 1717 Dec. 1 — Visitation of families not observed because the water could not be crossed.
> 1718 Jan. 26 — Weather so stormy that the people have now crossed the water three Sabbath days on the ice.[6]
> 1831 Dec. 11 — An evil disposed person having pierced the bottom of the Church boat in various places with a gimlet, the Session offer a reward of Two guineas for information so as to convict the delinquent.[7]

As I walk along the river, I continue these parish records into the present day.

> 2019 Mar. 31 — A heron was observed fishing on the Sabbath.
> 2019 Apr. 7 — The Minister lectured about the reservoir lifebelt which was set ablaze by miscreants on the north side of the Dee.
> 2019 Jun. 19 — A Day of Jubilation was declared on account of a newly fledged crow on Scots Pine Ridge.

Walking east along the Dee, over Cults Burn, I arrive at the rusting iron remains of Shakkin' Briggie. This suspension bridge, paid for by the Rev. Dr. George Morison, was built so that parishioners could cross in all weathers. Though raised high into the air on stone piers, the river may, during a freak spate, transgress the bridge in a dramatic reversal of crossings. Over time, the bridge has been progressively damaged and weakened by spates, neglect and the river's changing course. In 1893, questions were already being asked about its maintenance or lack thereof. An objection was also made to some kind of equine barrier.

> So far nothing had even been done to the bridge at Cults—it was not painted even. If it had been painted it would stand much longer. At one time a medical man on the Cults side was able to ride across the bridge, but instead of the county authorities helping him do so they put up an arrangement at the end of the bridge to prevent him going across on his pony.[8]

Close to a century later, not only were there medical women 'on the Cults side', but neither people nor ponies could cross after the bridge's decayed decking was removed as a safety precaution. Today, it stretches eerily across the water, its iron hangers devoid of any walkway, creaking in the breeze. The families who gathered here on blankets on the banks, eating sandwiches and pies, who swam and paddled and jumped off the bridge, have all grown old and moved on. Now, its uncrossability stands like a riddle. When is a bridge not a bridge? Each suspended hanger is about two metres apart and several are missing, prompting the onlooker to wonder what kind of creature might cross it now.

On guising night (Halloween), a woman in my street invites all kinds of creatures into her home, some of whom are children in costumes, to partake in apple dookin' (or apple dunking/bobbing), a tradition which she has carried out for many decades. She recalls another kind of crossing, that of a Labrador retriever belonging to a Mr Yule. This dog would swim across the Dee whenever her Airedale terrier was in season and she would escort him back down to the river and watch as he gave the appearance of swimming south and home. On returning to her house, Mr Yule's dog would be waiting as though he had never left. If reproduction is life's be-all and end-all, this unnamed Labrador's persistent crossings may well be the most authentic.

To cross a river then, it helps to have a good reason. A man tells me how he and his brother used to ride their pushbikes to the chain ferry in Bieldside, where they would cross to Blairs Ferry Tea Shop on the south bank and buy homemade apple turnovers and warm bottles of orange or lemon pop. They would then cycle along the river and come back across Shakkin' Briggie. The ferry stopped running in the early 1960s but the ferry tea room continued for another decade.[9]

BBQ Island

The warmth brings people out of their carpeted worlds. As they go about their business outdoors, they leave in their wake the large spent vessels of all that they have consumed. These bright objects give off the same distress signal: save us from ourselves.

> I wade to a shingle island where a BBQ tray
> pivots and morses like a great salmon among
> six-pack rings, dark fruit cider cans.

It's May when I collect these objects and more from the middle of the river. It becomes an uncanny midden of mussel-hinged sandwich containers, bloody freezer bags, and silver-gutted packets. When I find a plastic carry bag, I feel perversely grateful to have something to tow it all away in.

> The Tesco bag is printed with flowers and trees
> and birds. The lost things have been
> altered, put back, the way a pale lung
> breathes in and out, half in and out of the water.

What to do with the fury engendered by such desecration of place? Returning to the track beside the river, I breathe in deeply. The gorse's coconut fragrance is diffusing in the sun. Coconut fragrance doesn't do it any justice though, because I find myself wishing I could land on the keel of just one bright yellow flower to gain admission. Years ago, near the end of November, I watched an air show over the Swan River from the South Perth foreshore. Spectators sat in the river on plastic chairs and the sky filled with a haze of aerobatic smoke. 'This power of flight,' writes Shepherd, 'to take us in to itself through the eyes as though we had actually shared in the motion'.[10] Now, as I watch the aerial feats of breakneck birds with forked tails over the Dee, any remaining fury turns to awe. One day I will fall off the bank, having tilted my head back too far.

> Today, only small wings. Quick-low martins,
> red-winking swallows. Only the swifts,
> the swifts can bring me to my knees.

Inchgarth Reservoir

> The easeful surge keeps coming and coming.
> All things are adding to themselves.

Sprinkler days. These are the two days of the week (excluding winter when sprinklers are banned) when the people of Perth (Australia) can turn their sprinklers on (before 9.00 am and after 6.00 pm). The two days vary, according to the last digit of a person's street address. Here, water is unmetered (though charged at a fixed rate). Nan Shepherd enjoyed blocking a tap's flow with her finger as a child, but as an adult, she wished to go further and hold back a mountain spring.[11] In a way, though, she was holding back the river when she was a child because her drinking water was abstracted from the Dee, just as mine is today. The water that emerges from my tap is drawn from the Dee nearby at Inchgarth, as well as at Cairnton (just upriver from Banchory).

Maybe I'll eat the fattened air, too.

Sit here all the days. Heron, tell me, do I want to
leach back, or am I dying of thirst?

In her book *Water*, anthropologist Veronica Strang explores (among other things) how 'we 'think with water'.[12] Literally, because the brain is approximately three-quarters water, 'like a fertile, resource-rich wetland'.[13] As most of my daily water comes from the Dee, how startling it is to think (via the Dee) that in writing about the river, the river is writing itself. Metaphorically, too, we think with water. Psychologist and philosopher William James wrote that a 'river' or a 'stream' is how consciousness 'is most naturally described'; that is to say, a stream of consciousness.[14] The river was used by Barrow, Newton, and Gassendi to conceptualise 'the theory of absolute time', and has otherwise been used as a metaphor for time since antiquity.[15] In *The Living Mountain*, Shepherd diminishes mountain peaks, or 'the vertical sublime',[16] by describing them as mere '*eddies* on the plateau surface' (my italics).[17] Consciousness, time, the mountain – we reach for the river to explain what cannot be explained.

Walking east from Shakkin' Briggie in early May, the track is so low in places that it's almost level with the river. This brings about a strange sensation similar to walking alongside a moving walkway. Bluebells, bramble, wild garlic, cow parsley, stitchwort, red campion, comfrey, orange-tips, reeds and sedges, sycamore, heron, wych elm, song thrush somewhere, little bench, mallards, ash. Inchgarth Reservoir sluice gates. Midges, willow willow willow, boulders, great wall of gorse then avenue of gorse and broom, eroded bank where sand martins nest. A small male wolf spider crouches on a boulder next to the burnt-out remains of a campfire. Yet another 'disposable' barbeque in the river. A rapid ticking which doesn't come from the overhead power lines. It sounds like a cricket. This cricket is a small bird with a stridulating song, a grasshopper warbler. All of a sudden, it starts to hail.

Message rocks

> When I raised my head, I was alone in the universe with a few blocks of red granite.[18]

It's still May as I walk west along the track which runs along a high bank beside the golf course. The narrow clay track slants towards the river as it dips and rises. It has its own meander and in parts, where it has fallen away, it carves a new channel in firmer ground. The track is already beginning its seasonal disappearance beneath spring's burgeoning overhang of grass, ground elder, butterbur, cow parsley. It's while keeping my eyes firmly down that I first notice a river stone in the track's rut has been written on, in situ, with black marker:

SOMEONE OUT THERE LOVES YOU AND YOU
DESERVE IT!

On the way back, I read it again, this time upside-down. Spring is the season of love – maybe, in this instance, as-yet undeclared love, hence the 'someone' who purports to be 'anyone'. As the days pass and as I pass over the same message again and again, the message rock interrupts the flow of my thoughts. If I'm not imagining who wrote it and for whom, I'm trying to recall this kneeling-in-the-undergrowth-rock-scrawling kind of passion. It seems to belong to an earlier edition of my life. Suddenly the message rock is a small-scale billboard advertising things I no longer possess.

I change routes but when I walk between the field and river, I find another message written on another embedded stone which features this assurance:

YOU'RE NOT ALONE

I look around. My trusty canine and corvid companions are never far away. The river, too, is a companion of sorts. As I think about what it means to be not-alone, my actual and abiding aloneness becomes starkly apparent. The silvery Dee brings to mind that other silvery river, The Milky Way, and I recall how alone we all are in this impossibly vast universe. When rain and footfall finally wear the words completely away, I heave a sigh of existential relief. Later, it transpires that these messages are meant to be 'inspirational' and that there are more such rocks located east along the river. Though the messages have since disappeared, several message rocks can still be found in the digital hereafter, having been photographed and uploaded to Instagram.[19]

As the salmon swims

The river is 350 metres from my house as the crow flies, or five minutes by foot. But to walk there in a loafing fashion, *house to playing field / red pine ridge to river*, throwing the ball for my dog while greeting and feeding various crows known to me, takes much longer. At the river, the track branches east downriver along the deer field, past Shakkin' Briggie, Inchgarth Reservoir's sluice gates, to the eroded bank where the sand martins nest; or west upriver along the golf course, past Byron's watering place, BBQ Island, the quiet pool, to the end of the golf course (where Blairs ferry once was).

A short distance upriver is Byron's watering place. Although the poet Lord Byron spent most of his childhood in Aberdeen ('Thou sweet flowing Dee, to thy waters adieu!'[20]), this is the watering place of Byron, my Chodský pes. From the end of May to the end of August, this is also where I swim – and where a gravel bar emerges, large enough to lay a towel on. It's not as secluded or deep or clear as the pot I swam in upriver, in the Clunie Water (a tributary of the Dee), but it's much nearer. Let the Clunie come to me. The fifth hole of the Deeside Golf Club is close by and I frequently find golf balls in the water. On the other side, there's another golf course, but it's set back from the river and shrouded with trees. In spring, I hear a pheasant calling from its interior, sounding like a creaky Hills hoist slowly turning in the wind. And I see bright copper flashing through the gaps.

The way down to the river is a steep scramble. Byron deposits his ball in a large side eddy, formed by a boulder outcrop. For what seems like forever, I watch it endlessly looping upriver. At some point, the eddy will pass the ball into the river's fast lane and if I don't stop it, it will end up in the North Sea, eventually finding its way into the stomach of a whale, along with a hundred other artefacts. Sometimes it's hard to draw breath without feeling sorry for it. I teeter on the edge of the deep pool, where it loops, afraid to swim into it. I may subscribe to a poetics of submergence but actual submergence is too much; it's like swimming in a dam at night.

> Our toes imagined yabby claws, barbed wire,
> rabbit-trap jaws. But never how
> unlike ourselves we would become.

I spot a bunker rake lying in the shallows, thrown there by someone. I retrieve it and wade back to the deep pocket, inching my way in just enough. When the ball comes around again, I stretch out and rake it in like the river's croupier.

I swim in the medium lane, more or less in the same spot, *upstream/ nowhere*. If I swim too slowly, I'll start to slip downstream. When I've had enough, I put my feet on the cobble and gravel bed and lean forward into the flow, a fixed obstacle. The river purls in my ears, runs through my fingers so that I hope to be untangled. Whether Nan Shepherd ever swam here is unknown. Just as unknown is whether she could in fact swim.[21] Shepherd writes of the Dee, at its sources, in the Cairngorms, as having a profound clarity and brightness but here, in the lower reaches, the Dee is more 'golden amber', as well as Gerard Manley Hopkins' 'horse-back brown'.[22] As for brightness, apart from sunlight's dazzle, the river sand contains mica, which glints gold and far-away in the water's brandied hue. When I try to pick up these mica specks, my hands always come up empty and agleam with water only.

> I read about crows bringing gifts to a girl in Seattle.
> Crow gives me nothing until the end of June
> when he leaves one perfect feather
> which I insert in my hair, an insurmountable
> forward slash.
> It helps relieve this hurtling feeling.
> I wear it swimming upstream / nowhere, my push
> matching the river's. The clever river is always
> already gone, here all the same.

> Six boys float towards me in rings, beers in hand.
> *We came from Culter*, says one. Four miles
> as the salmon swims. In the fast lane,
> they carry past like smiling babies in stork slings.
> This sudden urge to caw / and caw,
> give to each
> a lucky gewgaw. A drumming stonefly, an almost
> thing with a tiny hole for wearing,
> a gleaming bone picked clean.

Apart from the boys who came from Peterculter in their inflatable rings, and the occasional shrieking paddler, it's unusual to see anyone in the river along this stretch. In decades past, far more people swam here, and drowned here as well:

June, 1930: the bodies of two students from Blairs Catholic College are recovered from a nearby pool in the Dee.

July, 1933: a thirteen-year-old boy is practising swimming with his friends, opposite Allan Park, when he loses his cork jacket in the current and drowns.

July, 1934: it's the beginning of the Aberdeen Trades holiday. A twenty-one-year-old mechanic drowns while swimming in a pool in West Cults. The river is higher than usual, due to rain.

Then, almost overnight, the unthinkable happens – a pandemic – and everyone is in the river. I see teenagers in boardies and bikinis. I have to pinch myself, where am I? Beach balls float past. In the flotsam and jetsam, I find a full bottle of sun cream, a camping chair, an inflatable turtle. With swimming pools closed and summer holiday flights cancelled, captive swimmers flock to the river, where they make a resort of last resort on the shingle island. I think it comes as a surprise to us all, the strange pleasure of being alive and chest-deep in the Dee's cold thrust.

Grass and rush and river

Arriving at Byron's watering place with a towel around my neck, I find an angler in grey waders on the other side. He stands where the grey heron normally is (I've never seen either catch anything). I don't disturb the angler, not because I know that he's paid to fish this beat, but because of that childhood rule which says he bagsed it first. I wrap my towel around my waist to protect my legs from nettle, thistle, and bramble, then continue to another spot upriver. The track is almost lost as I walk into a green blizzard. I would never walk through long grass and scrub like this in Australia. I'm unlikely to find a venomous snake here but I still stomp instead of walk – having been conditioned from a young age to alert all snakes to my imminent arrival.

The quiet pool is anything but. South Deeside Road swings in close by and the traffic is continuous. Unruffled and peaceful, this pool hardly appears to be moving, but when it mists over with insects, it takes on a life of its own as it spasms and sploshes with fish. On the other side of the river, a little further down, sits a modern house so large that I mistake it for a golf club house or a small hotel. Apart from a fishing hut, it's the only other visible building on the far bank along this reach. The very big house is surrounded by a wide expanse of luminous green perfect turf. Is it artificial grass? The consensus on this side of the river seems to be yes, it is. But I won't fully believe it unless I'm able to run my fingers through its spears. Until that unlikely empirical moment, it must sit – always greener, existing as both real and not-real, and, like so many things on the other side of the river, unverifiable.

Blackberries

> Self-so-ness in creeping bent and water shrew,
> algal down, autumn's dawning fog,
>   the river is a smoker.
>
> Broom stellified with tar-spotted stars of sycamore,
> mayflies from the riffle and dun-sparkling
>   drowning quiet, sharp-flowered
> rushlight, O the slow glide.

The best brambles are to be found along the banks. These must be imbued with secret springs because they taste so pure and sweet. Of course the easily reached ones have been taken but I have the advantage of being tall and my reach is further extended by my ball thrower. When I return home, my tongue is bramble-syllabled.

Lupin Island

Every childhood is in need of an island and Nan Shepherd had Lupin Island. Midway between Ardoe and Shakkin' Briggie, and made of shingle, hers was covered in blue turrets. The seeds of these Nootka lupins, native to the Pacific coast of North America, may have originally been carried down the Dee from Queen Victoria's gardens at Balmoral Castle.[23] Turrets, turrets everywhere. But the river takes what it brings and brings what it takes; and in the latter 1920s a spate stripped away the lupins 'and not one ever grew again' on Lupin Island.[24] It's possible to find the island on old maps, growing and shifting towards the south bank, and then vanishing as if an imaginary phantom island. Though nothing ever really vanishes, ourselves included; it is more a rearrangement. I like to think those lost lupins are still there, too, somewhere, like the ruins of a watery realm.

The new Muckle Spate

> My neighbour found the Dee in his garden,
> lifted schist pebbles like new potatoes,
> saying, *She came up to the crossbar once.*

It's already dusk at 3.45 pm, on Wednesday, 30 December 2015. I'm watching the Allan Park playing field from my living room window. Or at least I'm watching the football crossbar, the playing field having long since disappeared after days of unending rain. The river has broken its confines and every low-lying place is submerged: the golf course, deer field and most of Allan Park. I've seen the park flood numerous times but this is no ordinary flood. It is 'the absence of the world'.[25] The Dee has unmapped everything. It has made its way into the bottom of my long, steep garden, where it has effortlessly lifted firewood and a railway sleeper from my neighbour's garden like a Scottish strong person and floated them over the wall to my side. At 3.55 pm, I see the crossbar disappear altogether. The water eventually starts to recede but the rain never ceases. Five days later, the crossbar disappears for a second time. Hannah, the woman who lived here before me, must have watched countless floods from this same window.

>Hannah's pockets filled with cobbles
to keep from fixing to the ceiling like the sea crashed,
toggle pulled too soon.

>Green flaming willow moss in each grate, flues choked
with floe, sill-sucking lampreys.
This house in meltwater and outwash, unhewn.
Old Hannah or a premonition of her,
a dipper rafting on ice.

After the much-muchness recedes, we too might pause to ask, 'but river – / what have you left us?'.[26] Fish perhaps, as David Grant recounts in his twenty-four page poem about the Muckle Spate of 1829. 'We captured troots an' eels, / An' noo an' than a protty grilse / For weeks amo' the peels.'[27] After the floods, I'm walking to the river with my youngest daughter, when we spy dozens of small fish in a ditch beside the track. They are packed together and surrounded by ice as though put there by a fishmonger. Their world is shrinking fast and some fish in lesser pockets are already dead. The birds will enjoy this feast, though are probably already spoilt for choice by the glut of stranded and drowned offerings. We hurry home for a bucket, as I knew we would. We scoop as many fish as we can with frozen hands and then we give them back to the river.

Was it really higher than the Muckle Spate? Only the river knows – records of 1829 not being what they are now, bridges having since been built (which may have banked the water higher at certain points), and the river's catchment and capacity having also since changed. Four and a half years later, flood debris (fencing, pallets, straw) can still be seen wedged in the branches of trees along the banks. The flood line of wrack is so high, it's as though the trees are telling their own tall tales.

Deer field

In his introduction to *The Living Mountain*, Robert Macfarlane quotes poet Patrick Kavanagh, in relation to Shepherd's eye for the particular: 'To know fully even one field or one land is a lifetime's experience'.[28] The deer field, situated in between Loirsbank Road and the river (Loirsbank means 'lower bank'), was known, in a previous incarnation, as Tattie Thomson's field. Thomson's potatoes would float downriver when pulled from their drills by a heavy spate. Roe deer are always tucked away here, but the deer field could just as easily be the purple field (when thick with Yorkshire fog grass) or the buttercup field (when lit from within like a punched-tin lantern). Or the jackdaw field (when gleaned by silver-eyed jackdaws in their pale headscarves). This, too, is where we found fish after the floods – fish field would convey the unexpected, as well as the field's floodplain status.

A dress circle of eight houses perches on the raised north-east corner of the field, facing the river. There were 79 letters of objection to this development and years later, there still exists a collective *schadenfreude* among local residents; such as when house prices fell (these houses cost £1 million plus) or when the flood waters grew tantalisingly close. Prior to the development, an archaeological evaluation was carried out, which uncovered modern plough marks, returning the field full circle to Tattie Thomson.

Incursion

Byron's watering place, mid-morning on New Year's day. A mallard is flapping on the far side when something else catches the corner of my eye.

> A shining ball floats towards me.
> Strange how it crosses the river's drag,
> seems sewn with sealskin.

> Her tarry eyes lift from the flow. We stare
> at one another, our necks
> wrinkled astonished.

For weeks afterwards, I'm tripping over, my eyes glued to the river. Then, in mid-March, walking near the reservoir with a friend from Milltimber, I have segued into seals – how they can and do swim upriver as far as Banchory; how no one I've spoken to has seen one, other than on the coast; how lucky such an encounter is, unless if angler or fish – when we come across a woman who tells us she has just put her dog on a lead because, 'There's a seal around the next bend'.

The great freeze

Skating on the Dee was once a recreational pastime. In the winter of 1895, a young man and woman skated from Shakkin' Briggie to the Bridge of Dee and back. What must it be like to fly forward together on the frozen river? It must be like holding hands and stepping off a bridge. In such a moment, time must also freeze.

The river swishes past, thick with ice and grue. It sounds like granitas spiralling behind cafe counters in Fremantle in summer. Carols on the radio cause a similar disconnect (Christmas was never cold, let alone white). Ice was a large block bought from the bottle shop with a rope handle frozen into it, to be sledged down Monument Hill. Or it was a cube, to be slipped down the back of someone's shirt because they had just slipped it down yours. When I arrived here, something happened. The world began sliding from under my feet. Trust nothing, said a voice, not even the ground. Two years ago, the snow thawed and froze many times, compacting into something like a curling pond, on which cars and people spun. They spun this way for days. I keep Byron tethered, lest he ventures out and falls through. With his double coat, he's in his element. As if to prove so, he breaks open a puddle and laps the ice-cold water. He and I watch the river slow. Sunlight flashes off each mirrored chunk in sync. Upstream, the ice is unzipped, revealing a long V of flow. But here the Dee is grinding to a standstill, snowing over until river and earth have blurred together in a white-out of language. Sometimes it feels as though I have always been walking beside this river.

River Don Office

David Wheatley

On a back road near my house once stood a hand-written sign for the 'River Don Office', pointing to a nearby lane. To my regret I never went to investigate, though I liked to imagine a bucket of water on a desk, processing its paperwork on fishing licences and mulling cross-community projects with the river Dee. Since the sign's removal, I have reclassified a small portion of my brain as my own River Don Office, throbbing away night and day in sympathetic rhythm with the gurgle and flow on the other side of the park, halfway between where the Don rises in Glen Avon and its appointment with the North Sea.

Clambering into bed beside my son one night (we co-sleep) I am transported more dramatically to the river when I notice I've left the extractor fan on in the bathroom. Rather than get up to correct this mistake, I allow it to mutate into the outboard motor of a small boat, in which we set off, he and I, for a night cruise up and down the fast-moving river's tricky waters. We chug downstream in the direction of Aberdeen, shadowing then losing then shadowing the railway line again. Out to sea we spot the moonlit outlines of the tankers, which often rest at anchor for weeks on end, waiting for the price of their oily cargo to rise before they come into harbour. Fearing a jaunt to Norway may be beyond us we turn back, passing the village and heading west again.

In the mountains, there you feel free, even as they close benevolently round you, the high-sided pinewoods of Pitfichie and Clova Hill looming up in the moonlight as though about to pitch headlong into the current. Feet tucked under him where he kneels on the bow, my son stares into the silvery tide, with occasional glances over his shoulder to where I navigate. Soon we are closing in on the head of the Don, zig-zagging crazily in waters so shallow I feel us bumping along the bottom. Turning over where I lie in bed and brushing against the children's books piled high in the cot beside the bed I ask myself, "What is this, a magic-realist children's book?" A thin stream of drool has dampened my pillow, and by morning my carefully drafted report for the River Don Office (in fact, these words) has been lost overboard.

To the River Don

We came to a bend
        in the river
                where

a willow washed
        its hair in its
               double

and tangles of
        geese shadows
               shrank

    to a stickleback
           tide passing
                    under

    the bridge so that
           the reeds sprouted
                    eyes

    in which here too
           our reflections
                    swam

    and do they feel
           themselves
                    changing

    direction
           the fish or is
                    whatever

    way the tide
           goes merely
                    the way

The Don: A Sacred River

Ian Grosz

View of Bennachie looking northwards along the Don, taken from Pitfichie.
PHOTO BY IAN GROSZ, 2019.

Our lives are rivers, gliding free to that unfathomed, boundless sea, the silent grave!

Jorge Manrique[1]

There is no place that is not haunted by many different spirits hidden there in silence, spirits one can 'invoke' or not. Haunted places are the only ones people can live in.

Michael de Certeau[2]

Listening to rivers

Rivers have, from beyond recorded history, served as metaphor and spiritual inspiration for people all over the world. Just as rivers find their way back to the open sea where they may begin again, are reborn, renewed through the water cycle, our own lives run through the landscapes of our time, flowing between generations as memory and influence. It is not difficult to see why rivers are central to many world religions and spiritual practices. The Ganges is representative of the goddess Ganga. In Hindu belief bathing in the river washes away sin, liberating the soul from the repeating cycle of life and death that is reincarnation. Likewise, the river Jordan is made holy through the baptism of Jesus in the Christian tradition. In this way rivers have cleansed and nourished us, symbolically as well as physically, for as long as there have been people capable of story making.

The Nile, arguably the world's most famous river, carried the souls of the dead into the afterlife and in annual flood brought fertility to the soil along its banks by virtue of the flood god Hapi; while in Australia, the Yarra river has been a sacred part of Aboriginal culture since prehistoric times, being a major source of food and an important meeting place long before any European settlement. The Wurundjeri people, who can trace their ancestry in the Yarra valley through at least thirty-thousand years, named the river *Birrarung*, meaning 'ever flowing'.

All rivers might be seen to perpetually flow through the human narratives that attempt to make sense of life and death. They are themselves narratives, the stories of our landscapes and times. They serve as features through which we may unravel history and draw meaning from landscape. They help to show us who we are and from where we came. In Mia Couto's African novel *Woman of the Ashes*, set in nineteenth-century colonial Mozambique, the hapless Sergeant Germano del Melo arrives in Nkokolani by riverboat to be met by the central narrator Imani:

> We were walking along the riverbank when the visitor stopped and closed his eyes, asking me not to say anything. We stood there in silence until he suddenly spoke again:
> *Where I come from, we don't have this.*
> *You don't have rivers?*
> *Of course there are rivers. It's just that we have stopped listening to them.*[3]

By metaphorically listening to rivers, we may uncover the past and understand something more of the places and times that have shaped us. It holds true wherever we are from, wherever it is we live.

At the mouth of the Don

Aberdeen, known as the Granite City, lies at the coastal fringe of the land stretching between the Grampian Mountains and the cold North Sea in the northeast of Scotland. It is aligned roughly east–west between two rivers that have defined the way the city has grown – the Don and the Dee – and it is from this situation that the city takes its name. The original settlement, Aberdon, known in Gaelic in medieval times as *Obar-Dheathain* but now known as Old Aberdeen, lies squarely at the mouth of the river Don where it spills out to sea. Aberdeen may be translated literally to mean 'Don-mouth' since *Aber* is an old Pictish word meaning 'at the confluence of'[4], and is associated closely with watercourses. It is a prefix seen commonly in Wales and in remnant use elsewhere in Scotland.[5] The suffix *deen* has its roots in the ancient name for the river, first recorded as the *Devana* by Ptolemy in 150 AD and drawn from the word *devos* (god). Translating to 'goddess', this etymology more than hints at the river's once sacred status.

The Picts were descended from a race known as the Caledonii, and spoke an early Brythonic language close to the languages spoken by pre-Roman Britons to the south, perhaps resembling Old Welsh, or *Hen Gymraeg*. They occupied much of northern and eastern Scotland from the Forth–Clyde line up to the Northern Isles, and even into the northern Hebrides to the west, between the late Iron Age to the early medieval period. They later underwent a process of Gaelicisation under the influence of settlers from Ireland, who formed the Kingdom of Dál Riata in Argyll and the southern Hebrides. The name 'Pict' is popularly coined from Roman accounts where they are depicted as a fierce, warrior race painted from head to toe, loosely translating to 'painted people', but this Latin derivation of their name and subjective account of their nature is open to continued questioning and reinterpretation. Following the decline of the Roman presence, they became Christianised under the influence of the Gaels, and were ultimately subsumed into the wider amalgamation of Scots peoples between the ninth and eleventh centuries, living a pastoral life as farmers and herders. The story of the early Pictish people, language and culture however, is now reduced to a few Roman and Irish accounts, a few place names, a few enigmatic symbol stones, and conjecture.

A dedicated scholar of Pictish and Gaelic place names, Bill Nicolaisen, tells us that the river Don was:

> ... from a Pictish perspective, not just a river in which people might fish, on which they might travel by boat, which might provide water for washing and other household purposes, and so on, but at one and the same time a divine being which demanded some form of worship and adoration.[6]

He goes on to say that:

> ... there are likely to have been particular locations on these rivers where the worship of flowing water provided special cultural significance and, in addition to the religious nature of wells and springs, these locations appear to have been at confluences.[7]

Aberdeen's cathedral, St Machar, was founded in the early twelfth century. It is named after a sixth-century Irish monk who is said to have come to Iona with St Columba, before travelling to Aberdeenshire where he converted the local Picts to Christianity.[8] Much of what is known about St Machar comes from an early sixteenth-century text known as the *Aberdeen Breviary* – produced by the first press in Scotland – which contains biographies of the traditional Roman Catholic and Scottish national saints. These are drawn from stories and legends collected from the different diocese of Scotland by William Elphinstone, Bishop of Aberdeen and founder of the University of Aberdeen in 1495. The veracity of the Breviary is open to interpretation, but the cathedral can trace its roots as a place of worship going back to at least the sixth-century AD and, being closely tied to its position at the mouth of the Don, it seems likely that the location would have been an important and possibly sacred place for the Picts too, long before it became a place of Christian significance.

Today, I begin a journey to uncover the Don's layered meanings, its history and ghosts, at the source of the river out at the edge of the Cairngorms: a wild, wind-scoured range of granite domes shaped by ice and time, rising up from the fertile glacial valleys some 50 miles west of the city. Here, not far from the Don's humble beginnings on the lower slopes of Ben Avon, a massive, roundish mountain at the edge of the modern-day national park that makes up the Cairngorm range, traces of the old sacred ties are not hard to find.

The ghost of a holy well

Strathdon, the valley of the Don, from the Gaelic *Strath-Dheathain*, is a shallow agricultural valley changing gradually from the wilder, more windswept highlands to the peaceful rolling fields that characterise much of the river Don's course. The valley is awash with folklore and legend, and here at its upper reaches, where the river springs from its confluence with the Avon, records of holy wells are abundant. I have come in search of the Corriehoul Well, Tobar Vachar, popularly named 'St Machar's Well' in dedication to the memory of the saint, and situated somewhere near where the Corriehoul Burn – a stream at Corgarff – meets the Don.

In the London Folk Lore Society's Journal of 1889, Elliot Stock lists it among his survey of ancient wells and springs in the Strathdon Valley, and describes the old superstitions surrounding it. 'This well was renowned for the cures it wrought in more than one kind of disease,' he tells us. 'To secure a cure the ailing one had to leave a silver coin in it.' In another well, springing from a hollow beneath a rock on the nearby summit of Ben Newe, he found 'several pins, a small bone, a pill box, a piece of a flower, and a few other objects'.[9]

All over Scotland, in ruined churches and on ancient burial islands, coins and other small offerings can still be found: left at crumbling altars, in wells, or wedged into the trunks of old trees made sacred by association. Still commonly practised by tossing a coin into a 'wishing well', making offerings in this way goes back to pagan times, to bring luck, to heal or to curse, and in these small offerings are the long-lost deep-seated desires of the people who leave them. As I pull into the car park at the busy Goodbrand and Ross cafe near Corgarff, I think about this and wonder what hopes and fears were symbolised by the objects listed by Elliot a hundred and thirty years before me, and what I may find, or not, today. I carry with me in my pocket a small, low denomination coin in case I find the well still extant, to pay my respects to these old beliefs, if nothing else.

The well is said to be east of the eighteenth-century church at Corgarff, itself now long empty and abandoned, up for sale as a residential development at the time of my visit. It is a fate shared with a charming Catholic chapel hidden away amongst trees to the south, in the tiny settlement of Boilhandy. St Mary's – or 'Our Lady of the Snows' – was built in 1804 to tend to the local Gaelic speaking residents, themselves also now just a memory in the landscape, leaving only the chapel and the echoes of their language in local place names as testament to their existence. The surrounding burns and hills resonate with lost story and history: *Allt an Lin* – Lint Burn, where either lint was steeped or 'faeries lint' grew; *Alltan Mhicheil* – Michael's burn: had a Michael drowned here? *Allt Clach Mheann* – the burn of 'the kid's stone'; *Beinn a Chruinneach* – the hill of the gathering; *Carn Leac Saighdeir* – the cairn of the soldier's grave; and Corriehoul itself, which comes from *Coire ghobhail* meaning 'corrie of the fork', denoting the fork made by the burn with a smaller stream coming from the hill above the modern cafe. The place name 'Corgarff' comes from the Gaelic *Coire-garbh,* meaning 'rough corrie'.

The reappropriation of the churches signals the more general decline in Christian congregations seen across the country, but Corriehoul was once the centre of religious activity in the valley, with Stock's chapel and the St Machar well remembered through the folk record.[10] There is little surviving documentary evidence for its existence, but the well intrigues me: its ghost still present in the landscape through folklore and inherited memory even if its physical presence may be long gone. Collected by Stock in the late nineteenth century, the following story survives:

> Once there was a famine in the district, and not a few were dying of hunger. The priest's house stood not far from the well. One day, during the famine, his housekeeper came to him and told him that their stock of food was exhausted, and that there was no more to be got in the district. The priest left the house, went to the well, and cried to St. Machar for help. On his return he told the servant to go to the well the next morning at sunrise, walk three times round it, in the name of the Father, Son, and Holy Ghost, without

looking into it, and draw from it a draught of water for him. She carried out the request. On stooping down to draw the water she saw three fine salmon swimming in the well. They were caught, and served the two as food till supply came to the famine stricken district from other quarters.[11]

There is something more ancient in this tale than Christianity: the shadow of much older pagan belief hangs over it. The salmon, with its transformative power as it makes its journey from river to sea and back again, has long been a symbol of knowledge and wisdom in Celtic belief and the subject of several myths, including that of Finnegas and Fionn in Irish mythology who go to a sacred well where the Salmon of Wisdom was said to live, so that they might catch and cook it, and in eating it gain its powers. These old, lingering beliefs and myths led priests to keep salmon in holy wells across Ireland and Scotland into the sixteenth century, adding wisdom, or perhaps the symbolic power of transformation, to the divine power of water.

Standing at the side of the road and looking out across the rough fields and along the slow trickle of the Corriehoul Burn, which runs off the slope above the cafe and under the road down to the Don just 150 metres away, I am not surprised but nevertheless disappointed to find no trace of an old chapel or well. The absence somehow makes its folkloric presence even more compelling: the mystery of its trace in the record making its power in the imagination more tangible. Tantalisingly, what is here, on the far side of the road to the cafe occupying the corner plot between the Don and the burn, is a nineteenth-century burial ground enclosed by an old stone wall. I open the iron gate and take a stroll amongst the well-kept graves.

The earliest stones appear to be from Elliot Stock's time, with a few graves reaching up to the present day. There is no church, but the cemetery sits on an older burial site, perhaps also the site of the chapel. In the Historic Environment Scotland archive, an entry from a field report in the mid-1990s tells us that 'The oldest stones

Corriehoul Burn.
PHOTO BY IAN GROSZ, 2019.

all lie towards the lower, S end of the present enclosure, and appear to correspond with the area of a smaller, sub-circular burial ground depicted on the 1st Edition of the OS 6-inch map (Aberdeenshire, sheet LXVIII, 1869)'.[12] Elliot Stock himself tells us that 'the present graveyard occupies the site of the chapel'.[13] The well is supposed to be in the field somewhere immediately east of the cemetery, but all I see is a boggy plot of ground full of hummocky, grass-filled knolls.

The Don, audibly present above the noise of regular passing traffic and the occasional bleating sheep close by, is more of a large stream than a river here at its upper reaches; but I am continually aware of its steady flow as the water courses down the valley beyond the gravestones. I make my way back out of the enclosure and pick up a path that follows the burn down to the river. The place where the two courses of water meet marks the natural boundary of the field to the east where the burial ground sits. The time of Elliot Stock's survey and the establishment of the cemetery are contemporaneous, and I wonder if he in fact found any trace of the well when he tells us confidently that 'this is a fine well'[14] or simply recorded it from the folk record. The presence of the graveyard and the evidence of there once being a much earlier burial site however, leads me to give Stock the benefit of my doubt. Thinking of Nicolaisen's findings in his work on the Picts and the places where the river would have held significance, the position of the current graveyard – right at the place where the Corriehoul Burn meets the Don – leads me to think that there must be some truth in the story of this old well despite there now being no trace of what Stock recorded in 1889.

There are other wells to be found in the region, but the ghost of Tobar Vachar, with its tale of the salmon – pagan symbol of knowledge and wisdom easily transposed into the ichthys, the Christian fish symbol – spans the journey I will take along this river and time: from the roots of once pagan beliefs to the later formation of the region's Christian parish boundaries and my journey's end at St Machar's Cathedral. In the absence of the well, I furtively toss my coin into the burn, make a wish, and move on downstream: out of Strathdon into lower Donside, and to a village that will take me further back in time still.

Standing stones and burial cairns

Arriving in Monymusk, a slow and sleepy village originally built for estate workers but now with new suburban houses spreading out behind the small square of old stone cottages facing the twelfth-century kirk, I park outside the Grant Arms: a hotel and bar until recent years, but now a guest house and cafe. I will take a short walk that will lead me northwards past the new houses to a small patch of woodland in search of the trace of much earlier residents and the remnant of their ancient religious practices.

The river Don slides peacefully by the village, winding its way around to the east, past the thirteenth-century Grant family estate house situated at its banks through farmland from the direction of Pitfichie. There, in 1995 at a place called Greenbogs, half a mile to the north of Monymusk on a low gravel terrace along the banks of the river, a Neolithic settlement was discovered.[15] The site revealed was a regionally significant village of houses and huts that was in use from the late Neolithic to the early Bronze Age. Investigating archaeologists discovered a small cremation cemetery to the north of the site, with the remains of a partly cremated bone still inside an intact pot. South of this, there was evidence of a large building. A palisade and 23 large postholes were uncovered, as well as a deep burning pit close by with ash 20 feet thick within it. The existence of three further buildings – large round huts that each would have perhaps housed several generations of a family – was established by their postholes. One field away, to the south, are the remains of a stone circle contemporary with the settlement, and it is this that I have come to find.

We perhaps imagine that life in northern Scotland during these times would have been grim and colourless; but the climate showed summer temperatures reaching 10 degrees warmer than today, and it was much drier, something akin to modern south of France. Life would have been hard, certainly, but not without its pleasures. There was time enough to dedicate to the building of large stone monuments that would have required the cooperation of the whole community and a unified belief system. The worldview of these early Scots remains open to interpretation, speculation and sometimes, wild imagination, but the stone circle, and others of a type unique to the northeast of Scotland, do provide some clues.

I walk northwards out of the village and arrive at a small stone bridge at the edge of woodland where a burn runs down towards the Don in a steep sided, shallow gully. The branches of rowan trees, heavy with berries, hang over the sides of the burn. The stones are just visible from the verge at the side of the road, standing amongst large horse chestnut and beech trees. Rising up in the distance, above thickly wooded lower slopes, is the prominent summit of Bennachie – a popular local hill which dominates the landscape of the lower Don valley, and the site of a once powerful Pictish hillfort.

Access to the stones looks difficult, with the wildly growing verge, a barbed wire fence and the steep sides of the burn apparently standing in the way, but I walk a few hundred meters further along the road and find an open gateway giving access to the field that stretches northwards and eastwards along the burn and the edge of the woodland. The field has been returned to meadow and is full of cowslip, large-headed daisies, purple-headed thistles and red campion. I make my way across the field back towards the burn and the woodland's edge. Other visitors have been here – the landowners perhaps, estate workers, or possibly just other people curious about the stones – and I follow a trail of flattened grass through the meadow. The plot of fields and woodland here, known in Victorian times as 'Druid's Park', is now known as Deer Park, so the trail I follow could have been created by deer foraging at the edge of the field. The burn again becomes audible above the hushing of the breeze through the trees and the gently swaying grasses of the meadow, and as I pick up the field boundary by the burn the stones come into view once more. I have a rising sense of excitement, as though I am making some new discovery.

To get across to the stones I must leave the meadow and wade through chest high swathes of willow herb and nettle before emerging into the open woodland. The stones stand in a clearing on a low but prominent mound, under the shade of the horse chestnut trees and not far from the fence and the burn at the woodland boundary. Their silence is palpable, and perhaps the knowledge that they have been placed there by people long gone – people we know so little about – creates an atmosphere that is likely internally generated and projected out onto the environment: one that comes from our own imaginations, our own awareness of mortality and the deep mysteries of time. Nevertheless, standing in the stillness of the wood with its earthy smells, and facing the stones with the sounds of the burn trickling down toward the Don, the gentle wind through the trees, there is an ambience that is tantalisingly apparent. At the base of one of the stones, I find a small, inscribed stone heart with a message to a lost loved one. It adds to the solemn atmosphere and reinforces the sense of this place as one of remembrance.

Just three stones remain intact in this relatively little known and modest circle – two of grey and one of pink granite standing at about chest height – but there are interesting features to note about it. The most interesting, is that it is situated so close to the settlement and probably includes a burial – the low mound where they are situated. The time spanning the use of this small monument in its various phases potentially covers a millennium, and itself dates back to around the Bronze Age. The weight of this time hangs heavy in the woods around me, woods that were planted by much later land owners, who even planted trees in a circle around the stones to enhance the atmosphere of what Alexander Ogg,[16] in his estate map of 1846, denoted quite wrongly, though perhaps understandably, to be a 'Druid's Temple'.

Victorian imaginations aside, the stone circles that appeared at around this time all across the British Isles – from Orkney down to the south coast and across Ireland and Wales – are certainly places

Deer Park Circle.
PHOTO BY IAN GROSZ, 2019.

Deer Park Circle.
PHOTO BY IAN GROSZ, 2019.

of remembrance, ritual, and perhaps even worship. No particular or significant celestial alignments are recorded for the Deer Park stone circle, and its current three stones – though appearing deliberate in number and alignment – are thought to have once numbered at least four. An empty space at the northern end of the mound would appear to support this, and they seem simply to have been a way of more permanently marking the old burial cairn – staking a claim to the long-buried dead. Given the length of time the nearby settlement was in use, and its relatively small size, placing the stones would seem a way of also claiming the land for the small but significant group who occupied the territory along this stretch of the river. Here, the stones tell us, is where our ancestors lie.

Elsewhere in Aberdeenshire, people built more impressive arrangements, and with a feature unique to north-east Scotland. These monuments are known as recumbent stone circles, since they each employ a massive stone lying on its side between two large, upright flanking stones. The recumbent stones, acting as a false horizon, align with the arc of the southern moon, and in some cases the rising and setting of the moon in the 18-year cycle of the so called 'standstill moon', when it reaches its maximum southerly declination, or position in the sky. Observing and predicting the passage of the seasons, and of the years – of time – was possible only through the movement of the celestial bodies and the passing of each generation. The moon's standstill, above the fertile river valley and hills of Aberdeenshire, would have been a significant – perhaps even sacred and portentous – event for the people living along the banks of the river and the land surrounding it.

Further downstream at Inverurie – its name taken from the Gaelic *Inbhir,* also meaning 'at the confluence of' in the same way as *Aber,* and *urie* from the river Urie, a tributary of the Don – an impressive and intact recumbent stone circle surrounds an earlier ring cairn. The site is known as East Aquhorthies, where the Gaelic word *Aquhorthies* popularly means 'field of prayer', perhaps revealing a connection to the site as a place of worship that stretches back to the time of the monument. The Gaelic word for field is *achadh,* which may have become the phonetic 'aqu' in the place name locally. The prayer inference is drawn from the word *ortha*, which in fact means 'incantation', 'charm', 'invocation' or 'spell', giving a combination of *achadh-ortha* becoming *aquortha*, and so it seems possible that early Gaelic speakers may have recognised the ritualistic nature of the site and given it this name. It is one of the best known and preserved circles of the region, consisting of nine stones surrounding the older ring cairn, and a large recumbent with its two, flanking upright stones. The massive recumbent arrangement is a mix of porphyry and red jasper, with red and grey granite making up the surrounding ring stones, chosen perhaps for the perceived magical properties of their colours and the quartz crystals and veins within them.

Quartz is associated with all the recumbent stone sites in one way or another, and at East Aquhorthies evidence of burnt quartz residues have been found, indicating some form of ritual perhaps centred on this material, the dead, and the moon's glow at standstill. One can only imagine the impact the qualities of light at this circle, and the reflections in the river, might have had on such clear and auspicious nights when the boundaries between the two worlds of light and darkness, the living and the dead, must have become blurred. These are the roots of our beliefs, the beginnings of our worship: people, place, and the passage of time.

In the twelfth-century kirk at the centre of the village of Monymusk, incorporated into the interior walls much later and taken from its original position close to the river nearby, is an eighth-century Pictish symbol stone; but to pick up that thread, we will move further downstream to another old church at Dyce.

Symbol stones and the early churches

I pull into the little car park beside the ruin of old Dyce church. Below me the river bends sharply around the high terrace where the church is sited, while overhead, passenger jets, and offshore helicopters transporting workers to and from the oil rigs of the North Sea, make their approach into the airport close by. Despite the airport and the modern bypass routed round the airfield boundary, the church is situated at a surprisingly tranquil spot, characterised by the small settlement of quaint houses reaching down to the opposite river bank at Cothal. With open views north and westward, I can look far back along the river meandering through the surrounding cultivated fields and disappearing into the dips and folds of the land. In the gently rippling waters below, I watch a family of swans ferry-glide themselves across the ever-present flow.

The graveyard surrounding the church is still in use, but the church itself is now an empty shell of four ivy-covered walls and a bell tower. It is dedicated to St Fergus, a man possibly of Pictish origin, contemporary with an Irish monk named St Drostan closely tied with bringing Christianity to the north east of Scotland. There are several churches and a holy well in Perthshire dedicated to him, though his legend is probably a conflation of two missionaries living a century apart.[17] Abandoned as a place of worship in 1872, the church at Dyce dates back to the thirteenth or fourteenth century. Like St Machar's Cathedral, it has associations as a place of worship going back much further – to early Christian and likely pre-Christian times. These associations are corroborated by the Dyce symbol stones, now on display inside the ruin and representing this transitional period in belief and customs.

In my copy of *In the Shadow of Bennachie: A Field Archaeology of Donside*, the authors refer to the patterns of symbol stone sites, saying that 'despite the wide range of topographical features, the presence of water nearby is a recurring theme'. Of the Dyce stones, they speculate that 'the primary function of the site may have been as a cemetery or cult centre at the edge of a territory', and that 'the range of sculpture appears to represent its transition into a Christian burial ground'.[18]

Two of the largest Pictish stones housed here, each standing at an adult's height or more, date from 600 AD and 700 AD respectively. One stone, showing a large Celtic cross as well as other symbols, also has an Ogham inscription, thought to have been introduced to Pictish society by the early Irish Christian monks as they evangelised their way across the country. My field guide tells me that it is likely that 'the symbols and Ogham inscriptions are essentially serving the same functions as specific locations in the landscape, locations lying at the edge of territories'.[19] The stones show the full range of commonly found symbols of Pictish design: the so-called V and Z-rod, a crescent, a double disc and a mirror and comb symbol, as well as mythic beasts and other mysterious figures. Although thought to mark out territory by family and tribal names established through ancestral ties to the land, what these symbols mean is anyone's guess, and the Ogham inscription remains elusively un-deciphered; though again, my field guide offers an explanation: 'the symbolised inscriptions – the latter probably naming individuals or groups – visually identify the territories'.[20]

More widely, the Pictish stones, often located in their original positions along watercourses and associated with ancient burial grounds, are thought in this way to have shaped the later established parish boundaries. My field guide contextualises the occurrence of the symbol stones in terms of the transition to new beliefs: 'The adoption of new religious practices is likely to have elicited complex responses from the more conservative sections of Pictish society', it tells us. 'This in itself may explain the relatively sudden appearance of the symbol stones in the archaeological record; in effect a reaction to the threat posed by Christianity to traditional religious practices and their role in secular power'.[21] The river's sacred status, then, was changing.

I am reminded of the older features in this landscape – the stone circles, burial mounds and settlements – all occupying the same territories as these symbol stones. My field guide tells me that

> no single explanation may fit all the stones, but modern excavation is beginning to confirm that one of their functions was to mark out the sites of burials, either individually or in cemeteries. Furthermore, it has been shown that many cemeteries of this date [500–800 AD] include [much earlier] circular and square cairn barrows.[22]

One notable example of this is at the village of Rhynie situated to the north and west of Dyce along the Gadie Burn, another tributary of the Don. Two groups of stones close to the village are significant: one on a low knoll south of the village centre, Bell Knowe, with a Bronze Age cairn that overlooks a medieval burial ground, and the other group centred on the Craw Stane, or Crow Stone, so called because crows are often seen perched on it. The stone bears the incised figure of a fish — probably a salmon — and a typical mythic beast sometimes likened to an elephant. Stones from this location were incorporated into the original parish church, the replacement of which sits within the old burial ground on a terrace at the foot of the slope on the west bank of the burn. The Craw Stane stands at the entrance to a substantial earthwork enclosure overlooking the Water of Bogie, where human remains have been unearthed as well as evidence of substantial buildings and associated artefacts dating to the sixth century, revealing it as a site of high status Pictish settlement. The name Rhynie itself has a regal etymology, derived from the Pictish word 'Rig' meaning 'king'. To the south of the village and the Craw Stane, the remnants of two square enclosures are the probable remains of much earlier Neolithic to early Bronze Age barrows.

More stones can be found at Kintore and Inverurie, both villages a few miles further upstream from Dyce that have grown from the banks of the river. At Inverurie, where the Don and the Urie meet, four stones were uncovered from the fabric of the old parish church, which stood at the high ground above the confluence of the two rivers. At Kintore, three stones have been uncovered: two from the medieval Motte — the earthwork base for an early style of castle and believed to have once been part of a much earlier stone monument — and a third, again, from the fabric of the old parish church. The stones at both Kintore and Inverurie show early Pictish symbols, and were later re-inscribed with Ogham markings. Notably, the stones at these two locations were turned upside down before re-inscription, indicating perhaps that what had held true before, possibly for millennia, now no longer applied.

Many more Pictish symbol stones stand across the region, and in all, thirteen have been found in re-use in the walls of old churches or their kirkyards along the Don, the example at the old kirk at Monymusk being just another one of them. Many are likely to have originally been part of Neolithic stone monuments. 'There can be little doubt of some causal relationship between the placing of these symbol stones and the positions of parish churches in the landscape', the field guide tells us.[23] And it seems, from the coincidences of burial, monument and settlement, that there can be little doubt that it is the river – this old goddess – and the role she played in spiritual life for people stretching right back to the Neolithic, that has helped shape the region.

The river and the thread of time

Standing in the cool quiet of the old ruined kirk at Dyce surrounded by its graveyard, and gazing at these stones with their location close to the river – this goddess flowing through the land and time – reminds me that I am part of an almost endless thread of human life and memory stretching back beyond the horizon of my own imagining. It is a dizzying experience. When placed within the context of the time held in this landscape – the narrative woven by the river – I have a feeling of being untethered, as though losing my place, drifting free of the reassuring anchors of daily life that bring the illusion of permanence.

As we begin to see this remnant landscape, time seems to coalesce so that everything blends together in a ghost patchwork of eerie synchronicity: the shadow memory of prehistoric people burying and commemorating their dead, just as the modern minister of an old parish church passes the ghost of a funeral rite conducted by first-century Picts, who, in their turn, re-use the old sacred spaces marked out by their ancestors along this river two thousand years and more before them. It is a landscape neck-deep in remanence: in the residual memory of people stretching back further than you are able to see or imagine, a ghost landscape full of ghosts.

If the massive Pictish stones dotted across Donside and Aberdeenshire mark out the dead, then what could we make of the inscriptions? Does the commonly found mirror and comb remind us to be modest, warn against vanity; a reminder that the flush of youth and beauty are but short-lived and that the long eternity of the grave awaits? Is the equally commonly seen Z-rod representative of the lightning bolt of death itself, reminding us that it comes quickly, and to all? Whatever these symbols mean, they are ours to interpret as we wish, and in this way the Picts speak to us across the many centuries since their time.

I leave the church and walk down the steep track to the river below the terrace. Taking a seat at the fisherman's shelter opposite the old houses at Cothal, I hear a chorus of intermingling voices in the murmur of the gentle rapids: a garbled babble of lost language, echoes of the people that have been before. I almost feel that I am myself a shadow, conscious of being a barely noticeable moment, as though I have passed to memory already in the ever-flowing river of life that courses through and shapes this landscape.

Although not religious, when I later visit St Machar's Cathedral close to the mouth of the Don, taking a seat between the vaulted granite archways and beneath the wooden heraldic ceiling, feeling the cool indifference of the stone around me, I am moved to silent prayer of sorts: to the legacy of human strife and suffering; the search for meaning and our place in the cosmos across the times we inhabit. 'Our lives are rivers', wrote Jorge Manrique, 'gliding free to that unfathomed, boundless sea'.

The Cucking of a Scold: River Dee, Aberdeen, Scotland

Ashleigh Angus

The Old Woman Who Was Drowned at Ratcliffe Highway.[1]

> *Then was the Scould her selfe,*
> *In a wheele-barrow brought,*
> *Stripped naked to the smocke,*
> *As in that case she ought:*
> *Neats tongues about her necke*
> *Were hung in open show;*
> *And thus vnto the cucking stoole*
> *This famous Scould did goe.*

'The Cucking of a Scould' (c. 1615)[2]

I was shivering out of my shift, the water stretching it, pulling it down over my chest, as the seat rose up from the river. I felt the townsfolk's eyes on my loosened breast. Spoons hit basins; tongues hit teeth. They were laughing at me. They were shaking hands with my husband. Where was Marjorie? She was probably clinging to him, tilting her head back, stretching out her long pale neck, baring her teeth.

They lowered me down again, and I was under for such a long space, that I began to think the men had walked away from the cucking stool, leaving me rocking at the bottom of the river, the pain in my chest filling, filling, water laughing down my throat; but they jolted me back up again, very quick. The river tightened its grip on me as I rose, pulling at my hair and sucking my shift down to my stomach.

The townsfolk curved around the cucking stool, looking like rows of yellow teeth swaying as the wind whistled through them, like my husband's teeth did when he sighed deeply while looking at the hole at the back of our house: the hole heaving with filth and piss, filling, filling, because neither my husband or I would dig another, and when it rained, it overflowed; but it was good for the soil, my husband said, leaning towards me, his breath smelling the same as the ditch.

I was cleaner than all there, emerging free of dirt; teeth washed, eyes dry.

They lowered me onto the soil. The wind pinched every part of me, and my legs shook as I stepped out of the chair. The earth beneath me softened as I drooled on to the soil. I saw, at the corner of my eye, my husband moving back into the crowd. I thought I saw Marjorie's hand upon his elbow.

I gripped my shift at my knees with one hand and clutched my neckline with the other. I walked, head down, passed the smiling townsfolk, twisting my feet further and further into the ground with each step, and easing mud onto my feet with my toes.

I dressed behind the cart, catching my skirts before they fell on to my ankles so as not to disturb the mud I had gathered.

I held my feet like two upright shovels as they pulled me home, balancing the mud on top of them.

I kept them fixed there like that, the tops of my feet straining, as I lowered myself out of the cart, and I wobbled on my heels to my husband's door.

How soon I had stepped inside, when I saw Marjorie's pale mouth gaping at me, her eyes red and wide. 'I am sorry,' she said, fluid bubbling between her lips. She wiped her cheeks, 'I am so sorry.'

She stood, pulled her shawl off her shoulders, and draped it over mine.

I shrugged it off and sat where she had been sitting: in my husband's chair. It was warm.

'Don't be sore with me, Mary. I did not ask for this; what was I meant to do? I did not think they *would* put ye in the stool.'

I lifted my skirt, admiring the mud I had collected. It had dried around my toes but was still damp where it was piled high on my ankles. A little spit would wet it back up again.

'I am here, aren't I?' said Marjorie, stepping in front of me, touching her chest to assure me she was solid and real. 'I waited for you. I did not go. I did not want to see ye dunked, Mary – I didn't.'

'Will ye fetch me a bowl?'

She startled. 'Yes – yes – anything. A cloth?'

I shook my head. 'Just a bowl.'

'Anything.'

She walked towards the bench, saying all the while that she thought they would only warn me, only threaten me a little until I stopped. But of course, I didn't stop. I kept spreading such cruel lies and she did not know why – *why* Mary, why? We were friends, were we not?

'What was I supposed to do?' she said, handing me the bowl and sitting in the chair next to me. 'I had to clear my name; I *had* to. I couldn't have everyone going around thinking – Mary?'

I scraped the mud from my feet and into the bowl, gathering the wet bits first, then flicking the dry parts from my toes.

Marjorie slumped in the chair, stretching her legs towards the fire. 'I'm tired of fighting with ye, Mary; I *really* am.'

I spat into the mud and rubbed it in with my fingertips, mixing it with all the other fluids which wetted the earth beside the Don: the spit, tears, sweat, and frightened piss of all the scolds and witches who had been dunked there.

Marjorie cried silently. She was greasy, the strands of her hair thick and dark, her fingers calloused, tears cleaning lines in her cheeks.

I scooped the mud onto my fingers, balancing it carefully, and stood.

Marjorie looked up at me. '*Promise* ye will stop,' she said feebly.

I cupped her cheek with my clean hand.

She closed her eyes, wringing out a few more tears, and leaned into my palm.

I raised my other hand as if to cup her other cheek and slapped the mud across her face, smearing it down onto her mouth.

Marjorie's eyes and lips flapped open. She stood, knocking the chair backwards. 'Ye're mad!' She wiped away the mud. 'Ye're mad!' she screeched, flicking it at me.

It sprouted like moles on my arm.

'Mad!' She pushed me aside and fumbled with the latch on the door, coating it with dirt.

The door slammed. The latch rattled. Mud drooped onto the floor.

I washed my arms, feet, and hands thoroughly: scrubbing, scouring, picking, scratching until my skin was raw. The stone floor was cold and hard beneath my heels.

I cleaned the house, going and returning from the burn with several pails before I was satisfied. I did not use the street but walked behind the houses and along the corn fields, so as not to meet anyone on my way.

As soon as I finished cleaning, I began to shiver. My dress was heavy and cold. I pulled at my bodice weakly, stepped out of my skirts and draped them over my husband's chair. I sat. My shift lightened under the warmth of the fire, peeling away from my stomach and my breasts. I stared at the flames, not much caring that they were dying, and savouring the feeling of the cold as it swam into my lungs because it reminded me of the river water, and below the river I would not have to face my good husband as I had to now.

He stepped behind me, took my arm, and plucked me out of his chair.

I was not clean for long. Soon, I smelled of him. I slid out of the bed and over to a pail. I splashed water over my arms, my face, and more carefully now, my privie parts. I could taste the river on my lips. What would it be like, to rest my head there, in that pail?

Boils grew on Marjorie's cheek and the hand she had used to swipe off the mud, pulsing with fluid. I looked at it with satisfaction for my good husband did not call her to the house anymore, not as long as her face was so disfigured. But Katherine Lang came instead, and I wished I had not rinsed away all of the mud. My belly grew like a boil too, also filling with fluid, sometimes fluttering as though it were alive.

I visited Marjorie's mother, who was a cripple and a widow and needed someone to go to the market for her every Saturday. I had been going for her for two years now, as Marjorie had four children and could not carry any more from the stalls. I enjoyed going to the market for Marjorie's mother. I enjoyed accepting the first price asked for, even though it was always far too much, and spending all her money on it, and when she complained about how little I got for the money, I widened my eyes, looked at her blankly, and said that I had tried as best as I could but I was not so good at arguing; and she replied hotly that my tongue was as sharp as a whip and she was sure I would have no trouble at all if only I committed myself to the effort. I smiled simply in reply. The good woman added, quite proud, that her chopping knife was yet sharper, and that she would cut my tongue as small as herbs to the pot if I did not begin to use it on her behalf; and I thought she would do quite well at the markets herself if she had the use of her legs.

I had not taken one step out from the woman's door when Marjorie charged at me and ripped the coins from my hand. 'I don't want you going to the market for her anymore,' she said.

I stepped backwards, into the open door, but Marjorie stayed where she was, in the middle of the street.

'*I* will go for her,' said Marjorie.

'What's the matter with yer face?' Marjorie's mother cried out behind me, from her bed.

Marjorie replied that I had witched a boil on her cheek; and I wished she would not use the word 'witched', any word but that. People were stopping on the street and opening up their shutters to peer down at us.

I replied that it was but mud, and the boil would not have formed there if she washed her face as often as I, and then I asked if she would like to wash it in the river. The cucking stool was outside my master's house; we could strap her in and have her in the water in no time.

Marjorie's mother began making weak sounds behind me.

Marjorie assured her mother that it was all right. *She* would not occupy the stool; it was still warm from my base body and would yet be warmed by it again.

Heads hung out windows now like white plague flags.

Marjorie said, louder now, that it would do me good to be put in the river once more, for the first time had done little to cool my tongue. I had yet been sauntering up and down the town, pretending I was an honest woman, but slandering women far more honest than myself, and she said that I had not kept my promise (though I had never made one) to cease slandering her good name by saying to all that would listen that she was my husband's whore. Marjorie said her name was clean and that there were others who were guilty of whoring with my husband but not her, and that I knew exactly who she spoke of for I was head bawd, admitting several women into the house to satisfy my husband so that he may leave me alone; so that I might be freed from my own wifely duties, and that Katherine Lang does come to the house, as does Alice Young, who is a famous whore, and several other women who she does not know the name of. 'I am honest,' she said. 'And the only honest woman who has ever stepped foot in your good husband's house.'

A crowd had gathered now, all looking disgusted at me, as though it were *I* with the boil on my face.

'Ye are a whore,' I told Marjorie.

Marjorie's mother whimpered.

'And yer mother is a bawd,' I added.

Now her mother let out several cries. They were muffled, as if she had thrust the bed clothes into her mouth.

'And yer husband is a cuckold,' I added, stating these things like the facts they were. I did not want to appear flustered and desperate like Marjorie.

Marjorie reddened and said I was a filthy liar and that she had never lain with any man but her husband. She bade me step out of her mother's house, for she would not have her mother be seen with someone with as ill a name as I. Her face twisted so gruesomely, the skin around her boil growing more and more red, looking as if it might well burst with the force of her expression, and I imagined the fluid running down her neck and was almost sick with the thought of what it might smell like.

She said I was never to visit her mother again, and that I was never to sit on her pew in the Kirk, and never to borrow anything from her, or speak to her husband or her children.

I assured her that I would never be friends with such a brazen faced whore as she was. 'Ye are a glew whore; ye have stolen my life from me.'

I stepped out of her mother's house, brushed past her and stalked down the street towards my husband's house, telling all who had gathered there that it would not fare well for them to be seen in Marjorie's company. The folk banged their shutters and thrust basins against the wall to drown me out. Marjorie, with the townsfolk pressing up behind her, yelled after me: 'A cart and a basin *ting ting*, a cart and a basin *ting ting*, a cart and a basin if thou wilt not be quiet.'

The cart was outside my husband's house the next morn, blocking the door. I climbed over it, my skirt catching on splinters in the wood. I stepped down from the cart, but my dress had caught on a nail. I ripped my skirt away in anger, tearing it at the knee. I kicked the cart and screamed, so everyone in the street might hear, 'I will cut my throat!'

I made sure there was a clean pail of water in the house every night. Some three nights after my quarrel with Marjorie, I came out to wash myself and, reaching into the water, felt something rough and greasy at the bottom. I picked it up, feeling it slip and stir in my hand. It hung limply over my palm: a cow's tongue. I flung it back into the water, jumping back to avoid the splash. I swallowed and took several breaths. I could not be sick. It was too late to walk to the burn, and I would have no way to clean myself.

I paced all night, feeling my husband's grease thickening on my skin. I scratched at it, and it curled away from me like wax. I plucked strands from my hair, leaving them in a pile on the bench to bury later. I wanted to remove all of it, for it was coated in my husband's palm sweat, but the sun rose before I had even cleared out a good patch from my scalp.

The next day, I carried the pail down the street. Water slushed over the cow tongue and the knife I had rested beside it. I stopped at Marjorie's door, lifted the tongue out, lined it up with the centre of the door, and thrust the knife into it. It slipped through the flesh and wood with a satisfying *thunk*. Then, I wiped my hands on my apron, picked up the pail and continued to the burn.

When I returned to my husband's house, she was there. Katherine Lang looked loose and happy, tottering around the place unsteadily. I could not see my husband but could hear his laughter coming from behind the curtain of the box bed. His laughter was deep and hearty. I am sure it was I who was the source of it. Katherine's expression shrunk when she saw me, and my husband's laughter came to a quick end. The curtain of the box bed was remarkably still. I liked to think of him huddled behind there, tense and unbreathing, hoping I had not heard him.

Katherine turned very red. She began explaining that she was there for butter; she had none, you see, and I had borrowed from her not too long ago—did I not remember? She was only there for butter. Only butter. The woman's red face scrunched and folded this way and that. It looked to me like dough would if kneaded by bloody hands. Her mouth worked in fear, and it was my hands that shaped it.

She said she did not mean to disturb me, straightened her dress, and wished me a good day as she walked out the door.

I followed her out on to the street, asking her if she still wanted the butter. 'I'll be glad to give it ye, ye being *such* a good neighbour.' I raised my voice. 'That *is* why ye came to my house, is it not, Katherine?'

'Yes – yes. I didn't think ye would –'

'Ye look very red Katherine, are ye well? Anyone would think,' I paused, letting the heads slide fully out from their windows, 'that in your rush to leave ye had gotten what ye really came for; ye look quite hot, your skirt very creased. Well, one might think that ye had come to my house when ye saw me going out to the burn to play the whore with my husband – one *might* think.'

'I – I,' Katherine stumbled, looking at the faces above her. 'Butter – yes – ye just seemed so – *unwilling* –'

'Not at all. Please,' I said, turning towards the house. 'Did my husband not give ye any butter?'

'He is not home.'

'But he *is*,' I said.

'He said ye had none.'

I smiled. 'We have plenty. I will wrap some for ye.'

Katherine had all but confirmed her guilt in front of several townsfolk that day, but her husband stood up in Kirk that Sunday and publicly declared that he was not a cuckold and that the slanderous words going around town about his wife were nothing but filthy lies which came from the mouth of the notorious scold Mary Brown, and that was enough to absolve her of any guilt, for no one wanted to go against her husband who was an elder of the Kirk. I was sent for after sermon to appear before Katherine's husband and the Kirk session and answer for my continuous slander and abuse of honest women.

My scalding tongue was once again sentenced to be cooled in the river; seven dips this time, and I was glad of it, because seven is a good number. I paced in sevens; I washed my hands seven times before bed; I plucked strands of hair from my head seven at a time. But I did not show the session my delight at the charge, for fear they might make it six or eight; six being a very evil number indeed.

They wheeled me up the Gallow Gate, past the corn fields and the Gallow hills, past Spital hill, King's College, and, last of all, Machiar Kirk, which sat beside the Don. When we were on cobble stones, the basins tied to the cart laughed feverishly: on dirt ground they chuckled, on mud they rang, on rocky ground they simpered wearily. Townsfolk followed behind us, very excited at first, but tiring with the long walk. More folk joined us as we passed their crofts, mixing with the crowd and banging on their basins heartily, encouraging the crowd to start up their chants again. Some became so passionate in the drumming that they tried to leap onto the cart, only to have their feet flattened by the wheels, and I was quick to call these people the witless beasts they were. The cucking stool trailed behind the crowd, its seat nodding up and down like the head of a great bird, pecking at the heels of the townsfolk.

Katherine's husband said I was taking too long to remove my dress but did not want to be seen doing it for me, so he called upon his servant to. The servant boy did so excitedly, ripping it from my shoulder down to my feet in one long stroke, as though unveiling some new statue in the Kirk.

The servant then draped the necklace of cows' tongues over my neck. The tongues were cool, smooth – clinging to my chest like three drooping, disfigured breasts. I gagged at the smell of them – full and warm, sticking to the lower half of my face. One of the tongues had a great, gaping slit in its middle, one not made by the needle and string threaded through to make the necklace. No, this was the same tongue I had found in my pail, and the same tongue I had nailed to Marjorie's door. Where *was* Marjorie? Was that her hand flapping in the air, waving at her husband who was to work the cucking stool?

I sunk into the chair, relaxing as the straps were tightened around my waist, wrists, and ankles. The seat had the same straight back and wide arms as my husband's chair.

The seat lifted and swung over the river, dipping and jerking as it went, as though the men moving it could not hold its weight.

With a sudden, awful drop, I was in the water. It surged into my ears and my nose; it numbed the gaps between my teeth and cooled my eyes. The river was a grey, greenish black. White bubbles floated before me. These bubbles turned into the faces of the townsfolk, bobbing up and down, leaning close then pulling away from each other, trembling with glee; and then I was bobbing down once more, having not taken one breath. I could not tell if my skin was sinking into my chest or if the trapped air was pushing out from it, but I believed what I was feeling was the pain and confusion that accompanied death, and with this thought, the confusion turned into relief. I think I was raised a few more times after that, holding my breath each time. The men seemed to have little control over the chair, but I suppose I had grown fatter since last time, the strings of my bodice no longer closing neatly over my stomach.

The water forced me up, out of the chair, and I strained against the straps. The river would have expelled me if I were not tied down, and if the folk were to dunk me as a witch, I would float; and if I were to try and drown myself, I would need many stones to make sure I sunk. And if I did not run out of breath today, perhaps I could ask one of my husband's women to wheel the cucking stool to the river. I am sure Marjorie would gladly strap me in, lower me down, and walk away, leaving its great pecking neck buried in the water. I thought about how my body would first bloat, the leather stretching, cutting into my wrists, and then how it would shrink, the river ringing me out, squeezing, squeezing, pressing my skin closer and closer to my bones, my fluid leaking out of my pours, my skin wrinkled and sagging like a soaked shift draped over a starving maid; and then how my skin would be stripped from me, thinning, thinning, until my bones swam in the chair, bobbing against the leather straps, then slipping out of them, finally freed from endless sitting; stretching out as the river carried me down and polished my bones as they rattled along the rocks; I would settle like a skin at the top of the water, be lapped up by the mud, scooped up by others, and used to raise boils on open skin, and over time to be collected by black fingernails. Surprised by a sudden shock of cold air, I gasped.

There was Marjorie, standing beside her husband. She looked as disappointed as I was that I was still breathing.

The dark, the light, the river

Adam Kealley

Above the brig
The Chain Brig stretches its iron arms across the Dee, from Craiglug to Ferryhill.

Across the river, chimneys from the foundry and the brewery give the air an ashen, yeasty taste, like bread left too long on the fire. Beyond them lies the grand city of Aberdeen, with its forest of spires and smokestacks, its granite palaces and filthy tenements. Wealth and squalor cheek by jowl.

From his perch on the black rock, the boy gawks at the bridge, its length held up by giant chains slung between grey stone arches stood at either end. Each link is thicker than his two hands clasped together. It is a true marvel. At the far end, the eight-sided toll house squats like a blain on the road. He rarely has the coin to pay, but he knows a billie who'll let him cross in return for a quick fumble in the bushes.

He remembers the feel of those greasy hands on his skin, and pushes the thought away again. It is a little sin, he thinks, and worth it to escape the city. Here, he can breathe, the air not so close with smoke and sweat and stink. Here it is quiet, away from the constant noise, the press of people. The granite city is so different from home, a handful of bothies huddled by a bow in the river. But home is more than thirty miles away, where the hills rise up and springtime comes late. He'd go back there if he could, but knows he'd get a rude welcome. He is banished, ever since he took his eye off the bairn and he slipped in and under the dark waters, his da too trying to save the wee'un. Ever since his maw, wearing nowt but her nightdress, followed a fuath into the river one moonlit night to find them.

Blood-thirsty Dee
Each year needs three.

He shivers. All up and down the river, the old ways run deep as the Dee itself. Despite his cries that the curse were paid, they thought him marked by the faery fowk and turned him out on the road.

And so he followed the blackwater to the great city, finding a dozen others on the road all looking to labour in its factories or dig for the new railway. All full of heartache and hope.

Below the brig, the salmon fishers call to each other, one rowing his coble across the river, net shedding out behind him. The boy watches idly as, without stopping, the fisher loops back, catching up any fish unlucky enough to have tumbled through the narrows. Once back on shore, men haul in the net. A shout goes up as a clumsy hand loosens the pocket, and the wriggling catch spills onto the shingle. A laugh steals from his throat as several men splash about in the shallows, snatching at the quicksilver salmon while they flop and buck about. Some get away and he offers them a green-eyed prayer for Godspeed.

He gazes out again to the city, knowing he must return there soon. Past Craiglug, the Dee turns sharply, as if afeart to meet the cold, grey sea. Twice a day, the tide surges in, filling the harbour and turning the river mouth into a wide flat basin filled with boats, before pulling back to expose mudflats cut through with channels just deep enough for a clever pilot to navigate.

The tide is in now and at Po'cra jetty lies a fine three-masted sailing ship. A whaler. He has heard, on days he spares the tuppence for a mug of ale in the tavern, that these ships sail far away to the north, and hunt the great beasts in seas so cold they freeze right over. Sometimes a ship gets caught up in the ice, timbers groaning until they splinter like matchsticks. That's if the whales don't sink them first. Sailors like to stretch a tale, he knows, but Fitty the pilot's house has an ivory arch in the garden, made of two whale jawbones that rise much higher than he can reach. He can barely imagine such a creature, but they'd be a fair match for any ship, he'd wager.

The whaler has already unloaded its stinking cargo, and the boilyards in Fitty are belching clouds of greasy smoke. He has seen the vast kettles, full of boiling whale oil, and knows that ladies and gentlemen of a more delicate constitution will be walking with handkerchiefs clasped to noses, complaining of the stench. He takes more than a little pleasure in the thought.

The salmon fishers have folded their nets and packed their catch. They'll be bound for the sprawling fish market in Shiprow. The boy finds work there sometimes, knows the press of the crowd, the cobbles slick with fish guts and slime, the air thick with the cries of fishers and their wifies. It is loathsome work, and the fishermen are cheap. He earns pennies, despite being quick with his hands. But those quick hands he's trained to make better coin in other ways.

His empty belly cramps, and his eyes turn again to the Chain Brig, the Dee churning through the Narrows.

The sun is dipping lower in the sky, and soon the gas lamps will be lit. They bring a wondrous light to the fine streets of the city, but it is the shadows in between that quicken his breath.

It's there he'll earn himself a fine feed.

All for a silver coin

In the sunlight, Aberdeen granite glints as if flecks of precious silver are trapped in its ancient mass. But here, deep in the shadows under Union Bridge, the stone is always dark.

He has run all the way from Broad Street, dodging through narrow laneways and past the great Mither Kirk. On a Sunday, as the good fowk stream out of the church, pickings are always good. Especially from the well-to-do, those who mutter prayers for the poor whilst hoarding coin to build their grand houses. He won't take his tithe there, on consecrated ground. But once they walk through the kirkgate into the streets, the sermon fading in their ears, well, then he figures they're fair game. Them and their purses.

His nimble fingers are a source of pride. They keep his belly filled. But today, a loose cobble sent him sprawling, coins scattering. Were he not up so quick after, his brains might have joined them, the man's walking stick striking the stone instead.

In the gloom he crouches, squeezing his thin body into the smallest possible space. He is wedged between a tenement and the soaring bridge that carries Union Street above his head. He slows his breathing, mouth wide. He is pressed against the cold stone, green and slimy with scum. He scoops dirt and rubs it over his pale face, becoming one with the shadows. He knows to wait until he is certain of his getaway. He has been whipped round the Mercat Cross before, for a ha'penny loaf of bread, and he has no desire to renew his acquaintance with the lash.

He risks a glance. Through the great arch he sees the washer wifies at their trade on the Green, bleaching fine linens in tubs of steaming piss. He could slip amongst the hanging poles until he makes the trees – but knows to do so risks their irate shrieks.

The other way, the Denburn, little more than a stinking sewer, fingers its way to the harbour. That way, he thinks. He knows those streets as well as his own poor dead maw's face, better even. Which lanes twist to bewilder any that give chase, which lead to the bustling docks where he can hide amongst the barrels and crates, and where shrewd eyes are less likely to point him out to a pursuer. He knows better than to put too much faith in the dockers and fishers and whores, though. They'd as likely sell him out as save him. He is still a suspicion, a pale, fey thing of the Highlands.

A shout is raised nearby. His heart hammers against his ribs as footsteps approach. He tries to shrink further into the wall. The footsteps slow and voices call back and forth. *Doon here. Nae, here. Curse 'im! This way.* The granite seems to press down on him, squeezing out his very breath. His body burns, like when he had the sweating fever. The steps pause. He cocks his head, trying to figure out where the feet they belong to are standing. He hears only a horse clattering over the bridge, the calls of its driver.

He takes a chance and bursts out of his hiding place. Turning sharply, he heads for the docks. There, the town is older, standing firm as they tore down whole streets to make way for the great bridge. There, among the stores, the dosshouses and tenements, he will be safe.

A meaty fist closes around his collar and he is yanked clear off his feet. *Cotcht ye, boy*, for a mere boy he is. The constable says it with a sneer, and shakes him. The boy struggles, twisting this way and that until a hard slap has him seeing stars.

What've we here, then? A thievin' loon? The copper's rotten breath is in his face. The boy stays silent, knowing he is done for.

Clutched in his dirty hand, and damning him, is a silver half-crown.

Full of grace

The ship rears and bucks like a runaway pony. The great sails have been taken in and safely furled, leaving only the foresail to keep the *Shepherd* running before the storm. Cresting another mountainous wave, the ship pauses, pauses, and plunges downward. Yet sailors still clamber about the deck overhead, their rough-edged cries lost to the winds that howl around them.

He grips his bunk with all the strength his fingers can muster, and tries to hold on to the contents of his gut. The ship shudders, gains its keel and rises again. By his reckoning, it is mid-afternoon, but the storm clouds have beaten the sun into a sulking dusk.

The air is rank with piss, puke and the whimpering of boys. Those unlucky enough to be assigned the hammocks, strung down the centre of the ward, have long been tossed from their knotted cocoons. They cling to posts now, or to tables bolted to the floor. Some of the boys huddle two to a bunk, clutching each other tight in the gloom. But unlike in the long evenings, it isn't a haunted tenderness that draws them together, it is fear. Misery shines in every eye.

The Bibles used for their lessons spill from their shelf. They slide from one end of the ward to the other with each lurch of the waves. He wonders if this is the hour of their death, if they will drown, like the Egyptians who hounded Moses into the sea. As if summoned by the thought, the preacher bursts through the door from the next ward. His mouth starts to move, the sounds tossed about in the great roaring. The boy watches as the preacher's lips form words, and recognises the Absolution. Stiff fingers trace a ghostly cross in the air.

A shower of water plunges through the iron bars of the hatch and a wailing erupts from amongst the boys. The preacher disappears from the doorway, swallowed by the shadows.

He believes God forsook him long before tonight, but he whispers the Hail Mary anyway.

This strange place
They are held in a long wooden building, 28 wretched souls. It is stifling. Every breath sears his chest. He remembers a man he once saw, who staggered out into the streets from the great brick kiln with bloody froth dripping from his chin. He had breathed in lime and died choking as it burned away his lungs. He cannot shake the vision, and pushes through the bodies to gasp at the salted air that slips in round an ill-fit window.

He is glad to be clear of the *Shepherd*, his home for near on four months. Through the grimy glass he sees the ship at anchor, its three masts listing in the breeze. Its white sails are furled, and porters are loading on barrels of fresh water. In its belly, he knows, there are still more boys. Only some of them were taken off the ship here, the rest bound for Van Diemen's Land. After weeks of gruel and hard biscuits, of lessons and sermons until his head ached, of the constant shifting of the deck beneath his feet, he is glad to feel the steadiness of solid ground.

They are locked in the building. More than one boy has beaten against the door, begging for a draught of water, of air. The door, however, stays mute. He thinks it pointless they are so confined. There are only a handful of buildings in the town, scattered along a wide dirt road. There are none of the alleys and laneways down which he can vanish. There are no clusters of warehouses with dark shadowed corners. No tangle of crates and nets. There is nowhere to hide in this strange place.

At one end of the village, atop the cliff, is a stone building. It looks out over the wooden huts that cluster at its foot. It is eight-sided, like the toll house on the Chain Brig, he thinks, but it is fashioned of pale stone, so different to the dark granite half a world away. It is bigger than the toll house, but squat, like a tower begun and abandoned in this wicked heat. Its walls are windowless, and somehow more unnerving for it. Beneath it, the gaping mouth of the tunnel cuts through to the dock. The building was carefully pointed out to them all. It is a warning, a threat. It is a prison. Despite the heat, seeing it makes him shiver. He has seen too much of the inside of a cell already.

There is the rattle of a key. The door opens and he blinks in the sudden brightness. One by one the boys look up, misery plain on their faces. They are brought out into the daylight and made to line up. Despite the early hour, sweat soon streaks their skin and bloated flies find their eyes, their mouths. A wet stain appears down the trousers of the one next to him, and he shifts his feet in the sand to avoid being soiled. His throat burns, he is parched. A hollow-cheeked man ladles out water, but it is warm and merely makes his thirst more fierce.

The sky above him is frightening, burned almost white by a searing sun. It seems huge, this sky, a suffocating weight that presses down on his head. It makes him dizzy. He wonders if they have sailed all the way to hell.

Men arrive and walk along the line, sizing up boys like they're fattened lambs. Choosing one, they consult with a man in spectacles, who sits at a desk making notes in a green ledger. Then the men shake hands, and another boy is led away. They take the biggest ones first. Now there are just the youngest and skinniest left. The trouser-wetter and him.

Two men stride up. One stops before the boy, eying him suspiciously. The other hangs back, leaning into the meagre shade of the wall. A musket is tucked in the crook of his elbow. A grimy hand grips the boy's chin, his head turned from side to side. Next, his hands are examined, then his arms. Poked and prodded, he feels sullied and his cheeks redden. The man casts a glance back at the other fellow, who shrugs and walks on. After a final cold stare into the boy's eyes, the first spits at his feet and then follows.

These men are to be their masters. They are apprentices here, they are told, not convicts. Their sins will be washed away, pardoned in return for a one-way voyage to the Swan River Colony to work off their crime. But the men who arrive to inspect them look lean and hungry. Their clothes are threadbare and the boy wonders if they have the coin to pay the promised wages.

He wonders many things, but mostly he wonders what will happen when he is finally chosen.

The unseelie river
The boy groans as he pulls another neep from the ground. He sits back on his heels, trying to ease his aching back. He brushes dirt off the root. It is a stunted, malformed thing. He tosses it in the basket with a dozen others just like it. The ground all around this place is either swamp or sand, and only good for growing stunted, malformed things. Even the trees here wear strange, drab hues. He longs for the colours of home – the deep blue-green of the pine forests, the purple heather or the grassy freshness of the glens, even

the dark, dark waters of the Dee. He spits and stands to stretch, pulling his sopping shirt away from his skin and unsettling a cloud of flies.

The white sun is enough to drive him mad, a constant beating on his head that made him puke the first day he were put to work. It leaves him feeling wrung out, skin reddened and lips peeling. He is miserable each day until the afternoon breeze comes in to clear the worst of the heat. And he cannot get used to the sky, the vast burnished weight of it. It makes him feel small, too small for God to find him, maybe. He feels truly forsaken, even more than he did when he lost his maw and pa and the bairn, more than when his own fowk cast him out, and even more than when the iron doors of Parkhurst clanged shut behind him.

The river road leads into the heart of the settlement, with its handful of buildings huddled at the base of the cliff. Some fowk have built wooden houses along the road, but others still live in canvas tents. The whole town is pinched between two bays, one on the sea and one on the river. It is a place that seems barely held together. He has, during the meagre time off he is granted each evening, walked from one sorry side to the other. He doesn't go through the streets often, though. Too many cannot keep their suspicion for the likes of him from their faces, nor their sharp words. But no matter where he walks, the Roundhouse atop the headland is always visible, casting its watchful eye over the settlement – and the boys brought here to serve its needs. He knows the forked tongue of its stairs has already swallowed up one, accused of killing his master's son. There were no reason for the killing, he heard an old gossip telling his master, no reason at all, but the boy knows the maddening heat and the petty cruelties are enough to drive any to murder.

It's been weeks since he were chosen, his master striking a deal with the man who wrote it carefully down in his ledger. He'll not see his wages, though, they too will be written into the green book, and only given to him after he's served his time. For safe-keeping, they said, he'll only squander it. But how is he to trust that the Guardian won't run off with it? Or whether his master will even pay? His master is new here too, and still figuring out how to make things grow. If he doesn't figure it out soon, the boy broods, he won't make enough to feed him, let alone pay him his due.

One bitter thought leads to another. So much for the trade he learned, one supposed to make him useful to his society. He were taught tailoring by a quiet man who came to Parkhurst each day – he shudders to think of that cold island prison – a man who didn't hit them too often, not even when a boy broke a needle or cut the cloth wrong. But what use were a dozen tailor's apprentices in a place like this? It were bleeding obvious that most fowk were barely scratching by and weren't queuing up to be fitted for fine suits. One lad were taken in at the laundry, and another to help sew the coppers' uniforms, but the closest he has come to a needle and thread were to mend the master's fishing net.

The house he shares with his master is small, just a single room with rushes to cover the dirt floor. But there's glass in the windows and he has a pallet of his own to sleep on. It is, he admits on days when he feels less grim, better than the icy streets round Aberdeen harbour or the stairwell of a tenement with four families a floor, and a far cry from a bunk in the hull of a rolling ship. The floor is steady, even if nothing else is in this woeful life. It lies close to the river, and he leaves the basket of neeps inside and wanders down to the bank to wash.

The river is wide and seems at peace, a blue so deep it seems almost grey. Its surface catches the light like shivered glass, and he is reminded of the sparkling stone of Aberdeen. There, he was grateful for any peep of sun that danced upon the granite, but here it is a fierce and relentless beast. A pair of swans, for which this river was named, drift upstream. They are not the regal birds of home, but are painted a devilish black, their beaks red as blood. He crosses himself, and waits until they are out of sight before he slips off his boots and steps into the shallows.

The water is cool on his skin, but he is careful not to stray far from shore, lest it catch him in its slippery hands. It has a spiteful temper, whichever fuath lives in its depths. He has heard it drowned a man with nowt a wave to be seen.

He squints across to the other side, where the woods are thick and shadows deep. He sees faeries there sometimes, quietly watching him right back. He never saw the faery fowk of the Dee, nor their dark mistress, but those here are right queer, their skins burnt black by the fearsome sun. His maw used to sing of the Ghillie Dhu, the dark boy, a faery who lived by the loch where she were born. Others round here are angered of these faery fowk, but he knows the Ghillie Dhu bears no grudge for young 'uns like him. The masters, well, they are right to be afeart. Clad in leaves and moss, the dark boy is all but invisible and he takes poorly to those who tread unwelcome in his realm.

He hears a commotion and sees three lads running along the riverbank. He squints, the better to make them out. He knows them, they shipped together. He is surprised to see their like together, the masters usually stand in the way of the boys being friendly, lest past crimes become present ones. He gets to his feet as they skitter to a halt in the sand.

Have ye heard? one says, eyes alight with something that sets the boy's belly aflutter. He shakes his head.

It's John Gavin, says another, *he's set to hang. They're building the gallows right atop the hill.*

The people be crying out, the first says, *for all us to be locked up, that we can none of us be trusted.*

The third says nothing, but clutches the shirts of the others, breathing in short, hiccoughing gulps.

Their fright is catching, and the boy feels a chill settle deep in his bones. He steps back, the water clutching at his ankles. How long, he thinks, how long before he's dragged up the forked steps and tossed inside the pale stone prison? How long before he dangles on the end of a rope?

We're clearin' out. The third has finally found his words. *We're followin' the boats upriver.*

The sun feels too low in the unending sky, its flames licking at his skin. He cannae go upriver, he is not welcome there. Banished. Not even though the curse were paid in full. He still remembers the dark faces of his da's kin as they turned him out on to the road. He shakes his head. That were another river, another fowk. His head hurts, the light like red hot pokers to his eyes. *Nae*, the boy whispers, *I cannae go back.*

But he cannae stay neither. The three boys leave, pulling each other along the dusty shore.

He hears a gentle voice behind him, from across the water. It whispers his name. His real name, not the one he gave to the magistrate that cold day in Aberdeen. He does not know if it be the fuathan, the Ghillie Dhu or his dear dead maw. But it calls to him, singing softly of shadows and shelter. But first he must chance the unseelie river. He squints at it, its surface winking bright. His heart beats so swift he fears it will burst his ribs.

Nae.

The river beckons, laughing.

An Imaginative Map of Water in Seaton Park

Paolo Gruppuso and Simona Trozzi

Maps shape the world according to wishes, desires, needs and imagination. They make visible the invisible, thus bringing into existence states, borders, trade routes, lines of fire. By drawing sharp boundaries between the earth and the sky, between land and water, they reveal the shapes of the land abstracting them from the movements of life. The trouble with maps is that they hide their performative power; they conceal the mapping behind the map by selling models for descriptions, mirrors for snapshots. Deep maps reverse the process. They emphasise mapping over maps and movements over static forms. They reveal the hands that make the drawing, and in doing so they reclaim the value of imagination, subjectivity, experience, and creativity in making sense of the world we live in.

Our *Imaginative Map of Water in Seaton Park* incorporates embodied experiences as instruments of knowing. It is the outcome of an empirical subjectivity and it is poetically objective, as it aims to express and to share our gratitude and fascination for the river Don, for its ecology and for the myriad beings that bring it into

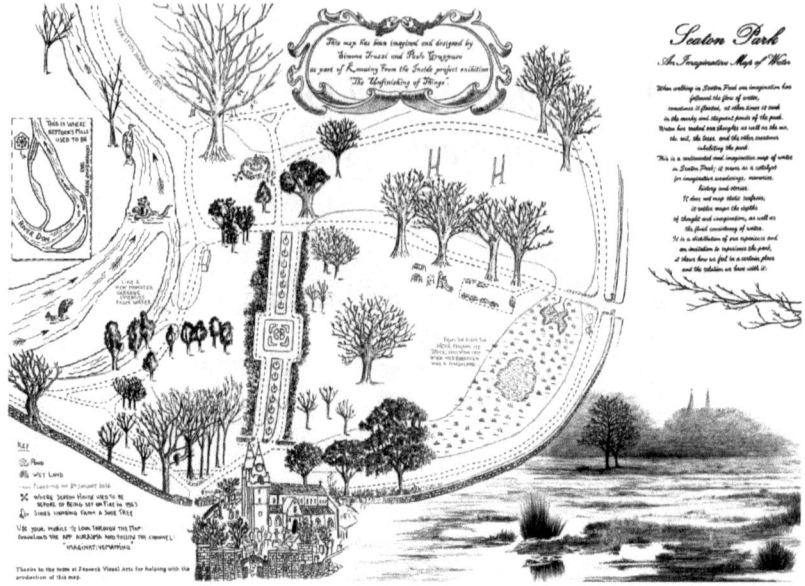

An Imaginative Map of Water in Seaton Park, front.

An Imaginative Map of Water in Seaton Park, back.

existence through their movements of life. Salmon, aquatic birds, otters, squirrels and deer join the river flow where things are fuzzy, unfolding and not yet given. We are with them, making kin, while walking with the river in Seaton Park, where stories and imagination congeal and dissolve. Sometimes they float, at other times they sink in the murky and stagnant ponds of the park that gather our thoughts, wishes, fears and hopes, as well as excess water.

Ours is a sentimental map that serves as a catalyst for imaginative wanderings, memories, and experiences. It does not describe static surfaces; it rather maps the depths of thought and imagination, as well as the fluid consistency of water. It maps the invisible landscape shaped by our experiences, feelings and embodied relations with water. It makes it visible by drawing, as a medium for transgressing the subtle boundary in-between our inner self and what surrounds us. As water storied the landscape of Seaton park, thus our stories inscribed the map itself. They are different ways of tracing lines, different ways of mapping the landscape and making it visible.

While I was in Aberdeen, working on my doctoral dissertation on the wetlands of Agro Pontino, Italy, Seaton Park provided a beautiful place for easing the stress of writing up. The wetland in the park unveiled their changes along the seasons: blossoming in spring, with wild ducks and swans breaking up the monotony of gulls and crows, which colonised the area during the summer in turn. There were misty days of autumn, red-coloured by the foliage of beech trees, and finally the silent days of winter, when a coat of ice covered the murky ponds, leaving out only reed and rush. Whereas I was attentive in following the changes of the area in time, my partner Simona amused herself spending her days in the park and exploring it by drawing. Trees, crows, gulls, plants and the different shapes of water soon started to populate her notebooks as much as the memory cards of my phone and cameras.

In those years, between 2014 and 2017, severe floods affected the area, changing the appearance of the Park and providing materials for our imagination to dive into a watery landscape. Water was indeed drawing her map, making visible Aberdeen's repressed past as a city born 'at the confluence of water'. Aberdeen's history, we discovered, inhabits the river, it flows in water, where it has merged with our stories, imaginaries and dreams. There, our mapping started, by following birds and looking for deer; by walking into the ponds and smelling the air; by mirroring ourselves into the water and getting lost amongst the roots of trees. The result is an imaginative map that exceeds time and reality, as water exceeded the river banks. A map that coagulates our experiences and that invites others to experience and map the park in turn. Thus, the story of this artefact, a deep map, is inscribed in the map itself.

Our process of mapping was made public at the final exhibition of the project *Knowing From the Inside* (or for short, KFI) based at the University of Aberdeen and led by Professor Tim Ingold. As an affiliated researcher, the project provided financial support for screen printing the map at Peacock Visual Arts in Aberdeen, and a beautiful venue to display it at Aberdeen university. The map was equipped with an app that allows the integration of a two-dimensional drawing with augmented reality such as videos and photos. The idea was for the public to participate in the mapping, uploading their own stories and materials. It is map to be used in anthropological research as well as a means to convey its outcomes beyond academia.

Sheena Blackhall

The River Dee

Woopeedoo! ! !
In the beginning I'm bubble-some as a baby in a bath
Frothy, flighty, a real live wire
Pure as dewdrops, mischievous as cuckoo spit
I'm a rollicker, a frolicker
I hoppity skip down the Bens
I am the broth of the morning without the bones

Cup me in your hands
I'll baptise your skin
Willows trail in me
Fir trees float their shadows

Paddler's fishers, swimmers
Even suicides I receive them all no question

Nearing the city, I'm a crone
A shawl of haars on my back
The weight of my long journey has wearied me
I give myself up to the sea
Lay down my oily burden

Oh Gently, Gently Rins the Dee

Oh gently, gently rins the Dee
Aside the clachan o Abyne
The blin-eed meen, casts doon a sheen
O siller, far the watters twine
Far twinty thoosan meens teet back
Frae watter's cup, aneth the pine.

The knowes aroon, sink saftly doon
The nicht pits on a pit-mirk plaid
A lanely echo, hyne awa's
The whaup, that wheels ower muirlans braid
The reeshlin birk far currents lirk's
A skeely clarsach, richly played.

Oh gently, gently rins the Dee
Aside the clachan o Abyne
The firs are newsin, burns sing sangs
The darklin watters jink an jyne
Here, tribbles, like the gloamin lowes
Slippin ower Mortlich, crine an dwine.

Tho I maun bide in steeny toun
Wersh is the taste o bitter wine
Oh bonnie clachan, reply loued,
My happy thochts will as be thine.

Dee Journey

A caller skelp o stane an storm,
Braeriach's sides are tempest-torn;
An in yon weety, derksome wame,
Whaur win is ice an sun's a flame,
The birlin Dee is born.

A sna-brig haps her growin tide,
Till, breengin up wi kittled pride,
She's heelstergowdie ower a crag!
A frichtsome drap — this wafter-hag
Cowps doon a corrie's bride.

Three lochs, disjaskit, dreich as dule,
She lies neth blearie Cairn Toul,
Till, necklet o the Norlan bree
She's glintin ower the Chest o Dee
A jimp an jibblin jewel.

Syne reemin on intil the linn,
Whaur warrior crags rise sterk abune,
An at their foun, an in aneth
Wi feint the whisper o a braith
o win, aa's dreepin, deep as daith,
As seenister as sin.

Ayont the gallows tree o Mar
She's lowsed an liltin fur Braemar
An ilkie burn, on ilkie Ben,
Will jink its cloudy, Heilan den
Tae jine her near an far.

Wi widded hills at ilkie gait
An salmon slidderin doon the spate,
She wallops neth a winsome brig,
Her waves, wud meers afore a gig,
Lowp up in touslie fete.

Atap her faem the kelpies ride,
The deer an eaglet rin astride
Till, pitten on a hamely goun,
She weary-wins a muckle toun
An, fair ferfochen, sattles doon
Tae coost her braws aside.

The Derbarl Yarrigan (Swan River) and Dyarlgarro Beeliar (Canning River)

Jo Jones

We're all in it together, this place, that one too: passing through, born here, born there, overlays and more:
[...]
I am never in one place when I am here. A composite.

John Kinsella[1]

Saltwater tears apart what freshwater builds. Every breath of wind blows this Country flatter. The ground is made of the broken-down mountains of an ancient interior, and one day this loose land beneath us will wash away. This is marginal Country, a temporary softness that clings to the edge of the oldest surface rock in the world. That ancient rock of the Wheatbelt has endured through the joining and separating of Pangaea and Gondwana, and it will prevail through all the ages of the Earth, long after the Swan Coastal Plain has eroded away. In the scale of Geologic Time this coastal area was formed yesterday and will be gone tomorrow. To the creator serpents this river is one glorious moment, where a black swan glides in to land with a splash, preens under its wing, then disappears. A fleeting moment, in Deep Time.

Cass Lynch[2]

It is difficult to know where to begin the story of the Derbarl Yarrigan (Swan River) and the Dyarlgarro Beeliar (Canning River) for many different reasons. Whichever route one takes, geographical or historical, there are ruptures, the explanation of which takes on a pressing shape in any story that attempts to meaningfully convey any aspect of the Swan coastal basin. Unlike Scotland's Dee or Don, the rivers of the Swan coastal plain do not have easily definable sources. Unlike the Don and Dee and other iconic rivers such as the Mississippi, the Nile, the Ganges, water for the Swan and Canning doesn't flow from mountainous regions, but snakes and bends, through interior flat lands and, eventually, through the arid dunes of the coastal plains. The sandy plain itself, the spills down from the plateau of the unfathomably ancient Yilgarn Craton, one of the oldest undisturbed continental masses of the planet, formed at its edge with the breakup of the supercontinent Pangaea in the Permian period.

Rivers in this place act differently

The search from the mouth to the source of the Derbarl Yarrigan will take you 200 kilometres inland, up the escarpment onto the plateau until eventually water disappears underground, through small town drainage systems and re-emerging a salt encrusted swamp 175 kilometres inland near the town of Yealering. Salt lakes are an inherent feature of the plateau and provide important bird and reptile habitat. There were no birds on the lake when I visited it a year ago. The encroaching salinity from a century of intensive agricultural production has changed many things. The Dyarlgarro Beeliar, again shaped by sandy flatness, converges with the Swan in a much-diminished form, for these days as, like many Australian rivers, it was dammed in the mid-1900s. Since the dam's completion in 1940 it has been the source of myriad ongoing ecological problems. Its source, again, many miles inland in the small town of Wandering.

Swan coastal plain and Darling escarpment.[3]

Comparative deep mapping: Swan coastal plain and Scotland's north-east

The fact that rivers in Western Australia work differently from those of younger (geographically speaking) landscapes is causally linked to the alarming state of river health. Our industrialised existence demands too much from them for water for agricultural production, as waste outlets for industry and as reclaimed swamp land for building. Most human occupants remain more or less blind to subtler forms of abundance. In my own childhood in the 1980s it was commonplace to catch fish, prawns and crabs on the river. By the mid-1990s after troubling mass death of fish and excessive algal blooms partly caused by fertiliser (nitrate) runoff from agricultural areas inland, families gathered around fires with prawning nets or fishing rigs were things of the past. Simply put, the rush to change this ancient landscape into an industrialised modern state – grasping at abundant resources and resenting the absence of others – has irreversibly and catastrophically altered the landscape and waterways. Of course, every modernised place on earth has undergone industrial and post-industrial reshaping and environmental damage, yet the rapidity and the scale of the changes in the Perth sandy basin are extraordinary.

It is useful here to return to the comparison to Scotland's Don and Dee. Industrialisation has obviously altered the waterways of Scotland's north-east, water is siphoned off for drinking, farming and food production. The mouth of the Dee in the port city of Aberdeen, for example, has undergone many reshapings, its surface oily and slick. This has occurred in stages over the last three centuries, gaining pace along the way. In Scotland, the ongoing effects of industrialisation have been shaped by sudden and traumatic displacement involving the mass (sometimes forced) relocation of people in events such as the Highland clearances, the endemic mechanisation of rural life and the movement into towns and cities, even onto oil rigs, in the search for work. There are, however, similarities and differences between these specific Scottish and Australian situations that are important to attend to. Both locales are home to teeming generations of human experience – of energised and generous working cultures, of cycles of pain and joy, of fast and slow changes, of remnants of ancient cultural practice that are both indigenous to place and brought from elsewhere.

In a deep mapping context, however, it is vital to recognise the precise patterns and shifting occupations – coming, going, staying and dwelling – in the north east of Scotland, and other many and varied nexus points of movement, trade and conflict in northern Europe have their own particularities. As outlined in the previous introductory material, the regions through which the Don and Dee runs have archaeological layers of human presence from Neolithic times to that of the Picts, the Romans and the Danes and the territorial disputes of the last millennia – from Scottish clan groupings, English incursions, the Norman invasion and onwards. It is vital to acknowledge here the fracturing of the Scottish clan systems during the Jacobite uprising and after and the extent of suffering and cultural erasure. The famous and romantic patriotism of Sir Walter Scott in the Waverley novels highlights the separate uniqueness of Scottish experiences attached to region and Gaelic and Scots dialects, and sometimes strange unexpected cultural inheritances, a small sample of which includes the diverse literary explorations of McDiarmid, Kathleen Jamie and Kirsten Norrie (clan name MacGillivray).

Deep mapping, history and Indigenous culture

The Swan coastal plan has Noongar artefacts that indicate that these people lived in this place from at least 45,000 years ago, long before the previous ice age. As is widely acknowledged, Indigenous Australians are custodians of the oldest living culture in the world, a culture driven in different places and different ways to the brink of dissolution through the actions of generations of colonisers (some of them Scottish). I do not mention these facts at this point in the discussion in any attempt to draw an inappropriate and insensitive comparison between types and examples of human suffering, rather to observe that the process of deep mapping encourages the consideration of time and place where the multi-dimensionality of time, place and culture are approached as the intricate stuff of infinite layering, and the layers are uniquely patterned.

Cassandra Pybus subtitled her book about the Indigenous Tasmanian woman Truganini[4] – *Journey through the apocalypse* – for good reason. While human history consists of so many modes of moving and dwelling that include bloody, violent actions and long-term suffering of others, the conjunction of the old world and the new involves a confrontation of cultures vastly and cataclysmically dissimilar. Above all other differences, colonisers had weaponry and force of numbers, the likes of which were absent from Indigenous story or experience. Of course these patterns repeat an echo in varied forms across the globe, particularly with the advances in technologies of navigation and sailing from the late 1400s onwards. While Indigenous Australians had encountered European seafarers for some hundreds of years – whalers, sealers, explorers, pirates – before the settlement of Botany Bay in 1788, knowledge of the realities of early contact have been important to confront as a culture and a nation, and have taken on greater urgency in the last three decades in the wake of the wide availability of revisionist histories. While the historical records includes many amicable beginnings,[5] British settlement in Australian was quickly followed by disease and an unimaginable scale of death for Indigenous peoples. Lanarkshire-born Scotsman Captain James Stirling led the Swan River Colony initiative in 1828, renaming his own land parcels along the Swan after his wife's home ground of Surrey – the town of Guildford and the estate of Woodbridge – rather than the northern region of his birth. A fraught and economically beset two decades saw the 'free' colony of Perth succumb to the economic necessity of accepting convicts from Britain for all the benefits of indentured labour. Perth's status as a thriving outpost of empire was sealed late in the 1800s with the discovery of gold, and Perth society has been obsessed with the state's mineral wealth ever since, shaping economic and cultural projects around mining's boom and bust cycles.[6]

After an expanse of at 45,000[7] years of continuous inhabitation, the occupation of European colonists was nothing less than cataclysmic for Noongar people and culture, not only the immediate effect of invasion but the prolonged, continuing outward expansion of settler land theft and the imposition of European systems of governance, law, punishment and land ownership. Indigenous people were systematically dispossessed of their lands as it was parcelled out and the settlers – Stirling, his officers and relatives – were given the prime areas. The Indigenous inhabitants identified themselves as Bibbulmen (from the land of many breasts); the land was the Mother, the source from which all life sprung and was/is nourished. These new ways of *owning* land for the Indigenous people, including the idea that the lands could be fenced off and animals or crop yield be forcibly defended, was deeply strange to the Noongar people. Until Australia's 1968 referendum, when it was determined that

Indigenous Australians had access to full citizenship rights, many Noongar people had no assured access to their traditional lands and the vital food and spiritual resources of the river (now prime Swan River Colony real estate). Over the 200 years of settlement they were moved from their traditional places further up the river, east and inland, many dwelling in 'camps' in the Swan Valley, further east out to Northam and the wheatbelt, or in what are now the outer suburbs north and south, where many Noongar families still reside.

As the signs of Noongar dwelling were erased and hidden in the coming centuries, there was a strange separation of time and place – the deep past or ancient culture overlayed by concrete and bitumen, sometimes laying unseen alongside the fence posts and early dirt roads that over time took up the routes of ancient tales, yet without the inherited phrases that were used to sing each place into being, acknowledging creator spirits and ancestors. With the distribution of hooved cattle and European farming methods, Noongar crops and hunting grounds were unavailable and, as the bloody history of the early colony shows, Noongar cattle 'theft' brought with it dire consequences.

In this far from complete account of the traumatic upheavals of colonisation, it must also be noted that settler experience was far from the idyll that some of them may have imagined when recruited for the scheme. The colony struggled to feed and provide for itself for the first two decades, only then agreeing, like most other Australian settlements, to take the free convict labour from Britain. European convict settlers, many of them English and Irish, some Scottish, suffered the forced displacement that has taken so many shapes since the event of modernity. Unlike the Noongar people, they could earn full settler rights after a time of service, depending on the severity of their crimes. Not all did. The famous outlaw, Welsh-born Joseph Bolitho Johns, repeatedly escaped from the infamous convict-built Fremantle Prison and famously wore a kangaroo skin cloak in the colder months – a *buka* – like Noongar people, and for much of his life lived 'rough' in the Avon Valley.

Considering the overlaying patterns of experience and inhabitation in deep mapping invites important comparisons that can be weirdly and unexpectedly congruous. The port town of Fremantle (Walyalup) is just one place, among so many others, that can be used to demonstrate the coexistence of so many songs, stories and lives. It echoes with the mingled resonances of lives gone before and, perhaps, to come. In traditional Nyoongar culture the mouth of the Swan River, Walyalup, had a number of symbolic and practical purposes. The sand bar that stretched between the south to the north shore, making the mouth of the river passable on foot, allowed people to cross along seasonal trails — *bidi* in Nyoongar — and traverse the paths and songlines[8] according to the seasonal availability of food and cultural patterns and observances. It was shared terrain where Nyoongar groups would meet, communicate, arrange marriages and enact courtships. Walyalup contains sites central to Dreaming stories of the Wagyl (river creator serpent), the crocodile, and the dingo.

The tail of the crocodile (the sandbar across the mouth of the river) was destroyed in 1892 to create Fremantle harbour. The harbour engineer, C. Y. O'Connor, died a decade later. A complex figure of great talent and energy in earlier years, O'Connor shot himself in 1902. He was under immerse pressure from state factions to complete an engineering scheme of pumping water 600 kilometres inland to the new goldfields, although Nyoongar stories maintain he was cursed after destroying the crocodiles tail and 'sang to death'. The mouth of the river was not only the site of initial colonial contact but of all that was brought in the following decades when Indigenous people were dispossessed of the area and disconnected from story and tradition. Many died from imported disease. It is clearly a site of profound sadness for the Noongar groups of Perth and a symbol of so much that has been lost.

Walyalup means, in Noongar, 'place of tears' and is where funeral rites were performed. It was believed that the dead made the crossing across the water to Wadjemup (now known as Rottnest Island), a place occupied by spirits. That European explorers and then British settlers made this reverse journey in from the 1600s onwards is sadly and oddly appropriate for nothing less than a cataclysm of worlds, a coercive recasting of lives, of realities.

Fremantle now, like so much of Western Australia, is a blend of culture that in one way is representative of Western Australian modernity, deeply entrenched in trade via the influx of imports and the export of our primary industries. It was the centre of trade unionism for decades. Its role as a centre of pioneering and shipping heritage is recorded in a number of large museums. For over a century its streetscape was dominated by the bleak outlines of buildings of incarceration such as the Roundhouse (built in 1831, 18 months after settlement, mainly used to imprisoned Indigenous men) and the Victorian-designed Fremantle Prison, used in its near-original state for criminal incarceration until 1991.

Also, significantly, the city has become a symbol for many migrations beyond the arrival of these first British settlers, both free and indentured. Fremantle was a first port of call in Australia for millions of migrants, many who settled here. Some of their names appear on the Welcome Walls, granite plinths with lists of names of individuals or families from abroad, particularly from Australia's 'populate or perish' decades of the 1950s.[9] There are many British migrants listed (including my own father) and many others who arrived in the great post-war scattering from places as diverse as China, Croatia, India, Sri Lanka, Pacific Island nations, South Africa, Zimbabwe, Somalia and Nigeria.

Fremantle has also been a transit point for many child migrants, from the Parkhurst boys from the famous Isle of Wight Prison (arguably Western Australia's first convicts), to participants in the child migration programs of the mid-1900s run by religious and charitable institutions. Many children suffered terrible abuse at the hands of their so-called protectors. It is where people and horses left for and sometimes returned from twentieth-century wars. These layers coexist. Now the town's earlier 'edginess' has been overlayed by gentrification and a vibrant arts scene. The Blakean energy of industry, creative communities includes many Nyoongar arts and culture initiatives, but also an unshakable presence of loss resonant concomitantly through each dimension of post-settlement newness.

The mouth of the river is clearly a site of profound sadness for the Noongar groups of Perth and a symbol of so much that has been lost. Sometimes, for settlers, the mourning for the land of their ancestors was expressed through the desire to Europeanise the landscape or pursue the riches they somehow believed their proper due as compensation for leaving and risk and work and making lives *elsewhere*.

This section of the volume includes responses Indigenous and non-Indigenous to the complex space of the Derbarl Yarrigan and Dyarlgarro Beeliar that range across academic disciplines and artistic forms. Some convey varied kinds of grief from fraught, often painful, imperatives to re-enter a space of ancestors through the settler experience.

Chris Fremantle visually responds to the diary of his ancestor, Captain Charles Fremantle, using a symbolic act of burning the words of his ancestor's journals into a nautical map as an expression profound rejection of the occidental lens through which Charles Fremantle recorded his observations of the colony with the eye of both a military man and colonial surveyor – people were often for subduing, the environment converted to capital value. Chris Fremantle's inherited artefacts – Fremantle's journal and a map of the naval port – are brought together as a material response to the violence of representation acts of colonisation some 200 years after initial settlement.

Samantha Owens' astute discussion of François Boniface Heirisson's Swan River expedition – a small section of the larger expedition headed by Nicholas Baudin from 1800 to 1803 – to survey, map and scientifically observe the western coast of Australia. The documentation of his observations conveys assumptions of colonial mapping as a point from which to reorientate perspectives. The practice of mapping in Owens' essay is a useful pivot from which to initiate the reorientation of deep mapping, in which the observer rereads and recalibrates according to a sensitised multi-perspective where different realities and worldviews, richly overlaid, operate simultaneously

Nandi Chinna and Cass Lynch are both acclaimed Western Australian writers and their poetry for this collection communicates very particular concepts of the Derbarl Yarrigan. Chinna's poems are part of a profound settler investigation of river as intimate space – in the detail of precise locations to the observation of microcreatures – an imaginative regression of the Anglo–Celtic settler psyche. For Chinna, as for many contributors here, these processes are inextricable. Her work summons ghosts of first governor Captain James Stirling and Dutch explorer Willem de Vlamingh, while inviting the presence of fish, frogs, turtles and serpents.

Noongar writer Cass Lynch takes the minimalism of the haiku form to invoke the vastness of time–space through the deep time dimensions of Indigenous cosmology. Cassie's extraordinary invocation of creator spirits and their elemental response to settler presence radically inverts ideas of the new and old world and those who move and those who stay – neither is the past ever behind us, it remains unalterably here.

Carol Millner and Maureen Gibbons experiment with literary and poetic form, reflecting complexities of life in modern Perth. Millner draws deep into memory – personal and historical – as she negotiates the shapes of inhabitation and notices patterns within and without. In 'Directions', she makes the apt and poignant observation that the human body itself contains its own rivers, big and small, 'sleeping street oceans of blood flow', and how the conditions of animal life form powerful invisible connections, whether one is a river, creature, part of an exploration party or a Noongar women gathering up food to sustain the flow of life.

In her poem, Maureen Gibbons writes of archaeological layers on a river bank, and planting and transplanting and, underneath, a different ancient agriculture of abundance that didn't/doesn't require the straight-line regularity of rows and staking.

Daniel Juckes and Qassim Saad reflect on the layers and complexity of migration, change and dwelling. Juckes' precise and poetic observations of a figure – Winnie – discovered in the paper ephemera housed inside an old copy of Nathaniel Hawthorne's *A Wonder-Book and Tanglewood Tales* lead to complex speculations about inhabiting a new place. The fabric of Juckes's text offers intriguing insights into the settler condition and the way one also inherits habit and patterns of culture shaped in ways that contain both displacement and longing. His discussion of the sweetly yellowed page of letters and responses to Perth's Sunshine League (a group of children who regularly write to a page in the newspaper) explores an interestingly British kind of 'cheerfulness' that, among other things, conveys the poignant unease of the migrant state – an at-home, not-at-homeness that, for Juckes, colours river encounters.

In 'Exile, Rivers and Design', Qassim Saad details an extraordinary global journey that negotiates difference and changing responses to notions of exile, home and a paradoxical state of in-betweeness that is increasingly permanent state of being that that is somehow, at home, within the perpetual longing for return. A type of solace for Saad (an industrial designer) is the supporting structures of bridges and their specific relationship with ancient and often famous waterways. Saad's journey leads from his family home near the Euphrates in Fallujah. The fabled locale of the birth of civilisation – site of old Mesopotamia – enters troubled decades in an attempt to decolonise and modernise. Over the next decades Saad lives in Jordan, Dunedin, New Zealand (Taieri River); Cairo, Egypt (the Nile); and Perth, Australia (Derbarl Yarrigan).

Susanna Castleden and Tom Wilson both embrace mobility and physicality as a vital element of river experience. Castleden's detailed representation of her cycle navigation of the Derbarl Yarrigan and Dyarlgarro Beeliar works through an innovative re-routing of the journey of a circumnavigation of Perth's rivers via the 'Don' and 'Dee' roads. The abundance of Scottish place names in the Perth region are explored through Castleden's rhythmic, embodied and representational work outlining a cultural overlay between geographically distant spaces.

Tom Wilson conveys his varied vigorous and immersive explorations into the water and surrounds of the Derbarl Yarrigan as a romantic journey not only crucial for the body, but growth of the whole self, nurtured and thriving, through numerous excursions often filled with Whitmanesque joy.

The work of Susan Midalia and James Quinton sends the reader inland, past the wide blue expanses of the coastal stretches of the Derbarl – the wide blue tidal water – into the eastern reaches where the river narrows, known for more brackish water, sedges, cool sinking river sands and hot, windy summers. Susan Midalia's work of a brief but resounding recollection takes to reader to the Bayswater Bridge from a time when river swimming was an intrinsic part of summer in the working class suburbs further from the beach. The material space is more than a site of reverie, but small bright fragment of cross-cultural connection shared through the openness of childhood.

Quinton has written many poems about the Bassendean river foreshore, the site of many family events, childhood exploration and adult experience and realisation. In the poems included here the Derbarl Yarrigan remains Quinton's canvas for the Chinese-box layering of consciousness and memory. At times, the exploration of the environmental destruction of the foreshore and wetlands lyrically conveys the ache of deeply felt connections to the non-human world.

John Kinsella and David Whish-Wilson write to us of water and children. The river is somewhere for youths to explore while not at school. They write texts about energised shiny, wet, white bodies immersed in river waters, but also of inner journeys from one place to another where there is no going back. Kinsella's upriver encounters with the agri-polluted waters spiral between the past and present in the faded shadow-figure of an out-of-temper ferryman: not so much the mythic ferryman of the Acheron, rather, a jaded old man, tired and out-of-temper. So too the damaged upper reaches are too faded to even echo the steps of Dante's inferno with any energy – too degraded, exhausted and effluvia-filled to show any watcher looking for their own reflection the true grotesqueries of settler practices that, in less than a century, degraded vast regions. To drive over the bridge now, the speaker 'accumulates the wastes as grief'.

Claire Jones' discussion of varied stretches of the Derbarl Yarrigan combines memoir with a series of sensitive observations about aspects of Perth's literary history. As with the work of the writers she visits – from prose writers Seaforth MacKenzie, Tim Winton and David Whish-Wilson to the contemporary poet Lucy Dougan – Jones reveals the river as a space of liminality where children encounter the depths of mature experience.

Whish-Wilson's poetic memoir conveys the use of a gill net in what begins as of youthful nocturnal escapes. Through the course of unexpectedly tender narrative of male maturation, the river transforms from a place of hijinks to one of deeper sensibility of dwelling. The ancient river reminds its human visitors of a primeval presence when the gill net is retrieved empty and gapes to mark the passage of the aggressive river predator, perhaps a bull shark, perhaps something larger, older.

The final two texts to this volume are vital for a number of reasons. The internationally renowned historian Anna Haebich contributes a detailed journey of the Dyarlgarro. The Dyarlgarro is a tributary of the Derbarl Yarrigan, but also a large river in its own right and, as Haebich articulates, is often overlooked in cultural and historical terms. After discovering the survey journals of a little known German surveyor Ludwig Preiss, Haebich traces the significance of his meticulous surveying and map making – his talent as skilled botanical observer and his disappointing complicity in the wider project of dividing up Noongar land to British colonisers – a process of fast-paced wealth-making from which Priess was eventually excluded. Haebich, however, doesn't leave the story here, but continues to trace the uneven response to settler history and memorialising of this intriguing river, the story of which hides so much of great importance to Indigenous and non-Indigenous relations – the varied ways in which Noongar story and ownership is silenced and swept into secret places. Haebich sees that one of the most vital forms of resistance in continuing traditions of story are performance of Noongar artists, recognising the potential of on-country story, embodied stories that go beyond words.

Haebich's essay explains the idea of solastalgia and how many Perth residents remember times in the recent past of cleaner, healthier river waters. To any sensitive observer, the ongoing environmental, archaeological and historical losses in the development of Perth spark profound loss, the 'homesickness you have while still at home'.[10] While some non-Indigenous Australians are deeply and genuinely affected by the pace and devastating breadth of environmental degradation and the continuing losses of it, many turn to Indigenous responses to the challenges of cataclysmic devastation as they have endured the cataclysm of colonisation and have seen people and place as profoundly, inseparably enmeshed, and sometimes find ways to witness continuality and recovery. The non-Indigenous turn to pre-modern wisdom is nothing if not ironic. The question remains if the recognition of multi-dimensional loss is somehow compatible with hope.

The final contribution here is by Wadjuk Noongar researcher, artist, elder and traditional owner, Vanessa Corunna, and is from her series that tracks European invasion, Indigenous response and resistance. The watercolour *Eagle Warrior*, painted in 2013, is a tribute to the spirit of Yagan that returned to Country after the repatriation and burial of his *kaat* (head) in 2010 close to the location of his body, buried in 1833. Corunna traces story and custom through her Noongar family who have maintained a close connection with country despite the challenges faced by the Swan Valley Indigenous community. Whether any of us return 'home' after all that has occurred in the last 200 years and the various manifestations of modernity is a question that is at best too large to answer and at worst impossible. Yet, Yagan returned after almost two centuries. He became an eagle and returned to his river spirit grounds.

The Diaries of Fremantle (an Ancestor) Burnt into Map

Chris Fremantle

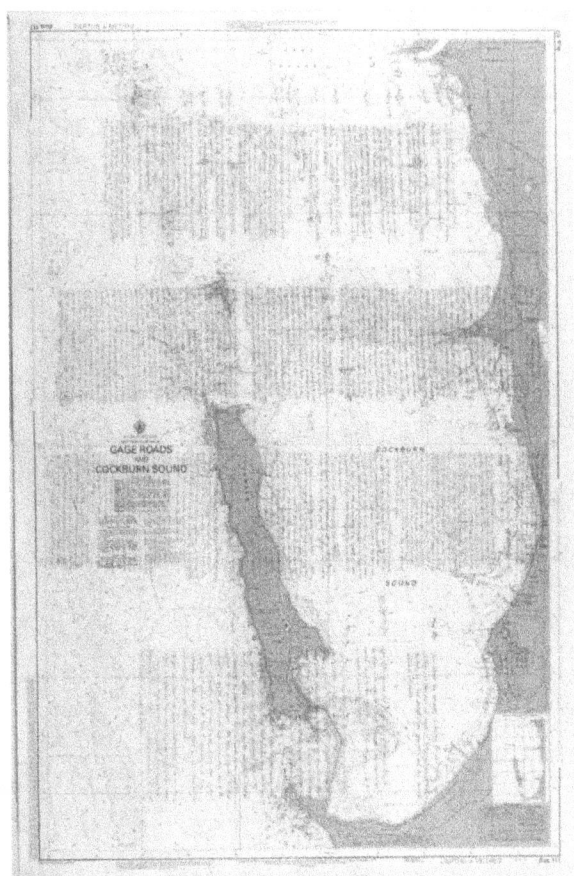

The Diaries of Fremantle (an Ancestor) Burnt into Map.
TEXT BURNT ON NAUTICAL MAP.

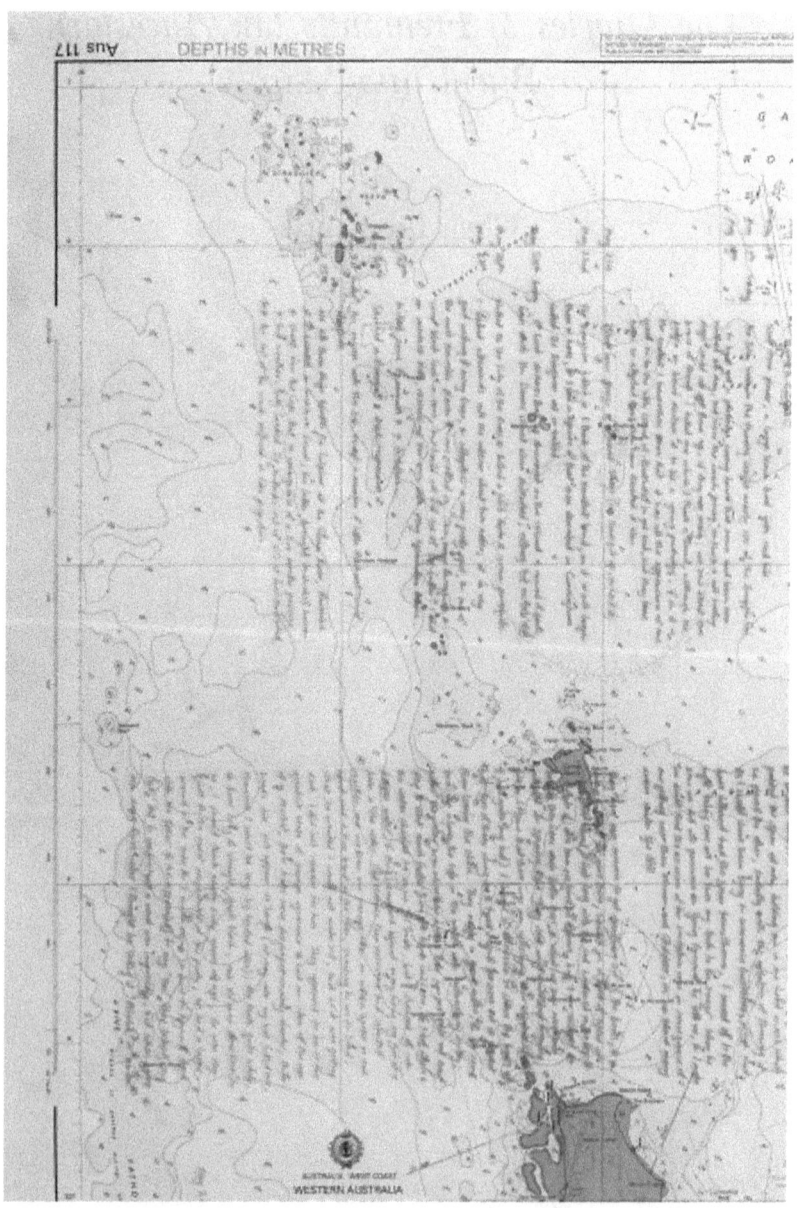

The Diaries of Fremantle (an Ancestor) Burnt into Map. Detail, top left.

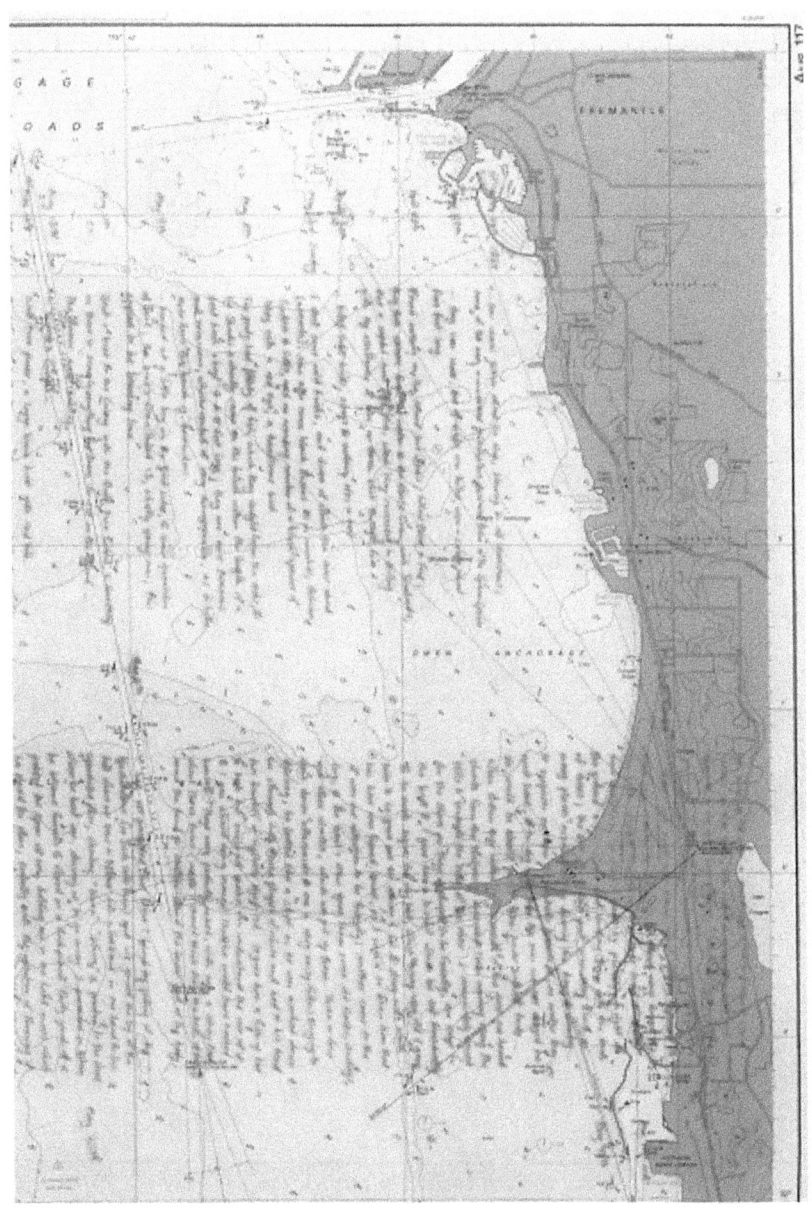

The Diaries of Fremantle (an Ancestor) Burnt into Map. Detail, top right.

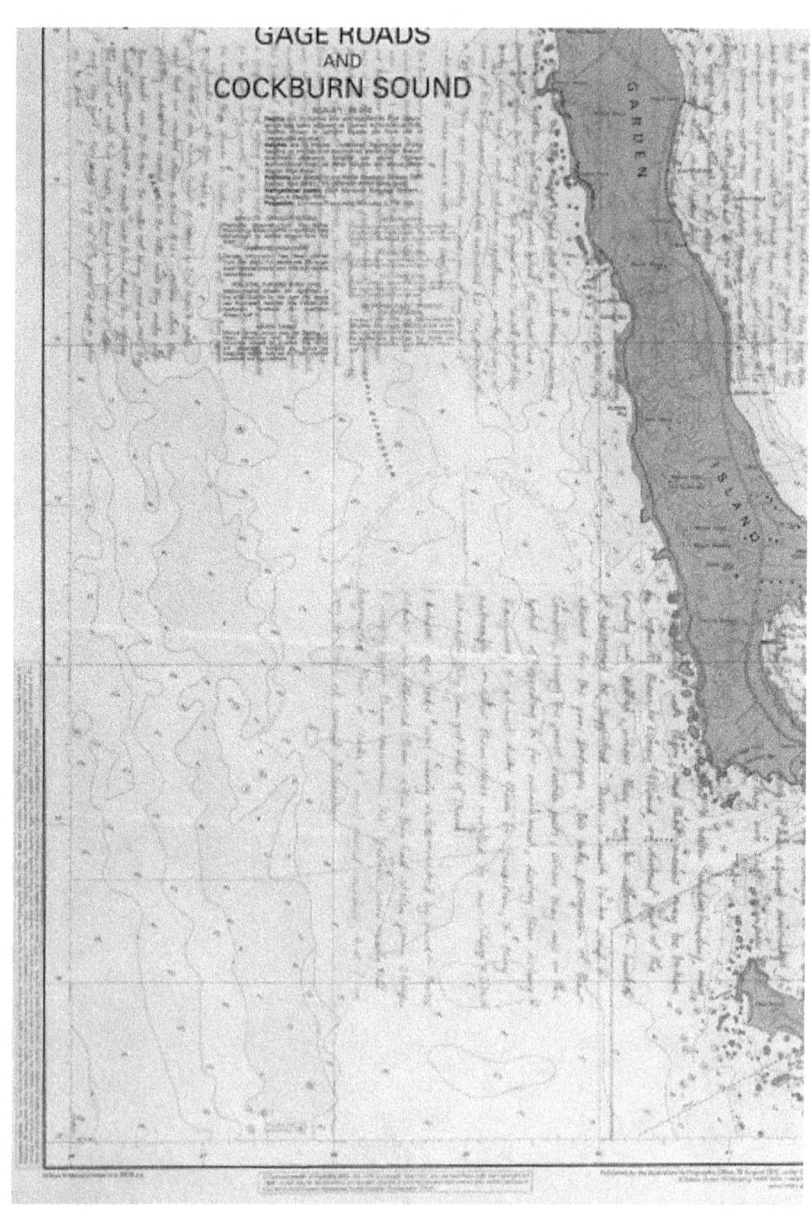

The Diaries of Fremantle (an Ancestor) Burnt into Map. Detail, bottom left.

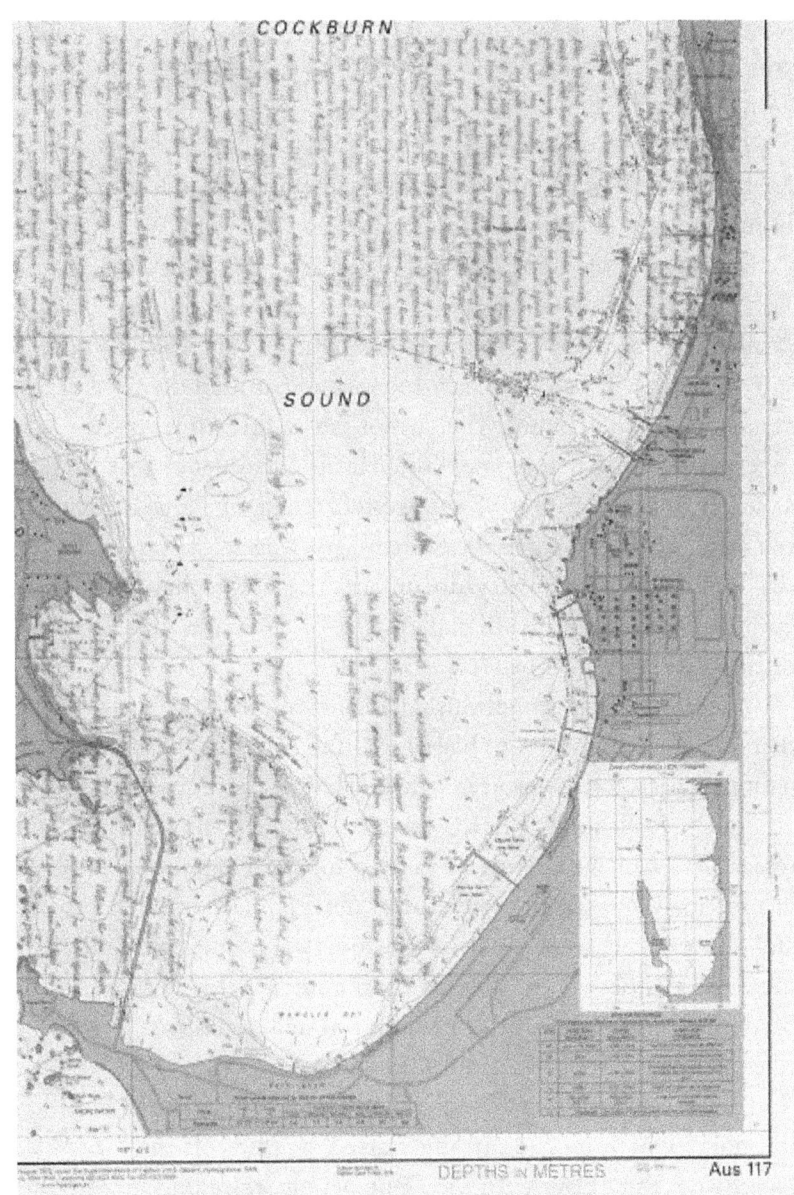

The Diaries of Fremantle (an Ancestor) Burnt into Map. Detail, bottom right.

I would like to begin by acknowledging that this artwork concerns Noongar people, their history of being colonised and their ancestral lands. I wish to acknowledge and respect the Noongar people's continuing culture and the contribution they make to the life of Western Australia.

I was born in New York, grew up in London and now live in Scotland. I grew up knowing that a member of the family had been involved in colonising Australia and that there was a part of Perth named after him. I inherited the *Diary & Letters of Admiral Sir C. H. Fremantle G. C. B. Relating to the Founding of the Colony of Western Australia 1829* from my father, who in turn had been given it by his uncle. It had been privately printed around the time of the centenary of the colony. The author is my four times great uncle (five generations before me). Fremantle (1800–1869) had in 1829 'taken formal possession of the western coast of New Holland in the name of King George the Fourth'[1] and he had of course planted the Union Jack. The diary documents the day-to-day activity of colonisation between April and August of that year, and his views during his return visit in 1832.

I developed this artwork using a nautical chart given to me by a member of the family who had visited Fremantle. I purchased more nautical charts for the project. I myself haven't been to Australia.

At Gray's School of Art, Aberdeen, where I am a lecturer and researcher, we have an interest in deep mapping. I became involved in practice-led research through the *On The Edge* research project, and the first phase of work which questioned the imposition of urban modalities of the arts on rural contexts. I was the director of the Scottish Sculpture Workshop, located 35 miles due west of Aberdeen in the foothills of the Cairngorms.

I met the artist, architect and researcher Gavin Renwick at the point where he had already started working in the Canadian Northwest Territories with the Dene people, travelling up through Yellowknife to spend often six months in the north. He was working as a cultural intermediary at their request on their land claim and was undertaking his PhD at the University of Dundee.

We undertook a live project with *On The Edge*, Gavin Renwick leading a team to explore the reconfiguration of life in the north-east Scotland landscape over 5,000 years as a way to think about coming changes. Renwick brought what he had learnt about understanding land in Canada to bear on that small part of rural Aberdeenshire. His decolonial practice enabled us to see the history of agricultural improvements and planned villages in the light of settler behaviours, particularly around reorganising life for economic reasons.

Deep mapping continues to be an important focus. What it means to be Indigenous, to be an incomer or a stranger are all of concern. But the family connection to the colonisation of Western Australia remains an unresolvable reality.

Deborah Bird Rose suggests that there are two violences of colonisation, one to the flora and fauna and the other to the indigenous peoples. She says:

> As I have argued elsewhere, we settlers, or settler-descendants, are the inheritors of the spoils of a dual war: one war was fought against the natives, and one against nature.[2]

Reading the diary with these two violences in mind – transcribing sections where fauna are killed and where Indigenous people are encountered, finding key passages which capture and clarify the violences – is all that it is possible to do so far. Putting this material onto a nautical chart seems appropriate – most of the rest of the diary concerns navigation, weather and ship management. This opens up a relationship with my predecessor and perhaps potentially also with people in a place I don't know.

There are a couple of questions, derived by Verlyn Klinkenborg from Barry Lopez that seem relevant:

> What if the perspective you could imagine for yourself, the foundation for your ethics and your politics, was not the condescending now of right now?' Here's another: What if you

were able 'to see the world from someone else's point of view without fearing the loss of [your] own position?'[3]

Beyond that as Audre Lorde says in *Uses of Anger*, '…it is very difficult to stand still and listen…', but that is all I can do now.

A Tale of Black Beaks: *Naturaliste* Explorers Encounter the Derbarl Yerrigan

Samantha Owen

Introduction

On 27 Vendémiaire Year IX, Nicolas Baudin, commander-in-chief of the *Voyage aux Terres Australes* (*Voyage*), sailed out of Le Havre. An *officier bleu*, Baudin joined the French Navy as a cadet following a stint in the French East India Company. Following the 1780 naval reforms, Baudin worked his way up through the ranks.[2] After a successful botanical expedition to the West Indies, Baudin was introduced to the *Institut National* and gained the contacts to propose the *Voyage*. On 4 Germinal Year VIII, Baudin noted in his diary: 'The reception [with Emperor Napoleon] was as I had foreseen, the voyage settled'.[3] Marketed as the greatest expedition since Jean-François de Galaup La Pérouse's 1785 voyage, Baudin and his second in command, Jacques Félix Emmanuel Hamelin, attracted a star 200-person crew, including Hyacinthe de Bougainville and Louis de Freycinet.[4] They were also assigned two artists, Charles-Alexandre Lesueur and Nicolas-Martin Petit, and 23 savants: draftsmen, engineers, gardeners and natural scientists – botanists, astronomers, mineralogists, geographers and zoologists.[5] An intention of the

Cover of *Atlas historique du Voyage aux Terres Australes*.[1]

voyage was to survey and explore the '*Zwaan* River'.⁶ They were successful and the *Naturaliste* shore party returned with what was cited as the first known map of the *rivière des Cygnes*.⁷

In this essay I shall explore the meaning of the trip taken up the Derbarl Yerrigan by François-Antoine Boniface Heirisson, the sub-lieutenant on board the *Naturaliste*, and his shore party. I suggest the surveying, charting, recording and mapping involved an act of possession. They wilfully misread or remained blind to signs of land cultivation and inhabitation and declared the landscape that was once classified as *terra incognita, terra nullius*. In doing so they felt at ease to name, kill, eat, destroy, remove and damage the plants, animals and ecosystems they encountered. In this essay I shall ask what can happen when we shift our perspective, when we dis *and* re-orientate? When we re-read our sources and try to see, hear and feel from the point of view of those being invaded, killed, removed, erased? I methodologically draw on the work of Diana Looser⁸ and ask what happens when the reader and 'viewer adopts an indigenous perspective of looking out from the land toward the arriving foreign visitors', in Māori the '*tangata whenua view*'.⁹ I do so in this essay as my argument is that by engaging from different world views to the hegemonic we can challenge the singularity of colonial perspectives that determine our landscape and how we view it and value it. I acknowledge that doing so is 'fraught, problematic and necessary'.¹⁰ In conclusion I raise the question of whether Heirisson's is the first map of the Derbarl Yerrigan.¹¹ How do we know and could we read otherwise?

Who prepares the ground for mapping?

The question of how we read and understand the mapping, geography and land-claiming of Australia has occupied more space in historiographical discussions since the 1960s, most notably marked by anthropologist W. E. H. 'Bill' Stanner's 1968 Boyer Lecture, 'After the Dreaming'. Stanner reflected on 'the Great Australian Silence', the absence of Aboriginal and Torres Strait Islander peoples from Australian history after European settlement and the denial of genocide and systemic abuse.[12] Stanner's lecture in the year following the 1967 referendum opened the floodgates for new research and new ways of seeing — as well as new denials.[13] Charles Rowley published the first systematic history of the dispossession in 1970, and in 1972 Henry Reynolds' work *Aborigines and Settlers: the Australian Experience, 1788–1939* tried to rethink the colonisation of Australia from a First Nations peoples perspective. He characterised colonisation as bloody and brutal, and asserted that colonisers met with resistance.[14] These massacres are still the subject of the research of Lyndall Ryan, who published the first account of genocide in *The Aboriginal Tasmanians* in 1981.[15] Also published in 1981 was Richard White's *Inventing Australia*. White argued that the 'idea of "Australia" itself is a European invention'[16] and that European views of First Nations people from the earliest landings formed an understanding of them as primitive. These views re-populated the explorers' understandings of what they viewed and recorded. They also informed their understandings of Australia as a *terra incognita* which, when mapped, could be owned as *terra nullius*: ready for European occupation.[17]

In *With the White People: The Crucial Role of Aborigines in the Exploration and Development of Australia* Reynolds tracked and traced — both the origins of those regarded as 'pioneers' and the very routes taken by these explorers. Reynolds' work expanded the definition of pioneers to include the Aboriginal people employed as trackers, pearl divers, nursemaids, domestic staff, and labourers, and made the argument that their labour was an invaluable contribution to the foundation of the colony. In doing so he complicated the histories which represent First Nations responses as only of resistance, and he raised the possibility that the tracks explorers followed to know Australia were made by First Nations peoples because they wanted to occupy the spaces they identified as most habitable. Enlightenment knowledge gave them the arrogance to justify an assumption of ownership.[18] These works were the subject of the History Wars and informed the tenacious High Court challenge by Eddie Koiki Mabo, a Torres Strait Islander who worked as a gardener at James Cook University. In *Why Weren't We Told?* Reynolds writes:

> Eddie [...] His face shone when he talked of his village and his land. [the islands of Mer (Murray islands), in the Torres Strait.] I said something like: 'You know how you've been telling us about your land and how everyone knows it's Mabo land? Don't you realise that nobody actually owns land on Murray Island? It's all crown land.
>
> He was stunned. [...] How could the whitefellas question something so obvious as his ownership of his land?'[19]

Mabo's case went to the High Court and won: the doctrine of *terra nullius* was overturned (Mabo and Others v Queensland (No 2)). The *Native Title Act 1993* codified the Mabo judgement and implemented strategies to recognise native title. Considering the Mabo case we are pushed to ask the question: who decided that the Crown owned the land? Who named the Mer islands the Murray Islands? Who assumed the role of mapping? Who presumed that doing so accorded ownership and land rights under a particular legal system? In *Making Settler Colonial Space* Tracey Banivanua Mar and Penelope Edmonds took these up and considered how colonialism engaged 'a profound extensive rearrangement of physical spaces and peoples' – historical space was remade to extinguish the presence of Indigenous peoples.[20]

In his tales set on the Great Barrier Reef, Iain McCalman addressed the mindset which made these dispossessions possible. He described Cook encountering the reef as 'a Scottish Enlightenment man of reason hoping to see the cultivated landscape of civilisation, a British imperialist scouting for economic opportunities for future colonists, or simply a nostalgic Yorkeshireman'.[21] In *Dark Emu*, Bruce Pascoe drew on this scholarship to assert that First Nations peoples were not nomadic and he called for a re-reading of explorers' journals by adjusting our 'perspective by only a few degrees'.[22] He suggested the explorers were using a speculative lens to calculate the value of that land and determine if colonisation was worthwhile. However, they were also misreading it. Pascoe made the argument that their 'cultural myopia' prevented them from reading the fertility as the result of 'careful management' by First Nations peoples.[23] Instead they chose to read the actions of those peoples within the paradigms of Enlightenment knowledge and nascent eugenics. Pascoe asserted that their wilful blindness led to the destruction of ways of life that sustain the people and the land and resulted in the destruction of the same people and land. However, it did allow the explorers to claim the land as *terra nullius* and to realise their speculative intents. In asking us to reconceive the explorers' accounts, Pascoe also asked us to reconceive the map of Australia – the invention, as White called it.[24]

Samia Khatun's *Australianama: The South Asian Odyssey in Australia* tackled the legacy of myopic vision that only recognises British settlers/invaders as colonials. She did so by reimagining the mapping of Australia to determine where South Asians disappeared to from early colonial and nation-building narratives and to thereby challenge the liberal multiculturalism that currently determines Australian diversity policy. She suggested treating language as a perspective: different languages open new narrative opportunities. Khatun argued that the mono nature of Australian colonial society has limited how we read, hear, feel and write history – has prevented the full complexity of Australian history being told and recognised. Specifically, she asserted that if our perspective is always defined by Western consciousness, as informed by Enlightenment narratives, we miss other perspectives and perpetuate the 'myth at the foundation of modern Western thought: the claim that the knowledge systems of Europeans are more advanced than the epistemic traditions of the people they colonised'.[25] Khatun's work started from an inquiry: why was a compendium of Bengali poetry books presumed to be the oldest copy of the Qu'ran in Australia?[26] To find an answer she adopted a pluri-cultural approach and thereby raised the question of how we restore Indigenous geographies.[27] Khatun used linguistic perspective as a way to reverse the 'discursive erasure of Aboriginal peoples and their geographical imaginations – an erasure which is foundational to settler mentality'.[28] Her methodology was to use non-Enlightenment historiographical traditions, to be open, as Looser also asserted, to narratives which are cyclical, circular – which do not follow the line of progress.[29]

These historiographies raise questions pertinent for understanding the *Voyage*. While the explorers acted as enlightenment emissaries, emboldened by a belief that they had the right to possess what they declared *terra incognita*, how can we read their accounts of the Derbarl Yerrigan? Who determined what they mapped and how they viewed it as they traversed the coast of Western Australia and floated up the Derbarl Yerrigan? Can we suggest that the map was made for them, the route was cleared, the sights identified? The Whadjuk people had prepared the landscape; it was just a matter of reading it.

Planning for the *Voyage* and a memorandum for a pleasure garden

The plan Baudin presented to Napoleon was to follow the path of Cook's third voyage and complete it by exploring and mapping the south west of New Holland. However, war with Britain necessitated a more modest itinerary, because of resourcing and strained international relations. The new plan was issued by the famous navigator and government minister, Charles Pierre Claret, Comte de Fleurieu, on 2 Vendémiaire Year IX: 'Citizen Baudin, post captain of the Republic', to undertake a 'voyage of observation and research relating to Geography and Natural History' and to examine 'in detail the *south-west, west, north-west* and *north* coasts of New Holland'.[30] The voyagers should 'study the inhabitants, animals and natural products of the countries' and collect and procure animals and plant-life 'unknown in our climate'. Claret outlined that from Edel Land to Leeuwin 'has not yet been examined', including the '*Zwaan* River which demands to be investigated'.[31] Reinforcing that the emphasis was on scientific endeavours and not political or land-grabbing exercises,³² the selected navy corvettes were renamed the *Géographe* and the *Naturaliste*. The passport 'delivered to Captain Baudin by the British Government issued to the crew by the British Govt' offered safe passage and use of British ports in recognition of the scientific nature of the expedition,³³ with the expectation that the French government would offer the same to their expedition led by Matthew Flinders. Five days later Baudin received a further request from Pierre-Alexandre-Laurent Forfait, the Minister of Marine and Colonies. As well as conducting the scientific collection, Baudin was to bring back a 'special collection' for the wife of the First Consul, Joséphine Bonaparte:

> You will make up this collection of living animals of all kinds, insects, and especially birds of beautiful plumage. As regards animals, I don't need to tell you how to choose between those intended for menageries and those for a collection for pure pleasure. You will appreciate that it must comprise flowers, shrubs, seeds, shells, precious stones, timber for fine works of marquetry, insects, butterflies, etc.³⁴

Forfait reminded Baudin that he was responsible for his crew and for ensuring a successful scientific expedition in the Age of Sail – there was to be no 'commercial speculation' and bartering was banned.³⁵ Finally, he ordered that 'those uncivilised peoples to whom you are taking nothing but benefits' have a positive view of France and to ensure Baudin's fate was not that of 'circumnavigators who have died under the blows of the South Sea islanders'.³⁶ Loaded with French and British maps Baudin, Hamelin and their crews set sail on 27 Vendémiaire Year IX for their first stop, the Ile de France.

The voyage to find the *rivière des Cygnes*

Baudin's *Journal de mer* records sight of New Holland on 7 Prairial, Year IX. Baudin's *Journal de mer* is heavy with recordings of the 'Soundings and nature of the bottom', constantly mindful of the assigned tasks to map and record the landforms. All journals recorded for the *Voyage* were dated by the 1793 National Convention Republican calendar, they used the Réamur thermometer, the French inch and French nautical miles, and longitude was calculated from Paris not Greenwich. Baudin named places as they encountered them, *L'Unique* reef for the calm waters[37], *Baie du Géographe*, *Naturaliste* reef[38], *Berthollet* Island, *Buache* Island.[39] The *Voyage* was scientific and the findings were on French terms.

They arrived on the south west coast at the end of the season known by the Noongar people as *Djeran*, the season of adulthood and ants. During this period the weather turns cool, the wind intensity increases and people prepare to move inland for the colder winter months.[40] On 10 Prairial, Year IX the voyage made their first 'discovery': Géographe Bay. A dingy was sent ashore and the scientists were eager to start exploring – and to find water sources. The corvettes continued up the coast to explore.

The weather changed with the advent of *Makuru*, fertility season, a period that is cold and wet with westerly gales. The corvettes met this weather head on and the journey from Cape Leeuwin was difficult and treacherous. On 15 Prairial, Year IX Heirisson returned from a shore visit reporting that he had found a river or lake. The following day a longboat was sent to investigate. The trip was a disaster; the longboat was grounded. Baudin watched it all through his telescope, recorded his worry that the crew, supplies and boats might be lost and his irritation that those he sent off did not follow the orders he issued to Hamelin – instructions on how officers should behave.[41] Hamelin managed to return to the *Géographe,* and after their meeting Baudin recorded in his journal his fears that despite having arms the men left on shore were 'at the mercy of the natives'.[42] The following day Baudin recorded seeing smoke coming from behind sand dunes on the shore and he hoped it was the lost men. However, upon seeing them on the beach he realised they were 'natives' and his concern heightened should they become 'venturesome'.[43] Some of his fears came true: not only was a longboat from the *Naturaliste* grounded, in the process of re-floating it all equipment was lost, boxes taken ashore for exploration were destroyed and one man, Timothée Vasse, drowned on 18 Prairial, Year IX.[44]

The speculative journey continued and both Baudin's mood and the weather worsened. The *Géographe* and the *Naturaliste* lost each other in the stormy seas on 20 Prairial, Year IX. Baudin noted in his journal that the *Naturaliste* caught up to them and Hamelin signalled their presence. However, Baudin did not stop. To escape the bad weather he decided to take the *Géographe* out of the bay to sea and, as the *Naturaliste* did not follow, he assumed they would next meet at their agreed spot moored at Rottnest Island or at the mouth of the *rivière des Cygnes*.[45] Baudin's decisions were to plan: on 28 Germinal, Year IX, Baudin had written Hamelin a letter telling him to head for Cape Leeuwin and continue north up the coast. If separated, which was likely as the *Naturaliste* was much slower, they should meet at Rottnest Island or Shark Bay.[46] Heeding the instructions, Hamelin continued on and anchored at Rottnest Island on 25 Prairial, Year IX to wait for the *Géographe*. On 26 Prairial, Year IX, the voyagers sailed into a large bay that Baudin assumed led to the *rivière des Cygnes*. The weather sent them away and the *Géographe* retreated and returned three days later. They attempted some dredges with the soundings to add to the Natural History collections and Baudin records with some disappointment that they found 'nothing very curious': jellyfish; sponges; and starfish.[47] On 30 Prairial, Year IX, Baudin's crew had their last sight of the mouth of the *rivière des Cygnes*, and they headed to Shark Bay leaving Hamelin and his crew, who only caught up to the *Géographe* almost three months later.[48] Hamelin noted in his journal a sighting of the *Géographe* from his mooring at Rottnest. Understanding that Baudin had come to their agreed meeting place, Hamelin felt assured until he noted that the *Géographe* did not set its anchor but sailed on, top sail flapping in the winds.[49] Hamelin could not follow as on 26 Prairial, Year IX, and while waiting for Baudin, he had ordered three shore parties. One, led by Louis de Freycinet, to Rottnest, another to islands sighted – Carnac and Garden – and the third, under the leadership of

Heirisson with the mineralogist Joseph Charles Bailly and François Collas, pharmacist, to the *rivière des Cygnes*.[50] It was the latter which was causing him the most concern.

Snatching the *cygnes*

Hamelin charged the *rivière des Cygnes* party to take a longboat to follow the river and search as far as possible inland for the source and to provide an assessment of whether it was a suitable place for vessels to rest. They were asked to identify land resources, fresh water sources and chart the river 26 Prairial, Year IX. The expedition was allocated six days of supplies: food, water and gifts for 'natives'.[51] They set off. Heirisson's log from 27 Prairial, Year IX records that passing Majarree, the river mouth, was difficult in the terrible weather and it took them three attempts to find their way around the sand and rock bar as the strong westerly gales of the *Makuru* season tossed their boat in the waves.[52] The crew worked hard to record what they saw, and to make sense of it: their interpretive lens told them it was a space different from the European one they knew and felt attachment to. Collas wrote a special report on his impressions of the land for Hamelin. He described the land to the right of *Majarree* as 'sterile: no plant life could be seen there' and he reported favourably on what he saw as the fertile 'left bank with flowery shrubs [that] tantalise the eyes with their myriad colours'.[53] Collas did not know that for the Whadjuk Noongar people Booyeembara, the limestone cliffs at the river mouth, indicated a traditional fishing ground and what Collas saw made 'sterile' by the presence of lime, indicated fertility: the lime was *goona*, excretion, which indicated that the Waugal, the rainbow serpent and their giver of life, had rested and fertilised there. Accordingly, the area was a major fishing spot.[54]

Once on the river they sailed through the jellyfish and alongside the pelicans, capturing one.[55] They did not realise that by taking a *nyer* they had violated local Whadjuk Noongar lore by taking a totem. They reported on the many new plants they saw and smelled.[56] Heirisson charted their journey continuously taking soundings by dropping a lead line with tallow in the base. The sticky tallow attracted sediment, shells and sand, indicating the flow and the depth, and the lead weight disrupted and dislodged all that lay in its path as the line was thrown and retracted. They immediately named what they saw, possessing it: the opening to the Djarlgara river was named the *entrée Moureau,* after a midshipman.[57] They assumed it to be a small inlet, recording it as such, hence disappearing a river and important water and food source, as well as home for an ecosystem. Noting the vegetation, Collas reported on this area as wooded and assumed it to be fertile. He then noted a change, which he interpreted as caused by poor fertility: 'Several [trees] were burnt, others were shrivelled and dilapidated with age'.[58] What his perspective sheltered him from seeing was the land cultivation along the river and that the dry vegetation had been purposely burned to encourage regrowth and to attract game for hunting in the drier seasons. The burn-off had happened in *Djeran* before the local people had moved inland for *Makuru* to avoid the rain and flood plains, which explained why they did not see and greet Whadjuk people on the well-used hunting and camping grounds they used.[59]

When they reached the beach below what is now called Mount Eliza they stopped to camp. Unequipped to read the land as anything other than *terra nullius*, they remained unaware that they were on or near the camping ground named Gooniallup, 'the place where the Waugal defecated'.[60] And so they slept where the rainbow serpent, the giver of life for the Whadjuk Noongar people, had also stopped to rest and fertilise. Nor did they realise the campsite was an important place 'associated with male initiation, economic exchange and a recognised trade route for red ochre'.[61] Hoping to get their bearings, the following morning, 30 Prairial, they climbed Mount Eliza. It is possible that the shore party took the track of the Waugal, Gooniallup, to the peak where they looked out to what their European eyes read as mountains.[62] There they noted the river snaked, as Heirisson's map is annotated by soundings replicated;

what they did not know was that the sharp rise of Mount Eliza was made by the Waugal as it came abruptly to the surface and then wriggled to the sea making Derbarl Yerrigan.[63] With limited sense the explorers could not appreciate it as a sacred place. Bailly records that after leaving Mount Eliza they saw *nyer* once again and they killed two more.

Shortly afterwards the party were grounded on the mud shallows near Kakaroomup which they named Heirisson Isles. Here they saw black swans on the *Zwann* for the first time:

> They were swimming majestically on the river. We killed several of them. Their plumage was entirely black, except for long wing-feathers, which were white; the bill was red, and the feet were black. We observed that a few moments after death, the bill (which was red) lost its beautiful colour and turned black.[64]

After, they killed the *maali*, skinned them, cooked and ate them, once again violating local lore. Sustained by a meal, and thinking little of the massacre and the profane disruption, they went on. A little further up they saw what is now called Claise Brook and were delighted to find fresh water. As they went up the river they passed – hidden in plain view – more campsites and hunting grounds.[65] Collas provided an assessment of the vegetation:

> The land is very fertile this far up and becomes more so as one continues inland. I discovered a kind of plant which seemed to me to be of a clover species. It was so abundant that it seemed to have been sowed by the hand of a man in a vast field, very spread out and in which one seemed to see furrows traced by the plough.[66]

Just as Pascoe noted in his analysis of the explorations of Major Thomas Mitchell, while the 'the peculiar furrowed nature of the land' was seen, it was not classified as 'a deliberate farming technique'.[67] However, the *Naturaliste* explorers were elated to find a native well and recorded that they saw no natives, just: 'a man's footprint of extraordinary size'.[68] Reading these accounts and regarding the vegetation patterns on the map Heirisson made, it is possible that this prime, flat farming area with river frontage was the land of the leader of the Beloo people, Munday, which also possibly account for the size of the footprint 'discovered'.[69] At Guildford they noted the salt-water river changed to fresh water.[70] They did not know of the Waugal sleeping in the neck of the river, *Nanook*. They were fortunate to pass unscathed as they were taking soundings and disturbing the river as perhaps the confusion they created meant the Waugal could not see them.[71] The dense forest Collas observed is called Mandoon by the people local of what is now called the Helena Valley.[72] When they reached Jagoolyoo, they reached a sacred place, a site for camping and for tortoise hunting. Nearby was a corroboree ground. Again they slept in a place associated with a Waugal.[73] The next day they went to present-day Henley Brook, which they recorded as a fresh water stream, 18 leagues, or 55 miles, from Majarree, the mouth of the Derbarl Yerrigan.

By now had been travelling for three days and low supplies and hunger forced them to turn back. As they went they shot water birds to eat and once again were grounded in mud shallows near Kakaroomup. That night, 1 Messidor, Year IX, they were terrorised by the wildlife. Sitting in the rain in the longboat they prepared to go ashore and all at once:

> ... we heard a terrible noise that filled us with terror; it was something like a roaring of a bull, but much louder, and seemed to come from the reeds close to us. At this formidable sound we lost all desire to go ashore; and though benumbed with cold we preferred to pass the night on the water, suffering continually from the rain and the weather.[74]

Their fear on the night of 1 Messidor, Year IX could be an indication that felt their presence was possibly unwelcome. It also confirms their inability to understand the place: they had not noticed that just up the river was Kooyamulyup, the place of the frogs and an initiation site for young men.⁷⁵ It is very possible the noise was a frog chorus greeting the *Makuru* rain or a bittern making a feeding call for frogs.⁷⁶

On 2 Messidor, the longboat returned to the *Naturaliste* and Heirisson, Bailly and Collas handed in their records of the trip.⁷⁷ All reported that the journey was difficult and the river depths proved a problem; the boat went aground several times in the unexpected shallows and they were forced to pull it through the marshes and mud. Their reports, and those of the other two adventuring longboats, contributed to the final determination on the Derbarl Yerrigan put forward in Péron's report:

> With regard to the Swan River, it cannot be considered suitable for supplying the water needed for a ship. [...] entering it is very difficult, and its course is obstructed by too many sandbanks and shallows; then one has to go too far upstream to find the fresh water required – if, indeed, this river is anything other than an arm of the sea running inland.⁷⁸

From the visit they collected plants, flowers, seeds, fruits, birds, shells and other specimens, all taken dead or alive. They were all boxed and ready to send home. Among them were two black swans, such as the Dutch explorer Willem de Vlamingh had taken to Batavia.⁷⁹ This time they were destined for the pleasure garden of Malmaison.

Conclusion: Locating the '*tangata whenua* view' at home?

On 18 Prairial, Year XI, Hamelin arrived back in Le Havre. Baudin's vessel, the *Géographe*, returned on 4 Germinal, Year XII, with frigate Captain Pierre-Bernard Milius in command. Baudin did not return to Le Havre with his corvette as he died of tuberculosis in Mauritius aged 46 on 29 Fructidor, Year XI. Also in Mauritius was Matthew Flinders, the captain for the rival British voyage. He had sailed to the Ile de France in Frimaire, Year XII, as his boat needed repairs.

Despite his passport, the governor in Mauritius took Flinders as a prisoner and he remained there for six years.[80]

The returned voyage was not celebrated. Étienne Geoffroy Saint-Hilaire from the *Muséum nationale d'histoire naturelle* in Paris came quietly to Le Havre and took back more than 33 cases containing tens of thousands of animal specimens, botanical samples, live animals and plants and the precious stones – complete detailed survey maps of the land they once classified as *terra incognita*, including Heirisson's first known map of the *rivière des Cygnes*.[81] He also dispatched to Malmaison the contents of Joséphine Bonaparte's pleasure garden: over 600 species of seeds and the surviving live animals.[82]

In 1807 the Imperial printers published the first volume of the official account of the voyage. The author was the naturalist, François Péron, and it was swiftly translated into English and published as *A voyage of discovery to the southern hemisphere*.[83] It was accompanied by an atlas by Lesueur and Petit.[84] Keen eyes scanning the medallion of Malmaison on the cover could pick out the black swans which were stolen from Western Australia, as well as the dwarf emus, kangaroos, wombats, parakeets and a lyre bird taken on the voyage.[85] The publication contains two notable absences. First, the atlas is a collection of engravings of animals, coastlines and 'natives'. There are no maps. Second, there is little to no mention of Baudin in the official account. Relations with Britain were strained and a possible suggestion is that the aim of the voyage, to be the first to publish these maps, was strategically supressed while the political crisis was resolved.

As the maps were disappeared from official memory for the time being, so was Baudin. It perhaps suited the narrative better for him not to be the heroic captain who returned a voyage to France first, and with considerable spoils. Thus Péron was made the official reporter and the focus was on the treacherous journey and the high attrition. Such a trope was made clear in the Preface written by the *Institut de France*: 'some of them being too disgusted with their employment, were landed … others remained in ill health … but the rest are no more!'[86] The reason for these losses was directly squarely at Baudin. Named 'Nicolas the Incompetent, the archetypal loser',[87] it was reported that his anxiety led to bad decisions – to delay departure from the Ile de France, to limit exploration, to micromanage his crews and corvettes.[88] It was in this manner that the voyage remained reported and the significant gains and acts of possession quietly populated Joséphine Bonaparte's pleasure garden and enriched the museum collections. Flinders returned home to England in 1809 and was feted.[89] The first detailed map of the *rivière des Cygnes*, cited as the first known map of Derbarl Yerrigan, was published in 1811 in Part II of the *Voyage* atlas.[90]

In this essay I have methodologically adopted '*tangata whenua* view' to read the accounts of Collas, Heirisson and Bailly and their Derbarl Yerrigan exploration. In doing so the accuracy of Heirisson's map comes into question, as does the possibility that it is the first. The longboat travelled the Derbarl Yerrigan aware of the local inhabitants and wildlife. They explored with the expectation that they would see and greet Whadjuk people. The land to them as *terra incognita* was inhabited and they carried gifts for and had instructions not to 'shed the blood' of those they may meet.[91] Their fear on the night of 1 Messidor, Year IX speaks to their awareness that the land was occupied, and that they were possibly unwelcome. However, their Enlightenment lenses skewed their vision and while they could recognise the possibility of inhabitants they could not conceive that the space they were mapping was a functioning society. That land was cultivated, farmed and maintained. That animals, plants and sites were sacred. That a cultural and spiritual life was established. That the different seasons demanded different occupation patterns. To that society the shore party brought disruption and dislodgement, fundamentally shifting the meaning of the land to Whadjuk Noongar people, erasing local knowledge about land fertility and resources and fitting the landscape into a European vision to be conquered, owned, occupied and stripped of natural resources.

Appendix – Dates

25 March 1800 – 4 Germinal Year VIII of the French Republic
24 September 1800 – 2 Vendémiaire Year IX of the French Republic
19 October 1800 – 27 Vendémiaire Year IX of the French Republic
18 April 1801 – 28 Germinal, Year IX of the French Republic
27 May 1801 – 7 Prairial, Year IX of the French Republic
30 May 1801 – 10 Prairial, Year IX of the French Republic
4 June 1801 – 15 Prairial, Year IX of the French Republic
7 June 1801 – 18 Prairial, Year IX of the French Republic
9 June 1801 – 20 Prairial, Year IX of the French Republic
14 June 1801 – 25 Prairial, Year IX of the French Republic
15 June 1801 – 26 Prairial, Year IX of the French Republic
16 June 1801 – 27 Prairial Year IX of the French Republic
17 June 1801 – 28 Prairial Year IX of the French Republic
19 June 1801 – 30 Prairial, Year IX of the French Republic
20 June 1801 – 1 Messidor, Year IX of the French Republic
21 June 1801 – 2 Messidor, Year IX of the French Republic
7 June 1803 – 18 Prairial, Year XI of the French Republic
25 March 1804 – 4 Germinal, Year XII of the French Republic
16 September 1803 – 29 Fructidor, Year XI of the French Republic
December 1803 – Frimaire, Year XII of the French Republic

Nandi Chinna

Stirling's Garden

By the formation of gardens and by leaving stock, I performed Acts of Occupation upon which at any time a just claim to the Territory might be founded and maintained.
James Stirling, report to Admiralty, 31 August 1827

It is the month of March,
too early for autumn rains
in Swan River country.

Forged metal slices river loam
like a knife through dark cake.
Picks and spades tear holes,
scrape trenches and mounds,
and into this mixture is sown
the simple act of occupation,
the seeds of peas, radishes, and cabbages

the soft stones of precious potatoes
and carefully wrapped cuttings
of English peach trees.

Homesick in unfamiliar soil
the seeds seek the things they know
clouds, humus, water,
and in the absence of these
split open and abort
their mutation onto the hot ground.

The green of a garden
is indifferent to cartography;
lost amongst a tangle of wild grasses,
the colonised have eaten the invaders.

Rivière des Cygnes (Swan River)

de Vlamingh's expedition January 1697

All were very shy, the men, the birds, the swans, the Brent Geese,
Crammed-gees, the cockatoos, the parakeets ...
      Mandrop Torst, Nijptangh diarist, 13 Jan 1697

At every turn of the river
smoke from small fires drifts through trees,
a dark shape snags at the edge of sight,
birds wheel in the sky,
shouting at nothing.

In a pit on the river bank,
sprigs of a pungent herb,
reminiscent of thyme,
float in brackish water.
Nearby, the marks of a thumb and fingers,
a fresh footprint in sand.

A fire, recently lit, collapses into itself,
and three huts shelter soft bark
placed carefully
in the shape of sleeping bodies.
The sailors call out hallo, goedemorgen,
awkward notes, dissolving into the absence

of streets, towns and horses,
bicycles, gates and fences.

It was only the swans, black as coal,
so many swans, to turn the idea of a swan upside down,
watching cautiously, the first bow of a boat
to slice the surface of the river.

The sailors press lead into steel,
aim and fire across centuries,
black feathers percolate the spume.

de Vlamingh thought he heard a nightingale singing
but there were only banks of Black Swans.
He shot nine or ten.

Derbarl Yerrigan (Swan River)

I do not know much about gods; but I think that the river is a strong brown god — sullen, untamed and intractable.

T.S. Eliot, The Dry Salvages, Four Quartets.

There are so many misunderstandings about a river:
Is it a turtle swimming towards the sea
dragging the world on its back?
Is it a dark blue road, a winding highway
green lights to the starboard, red to the port
a confluence of ideologies,

to be demolished, then rebuilt
with rubble torn out of the horizon,
its wild sharp edges carved
into passive moorings for boats?

Is it there to throw yourself into?
Briny skin, hands colliding
with jellyfish as you swim out
recklessly into the paths of ferries and yachts.

Or is it about the beloved held close,
impressed with your knowledge of fish and pelicans,
dolphins, turning grey cartwheels through the backwash
as the sea breeze dents itself against bridge pylons
and drapes you with an imprint of far off places?

Is it a mixing of sweet water with salt,
turning back upon itself, mingling interior and exterior
estuary nibbling at river, river hemorrhaging
into the widening space.

FOUR RIVERS

Is it the flick of a serpent's tail,
or the wake left behind as its rippling skin
cuts swathes in limestone hills,
or an ancient trail along which people walked
following tributaries and at each place
re-telling the story of every drop of water
that seeps from the ground, high dives from stony ledges
and cleaves relentlessly westward?

It unsettles me as I stare into its darkness
but I try not to turn away, I keep looking
as long as it flows, parting from itself
and meeting itself again
in a quiet cove where it will rake the beach,
shells lifting and settling like breath.
And if I am lucky enough to see black swans
moving in pairs, returning home,
I wonder if a river could break,
I wonder if it is a snake, or a turtle
or if is it a god.

Rocky Bay (Kairp Ngungar)

I've often wanted to sleep in the cave myself
but every time I come here there is already
a crumpled blanket, a pair of shoes, and some trousers
hanging on the rocks to dry. Today is no exception,

two Noongar boys are riding their bikes
around and around the limestone column
that holds up the roof of the cave
their tracks like thin snakes crisscrossing
entwining, carving the sand into fish bones.

The ashes of old fires lie metres deep,
black smoke murals depict the night
a serpent camped here,
exhausted after creating the whole river
and then having to fight
to keep the land the river passed through.

Curled up around that central pillar,
who knows how long he slept, regaining his strength,
dreaming up the prawns
the crabs, the particular fishes,
humming in his sleep, the melodies of songs
about women and kids wading in the river
driving fish into the bay, where they are caught
by men waiting with spears.

Did he dream up the newcomers, burning lime,
scarring the walls, blasting holes in the ceiling,
a drain cut through the rock below
still sticky from the effluent of the soap factory
when the cove is called jokingly *Soapy Bay*?

All we know is that the big snake did move on,
tonight someone else will sleep here
curled up in blankets, the dark river
winding westwards, the ocean in the distance
infiltrating their somnolence
with a barely perceptible hiss.

Writing on Water

First you must wade through the minutiae
copepods, water boatman, and backswimmers.
You may be bitten by fleas
reborn after aestivating for two hundred years.
Remember frogs cannot swallow
with their eyes open so they may not see you coming.
Sift out the sediment. (This can be achieved
by taking off your shirt and straining the water through the cloth.)
There is a lot to know before you can start:
water can kill as easily as quench,
water can be very old;
water makes ink run,
will dissolve paper.
One letter too many or too few
can change the whole meaning.
Until it dries out you may not be able to understand
what water has to say.

FOUR RIVERS

Swan River Canyon

Australia's largest canyon, larger than the Grand Canyon, lies 45 km west of Perth, carved by the ancient path of the Swan River.
                                                                         Amy Middleton.[1]

Before the river had a name,
before there was a person to name it,
it swallowed itself whole, pebble teeth
and scouring palate eating the miles
that were not yet miles, excreting alluvium,
building a country onto the end of its tongue.

Submerged mountains sheer into opaque shafts
where galaxies of shrimps glow in mobile constellations.
Deep-sea squid strobe their blue lights.
Star fish weave themselves into baskets.
Crustaceous spiders scutter in rock dust.

One hundred atmospheres deep
crevices wait for creatures not yet invented
to stumble into them and drown.
An ocean rising engulfs an intaglio of footprints
stepped out there when the world was soft,

before the land became the sea,
before the dead were reborn as helical shells.

The Eye

At night the river hones its craft,
creaks and groans as it scrapes the hulls of vessels,
tugs at moorings and deposits versions of itself
further and further out to sea.

The woman is wandering along the river bank.
She stares across the dark mass of restless water;
the light on the automated toilet block
beams constant vacancy from the opposite bank;
a single green eye blinking
through a confusion of riparian fringe.

She thinks she hears a boo book owl
haunting a street tree
but it is only a small dog howling
behind a locked gate.

The rufous night herons shuffle in the pine trees
uncomfortably close to the eaves of houses
where thoughts gather, trapped in ceiling cavities,
isolated from the stars.
She feels the pores of the overheated ground
opening like manifold breaths inhaling,
as cool air falls into the earth.

Haiku[1]

Cass Lynch

The weeping river / gathers salt from the earth / to embitter the sea
Waliny bilya / baal wedjan djalam boodj-ool / warn wardan nyorn ngibart-abiny
Crying river / it gather salt ground-from / make ocean sad poison become

Did serpents make the lands of Britain? / do they wonder / where their people went?
Wagyl warn moonboorli-wardan-boodja unna? / baalap kaadatj / windji baalabang moort koorl?
Creator Serpents make beyond-ocean-country yeah? / them know / where their family go?

The river flows from the hills / through my cerebellum / then out to sea
Bilya baal koorl yal karda mord-ool / koorl boora nganyang nyit noorakoort / ngoowal wardan-koorl
River it go from hills-out-of / go inside my little-brain / then sea-go-to

Carol Millner

Directions

You probably aren't thinking
about it now, as you read this poem,
stirring a cup of cocoa with your
other hand,

you probably haven't thought about it
for days, weeks, even months, yet all
the while small doors are opening and
closing deep

inside your chest. And inside mine
and inside everybody's that you know.
All along the sleeping street oceans of
blood flow—

while my poor poem sails out
across the paper like a nineteenth
century explorer making serendipitous
observations on
the flora and fauna
(loggerhead turtles) and the heat.

Soon we will sail around the point and find
a group of Noongar women gathering or
an Englishman picnicking on the beach.

We will have to ask someone for directions.

Your directions

> After reading T. A. G. Hungerford

I tried to follow your directions
but the market gardens are gone now.

I went looking for the jetty
you jumped off at Como, your father's shop,

your mother's kitchen, your sugar bag
for mullet behind the door. I went looking

for you holding a canoe on your head
and a piece, smothered with lemon

and melon jam, in your other hand.
I went looking for your river.

Weather Words

A few years on and I look up like a local,
number the seasons, as my children have been taught
in Noongar language—

djeran   makuru   djilba

kambarang   birak   bunuru

I calculate lake levels against desal.
enumerate drops in a cloud; conserve
weather words—

cumulonimbus   cloud-burst   storm

plash   patter   petrichor

The way I go[1]

Reimagining Fanny Balbuk (1840–1907)

You come down from Matagarup
with me. I show you how to walk
straight. Straight's the way I go.
You see this wanna? This wanna
love to go digging with me.
Put a fence on my path this wanna
gonna break it down.
My people always used this path
till they took the lakes and built
that station. No more jilgies there now
No more feed of warran. Just trains
trains, bloody trains.
Not only me sad to see those
yam beds go. Somebody's
planted veges all around the
Art Gallery.

CHOGM week

Driving down Barrack Street
I stop at the lights, watch a mother
and her four Japanese children
cross the road. Behind them

the road rises, the wind is at their back
and the Swan Bell Tower stands tall
in a dress of turquoise
practising her royal wave.

I try to recall that were I walking here
before the city I would simply
be climbing a small rise
between two lakes before
dropping down
to the river.

CAROL MILLNER

Derbal Yerrigan

D   e   r   b   a   r   l

Y   e   r   r   i   g   a   n

(Swan River)

Derbal
D-e-r-b-a-r-l   new word

Yerrigan
Y-e-r-r-i-g-a-n

Derbal Yerrigan

this land speaks

Maureen Gibbons

here on this river bank, the flora is familiar: the creeper with
the violet-shaped leaves, the one I transplanted into a chipped,
green-enamelled bowl. my first garden. no flowers, yet the leaves
multiplied, grew larger, and over-flowed the bowl.

in today's winter light, the creeper weaves through clumps of
reeds with vertical criss-crossed shadows. and here, the weeping
melaleuca—tresses teasing the water's surface, bark shedding like
unwanted chapters of a life's story.

on the far side of the canning, mounsey's cows were not seen or
heard until dusk: udders pink and bulbous. their lowing—plaintiff.
no cows today—but look, a shag, black satin feathers flipped open
like oriental fans and the river itself—tannin-stained, the surface a
body of resistance yet teeming with unseen life.

splashes of blue-green feathers, the screech of rainbow lorikeets, not catalogued in my childhood. nor ibis, their curved black beaks etching invisible semi-circles into the soil.

on the river flats, look-alike houses with clipped lawns and sculpted gardens replace our furrowed orchards.

no tang of oranges,

lemons, mandarins.

no skin bloom of santa rosa plum.

no rows of spinach.

no staked runner-beans.

no thwack of axe—no headless fowls

spinning like catherine wheels

on guy fawkes night.

beneath our feet a history: an archaeologist's dream. middens belonging to the beeloo, first nation people, who lived off the land and the river's bounty: fresh-water-mussel-shells, gilgies, birds, possums, kangaroos. buried under detritus of colonial settlers, my ancestors: timber winches, horse-shoes, steel harnesses, milk churns, plough discs, harrows, fence-posts…

i listen, land. you uncover my heart. soften my tread.

The Wonder Book

Daniel Juckes

The book is red, hard-covered, and anonymous; its paper thick and rough. The cover creaks as it opens, and when it does small pieces of paper flutter out: they are newspaper clippings, held together by a rusted pin, and marked with pencil wobbled underneath the typescript. Where the book itself was glued when it was made the paper is no longer cream but brown and speckled, and the tabs holding down the cover and pages are visible lumps. Three spots of foxing, decreasing in size, fall down the title page in constellation; the font of the title is dark, serifed, and thick lettered, and says, *A Wonder-Book and Tanglewood Tales*. On the next page is a small rip, torn a week ago, a decade, or fifty years in the past. Here the fox-spots have seeped through the paper, and are the colour of dried blood.

The book was written by Nathaniel Hawthorne. This edition was published in London, by George Harrap, in 1925, and had come a long way in order to reach the second-hand bookshop in Fremantle where I found it. There, as I looked more closely at the clippings which fell from it, I saw that someone had deliberately chosen to place those crinkled bits of newsprint inside its pages:

they were two years older than the book itself. This was more than enough to convince me to buy it.

For a while it sat on its shelf. Occasionally I would pull the little pin from its place within the clippings and read again what I was beginning to remember. And each time I did, I had to be careful – the paper is fragile, like old skin. When I finally read the wonder book I picked through it like an archaeologist, noting all the quirks and spots and time-tattered detritus inside – I recorded all the rips and tears, the marks, the things trapped between words and pages. As I read, the paper began to turn my fingertips white, and a musty smell seemed to lift and wind around my head and hands, growing stronger the deeper I buried into the stories (which are syrupy retellings of Greek myths). As I read, I kept notes on what I found:

> Pg. 21. A hair, caught between page and spine.
> *You will think, perhaps, that they were afraid of being stung by the serpents that served the Gorgons instead of hair, —*
> Pg. 45. A small red-orange blob, squashed flat, the size of one letter 'a' on the page.
> *But children have no mercy nor consideration for anybody's weariness; and if you had but a single breath left, they would ask you to spend it in telling them a story.*
> Pg. 53. 0.5cm rip at foot of the page, continuing through to page 59.
> Pg. 128. A strange thing, bent like an insect's leg. Black.
> *"Mercy on us!" whispered Baucis to her husband.*
> Pg. 177. An indentation at the foot of the page. Curved like a fingernail.
> Pg. 195. A flat, furry splodge; brown and white. Crusted over the 'p' of 'prince'.
> *"No, prince; but I have seen it before," answered the master. "It came from Talus, I suppose."*
> Pg. 203. A fox-spot. Gradually fading. Visible until pg. 214.
> Pg. 214. A bookmark! Plain white paper, edged in blue (paint?). Completely hidden until the page was turned.

Pg. 276. Wisps of something caught between the pages.
At this intelligence all the voyagers were greatly affrighted.
Pg. 346. A bug, grey now, wings split from its thorax. Trapped.
Their breath scorched the herbage before them. So intensely hot it was indeed, that it caught a dry tree, under which Jason was now standing, and set it all in a light blaze.

The wonder book, when read like this, was its own paper stratigraphy. And the insect inside, so brittle that it cracked and split whenever its page was turned, was a silver fossil. Did it crawl in unnoticed to be sealed off from the world? Or, when it was wet and warm and breathing, did an older pair of hands close the covers to shut it in? The presence of somebody, in the paper slipped between pages, or the pressed half-moon of a fingernail, was tangible – and perhaps even more so than it might have been, because I knew her name: Winnie. And because I had seen the way her fingers wobbled a line of pencil across thin, old paper. The wonder book was one piece of one strand of the string of things that made her.

The clippings I had from Winnie showed a date, but I did not know which newspaper they came from. I felt, though, that I wanted to. I wanted to know more about her, even if I was not quite sure why. (This was the summer in which Perth was a workshop; when the walk from train station to library was little more than a city-shaped noise, and the tracks themselves were being ripped up and pushed underground. Perhaps that was some kind of reason?) In any case, I could hear the great machines at work until the very last moment, when the elevator doors closed and the lift began to rise to the third floor – to the J. S. Battye Library of West Australian History. There is a ritual in places like this; an order of things which manages to identify the uninitiated. It was in the Battye that I finished reading the wonder book, and, once I had noted down all that I found, I remember watching a while the city from there, through its wide windows. Perth was silent; all mirrors and steel, and – in the distance – the river was much the same: made of glass and strange metal. And I thought on the wonder book as I watched. Inside was

APRIL 27, 1923.

Winnie Dawson.—What a charming garden you must have. Quite an orchard, in fact. It must be lovely culling the fruit in the early morning.

COMPETITION FOR SATURDAY, APRIL 21.

QUOTATION FROM SHAKESPEARE.

A well known quotation from Shakespeare is hidden in the combination of letters given below. If you start with the right letter, and then take every third letter you will easily discover it.

HOUSE, CANOE, AFTER, HARE, OUR, ARE, AFIRE, SAGA, AND, FREE, AS, ATTIC, IRON, ANY, TATTA, HENA, MAT, IT, SAW, HOLA, APPLE, EAR, SCHOOL, UEN, RAGE, CONRAD.

AUNTIE NELL'S POSTSCRIPT.

ANSWER TO TO-DAY'S PUZZLE.

QUOTATION FROM SHAKESPEARE.

"There is a destiny that shapes our ds."

PRIZE WINNER.
WINNIE DAVISON.

---

9 Fraser-street, Swanbourne, April 16.
Dear Auntie Nell.—I am sending my solution to Saturday's competition, and I hope I have obtained the correct answer. My mother, sister, and I have just returned from a motor trip with a friend of ours. First we drove along by the sea, and then we returned home by Peppermint Grove, and we enjoyed the drive very much. We have had a very good crop of fruit this year, including figs, grapes, and mulberries. We also had a few pears, but they were not very nice. It is nearly 9 o'clock, so I will have to post this letter now, in order that you will receive it in time for me to enter for the competition. With lots of love and good wishes.—From your loving niece.
WINNIE DAVISON, aged 14 years.

Clippings from *The Daily News*, taken from inside the wonder book.

the story of Cadmus, a prince, who, after years of wandering in search of his lost sister, finds a spot where, he is convinced, his home will be: 'It was a fertile and lovely plain, with great trees flinging their sun-speckled shadows over it, and hills fencing it in from the rough weather. At no great distance, [he] beheld a river gleaming in the sunshine'. But I also thought that, even though this place feels to him like home, there is also the threat and throb of danger, because a dragon lurks. It guards a fountain of water and is threatened when Cadmus's companions approach it. Then the dragon devours each and every one of them, so that Cadmus, incensed, leaps in turn at the creature, leaps down its throat, in order to kill it. Later, he uses its teeth to grow a city on the plain he saw below him.

The day after I finished the wonder book, I poked my head through the door of the microfilm room. There was a woman inside, reaching into one of the thin, metal drawers – there are rows of them there, piled up into dentine columns and stacks all taller than I am. The drawers seem the size of envelopes until you pull them open – then they stretch, like the arms of a magician. The woman pulled out a case and walked past me into a darkened viewing area, where machines made odd, mechanised noises.

I worked my way along the columns to the years I needed, took two cartridges, and found a reader close to the woman I had seen. The films I had chosen covered *The West Australian*, from 9 March 1923 to 23 April 1923, and *The Daily News*, 6 March 1923 to 2 May 1923. It was difficult to thread the newspaper negatives through the winding brace: it's an analogue skill, like poking holes in a cardboard disc in order to program a computer. And even when the film is threaded, you still have to coordinate its projection onto the track of light that is your screen. Only then does the microfilm flash weeks into seconds and do days clack past in a blur – the click-clatter as stories spin is a cream smudge of sound and light, mimicking print runs in old newsreels.

I found no trace of Winnie in *The West Australian*, so changed the cartridge to one made from a newspaper which no longer exists. The layout of *The Daily News* took a little getting used to: the paper seemed to work back-to-front, with the personals first — a patterned mesh of repeated words designed to attract attention — followed by sport, and then sub-headed pages on trade, 'The Land and its Culture', cars, and (on Saturday), the women's and children's sections.

'The Children's Page' was at the back of every Saturday paper. It held games, puzzles, stories, letters, and illustrations, and children were invited to join a club run by the newspaper, 'The Sunshine League', presided over by the editorial presence of Auntie Nell — she would write a weekly column and receive mail, charitable donations, and entries into quizzes from the children the page was for. The league's goal, according to the paper, was 'to train children in acts of kindness and love, believing that such acts bring blessings to themselves and others'. They also aimed to raise funds for the Sunshine Cot, a sponsored cot at the children's hospital; this bit of charity was kept running by donations from the letter writers — Winnie donated once or twice. And all this sweetness seemed to me to fit with Hawthorne's prose — even though there were seventy years between his book's first edition and Winnie's letter, dated April 21, 1923.

In the end, it did not take too long to find her there, on film in the library — though, I can still sense the exhilaration I felt: she was *true*, proved by a record. After that first hit, a trickle began, and as the microfilm turned I found her again and again — perhaps it was because I did not know much at all that anything discovered felt monumental? In any case it seemed as if she was a living puzzle, her traces once built of axons, heartbeats, and bones. From then, that summer, I followed her as best I could, through all the places she said she knew. I went to the houses where she lived, the parts of Perth she mentioned, and the books and films and people she named filled all the time I had: her brother was a wool classer in the north west. She donated to the cot fund when she could. She was well read: ghost stories were a particular favourite, along with *A Tale of Two Cities*; *Jimmy, The New Boy* ('Bonzer!'); *Three Men in a Boat*; and *The Innocents Abroad*. She painted and wrote. She moved house from Swanbourne to Mount Lawley, and then to another address in Mount Lawley. She went to the cinema and saw *Monte Christo*; *Orphans of the Storm*; and *Little Lord Fauntleroy* (starring Mary Pickford); she visited the Theatre Royal, in Perth, on Hay Street, to see Odiva and her performing seals, and she took exams in the month of June, 1923 (the same month Auntie Nell scolded her sunshiners for spinning glass and stones from their shanghais, 'a very dangerous practice, [which] during the week nearly resulted in a little boy bleeding to death. He was struck on the arm, and the glass penetrated very deeply into the flesh, and cut an artery'). Later in the year, Winnie went swimming in Mosman Bay – on 10 December, 1923. When I went to Mosman Bay there was no one swimming, though I could see some people walking out on the sandbank across the bay, and I could see the city shining in the distance. I could hear the sound of lawnmowers.

Nell's columns give snapshots of possible lives. They pick up on themes from the newspaper, and ask the children who write in to tell how they spent their week – she seems, perhaps, an agony aunt for children who have no problems beyond school or sickness or inclement weather. The same sort of children are present in T. A. G. Hungerford's short stories, living idyllic little lives in a city that was, then, semirural. But, in Hungerford's stories, the rough bits do show through. There are boys who yank feathers from peacocks, there are men ruined by World War I, and vagrants drinking methylated spirits in abandoned, convict-built buildings. Tom, his young narrator, says they 'were so poor and the people so hopeless and ashamed and sorry about it all'.

I began to see Nell as a vague, even condescending, presence, lecturing and hectoring, and rather fond of Dear Old England. It was complicated to acknowledge this. And there was something about her which felt untoward: in an earlier column, 'Auntie Nell' – this time in inverted commas – berates the children who did not write to her. She says, 'I was rather disappointed in not receiving more letters about your holidays, and hope that next time I give you an essay, you will respond more loyally … In a few cases the essays [that she did receive], though very good, showed signs of haste, and blots and incorrect spelling were the result'. She was preternaturally concerned with how those texts appeared. In their letters, all the children who wrote to her seemed to know her – some even claimed to have spotted her around Perth. But I am not sure she existed. Maybe they saw something similar to the red rosette of the Sunshine League pinned to one chest as they walked through the city they knew.

Before Auntie Nell came Uncle Tom. He founded the Sunshine League in 1907, and, even though World War I meant less space for children in *The Daily News* – there were paper rations and stories of the conflict were highly sought after – from the early 1920s (when Winnie was writing) they had an entire page again, printed in black and white, with poems and stories about fairies and school squeezed into needle-tight columns. The children ranged in age from quite young (seven, eight, or nine) to teenagers – the oldest I found was 16.

It was hard to warm to most of the people on the page: they were themselves syrupy, like the wonder book. I found myself, over days and weeks of reading their letters, forming impressions and imposing personalities, so that the names of probably-dead people condensed into tiny shapes, and Winnie seemed to be the only child I had difficulty imagining, the only fuzzy one – I don't know if this was because I had invested more in her, or if I felt I owed her more than invention. But, the others – Indie Ducat, Jean Trezise, Ray McLintock, Merwyn Fogg, Olga Porteus, Myrtle Sims, Fred Dempster, Ruth Fitzgerald, Mervyn Ptolomey – I couldn't help but make up. I had to, even though these were once the names of people, writing with pens held in hands attached to bodies. Ruth Fitzgerald, for instance, who lived in an hotel, seemed to send too much money to the cot fund; she boasted too, and her stories and letters seemed always to be published – I remember laughing, in the silence of the library, when Auntie Nell rebuked her for forgetting to include the money she had mentioned in her letter. But Ruth and Nell still did not feel real – not really. The children's page was some kind of facade, behind which the past threatened occasionally.

Despite this, their sunshine world seemed to follow me. Rummaging in another second hand bookshop (this one proper and crooked, bent into strange corners and nooks by books settled on their shelves), I found five issues of *The Sphinx*, a student magazine from Perth Modern School. They ranged in date from 1915 to 1926. Winnie wasn't there, but I did find a McClintock, one 'C' away from Ray, and 'n-i-e' away from Winnie: Winston was photographed, in August 1924, standing on the far left of the middle row in the school's first eighteen football team – 'A reliable kick, but should learn to run the ball the full ten yards before bouncing'. In that issue he wrote a poem about insomnia too, crunched by more 'cansts' and 'arts' than were necessary, and caught somewhere between a deep melancholy and a throwaway glibness:

'INSOMNIA'

(Inspired by a crayfish supper, the com-
      ing exams, and Wordsworth's
sonnet, 'To Sleep')
Come, vagrant sleep, and close the lid
      Upon the casket of my thought!
Come, truant, come when thou art bid,
      And let thyself be caught.
For lonely is the night, and still,
      And, save my own, no breath I hear;
No other mind, no other will,
      Nor heart, nor hand, is near.
Thy waywordness what prayer can move?
      Canst thou by any lure be bought?
Or art though, then, like woman's love,
      That only comes unsought?
Up! Where's my novel now? My gown is here,
      Slumber be hanged! Now for a book and cheer.
                —W. Mc

He was a prefect in 1925, aged around 15 or 16, and was also champion swimmer of the school – at the Claremont swimming baths he recorded times of 6:45 in the 440 yards, 2:39 in the 200, and 68 seconds in the 100. (Later, after all this, the pylons from the Claremont baths were discovered underneath a carpark next to the river where they had once been planted – they had been used as infill since 1936. After their discovery, the pylons were kept 'in the [Freshwater Bay] museum's gardens under hessian wraps to keep damp and prevent rotting'. The museum coordinator made sure that they were watered each day, until a decision could be made on how best to preserve them – whether by drying out or fungal treatment. I sometimes walk past the museum to see if I can spot them. It takes about an hour to get there from Mosman Bay.)

In this sporadic way, I took myself into homes I could never know, placed myself in kitchens I couldn't trust – rooms which blurred at their edges – all the while watching invented, real children plead with parents for the last page in the newspaper. They'd jump and stomp like normal kids, like people I know, and then they'd sit down and write, like tiny adults, something along the lines of, 'I remain, your loving niece. WINNIE DAVISON'. It was, perhaps, a trick of the print or their phrasing that I saw these children as too proper. Maybe their handwritten letters, blotted and run-through with the spelling mistakes so castigated by Auntie Nell, would have brought me nearer? I do not know. I kept learning more about Winnie though – even things she didn't mention, like the weather in certain weeks, or when the Prime Minister came to speak in Perth, or the results of a boat race she could have attended, which ran on the river where she and Winston had swum. I held tightest to the things she told me, but every time I thought I could say something certain, I found more questions to ask. In the end, I found it exhausting to try to keep all the facts I found in order. And anyway, the details were colouring a life I still had no idea of – I didn't know, for instance, what colour eyes Winnie had, or who her mother was. I couldn't tell you what she dreamed about, or if she was in love. Details can be deafening when they come randomly, spattered occasionally on microfilm.

One day, I bumped into an old high-school teacher, and, without meaning to, asked if I could use one of the school's microscopes. I had to remind him of my name even though we had once spent weeks together, in Vietnam, on a field trip.

The high school I attended is not far from where I live. And, as I walked into the front office, where the carpet and the desk and the blinds were the same as the first time I saw them – an afternoon spent patrolling new schools with my parents and brother, a week or two after arriving in Perth from the UK – there was a pile of yearbooks on a small table. I found pictures of me in at least a couple of them, but all the others, the ones from before and the ones from after, didn't know I had ever been there at all. I had to pin a badge saying 'Visitor' to my shirt.

The teacher I'd arranged the visit with was in a meeting, so I was introduced to Poonam, the lab technician. I have a soft spot for lab technicians – it was my dad's first job after graduating from university, and I always imagine him doing the sort of things they do. Poonam was new. The technician years ago was Barry White, who had hairs spouting out of his ears and dispensed test tubes and specimen jars in spectacular silence.

Poonam took me into the science offices, backstage, and set me up on a computer. Something that looked like a torch dangled from a curled-around wire and was plugged into one of the ports. 'We've got two different types of microscopes, you can take some photos with this one and then get a closer look with the stereo one.'

It took a while to get used to the first microscope. I had to use both hands, one to focus and hold the slide, the other to click the mouse to take the photo. Every little jolt and quiver made tiny movements monstrous, but after a few less-than-impressive attempts, I managed to focus on the hair from page 21 of the wonder book. The slides I'd made, up close, were terrible, full of air bubbles and bits of fluff. (I'd made them at my ex-girlfriend's house the night before, trying to avoid the flapping tail of her not-quite-puppy, and hoping that she didn't need her tweezers that evening. I'd bought the empty slides from Toys 'R' Us after spending a long time trying to source them. In the end I'd had to buy a toy microscope; it wasn't very good, but I only needed the rectangular bits of plastic and the little, circular covers that came with it. I kept the slides in a soap tin, and they had rattled on the drive to school. The dog is much older now.)

Through bubbles and lint I saw the hair. It was blond and smooth, probably from an arm or a leg, and it was so slender that it tapered completely to a point I couldn't see even under magnification. Next under the torch was the small splodge of something orange from page 45. It was shaped like Africa and I still couldn't tell what it was, but I imagined it a crumb, something fallen. In any case, it had been stuck to its page in the book, and I had wiggled it free.

The insects, though, were the most interesting things to look at – and there were more now, as the blob from page 195 was not just a miscellaneous splodge, but something. As both creatures grew larger on the screen they became more and more alien, covered in hairs, limbs lost off the edge of the picture – sometimes I wasn't sure if I was looking at limbs or antennae, or just something squashed into badly built slides by my shaking fingers. I took what photos I could with the torch and then moved onto the stereo microscope.

The sub-ocular world is nightmarish. It grows and grows and whatever we can see with eyes or touch with fingers is nothing compared to the close-up or the close-in. Every surface is a strange map, cracked and broken. The winged-insect, so much like a fossil, all grey and brittle and seeming fragile on page 346, was clear and clean and beautiful. And you can see, up close, the point where its wing ripped from its body; there, the pale paths of tiny veins and joining exoskeleton seem a river plain caught through a satellite lens – like a picture of Perth seen from above. I tried to imagine Winnie walking around Lake Monger with Towser, her dog, as she did on 1 December 1923.

Poonam, coming back past where I was sitting with a stacked-full trolley, suggested I hold my phone up to the lens and snap a picture. The odd, murky images – the result of a shaking hand – made a strange impression on me. What used to be a fossil – perhaps a famous, wrecked archaeopteryx, squashed and kept in rock – now, with eyes and mouth frozen forward, lived. Or once-lived, something I can never quite sense in bones. The space close to it was full of colour and covered in hair and the crushed parts of itself, a body made of maps made of cells.

The suspected bent leg from page 128 was a dark and spiny shadow, and the only patch free from spiked hair was the bent part of the limb. The hair from the join between pages 20 and 21, under this new lens, was pristine: cracked, but only like a painting cracks. It was a masterpiece, pointed to a tip I still couldn't quite see, some kind of pale-blond singularity. But the blot across the 'p' of 'prince' on page 195 was the strangest under light. Like an illustration by Ralph Steadman, made of hectic lines and crazed personality, it stared through the lens past a chin pricked with sailor's stubble, each tiny hair of which was tipped like an arrow.

Leaning back from the lens was daunting. The room felt loud, and everything I could see seemed larger and deeper.

As the summer went on, I began to spend more time than I perhaps should have in Mosman Bay. I still do – even now it is a place I cannot let loose. There was, of course, and is, no trace of Winnie or Winston – even though it was one of the few places she named in her letters. But then, there seemed no trace of anyone at all, really. It always seemed so silent – a strange and glorious place perched, somehow, where it should not be. And still, while I am there, I feel resentful of the grand houses on the lip of the river, sprung as if from old dragon's teeth; then there are the Porsches flashing round corners, and the stillness of the water – though I feel too that the view of the city from the top shelf of the cliff is perhaps worth that sense and more, something like an inverse, perhaps, of what Cadmus may have felt on waking and seeing the vast marble domes and pillars of his home newly 'grown up out of the earth'.

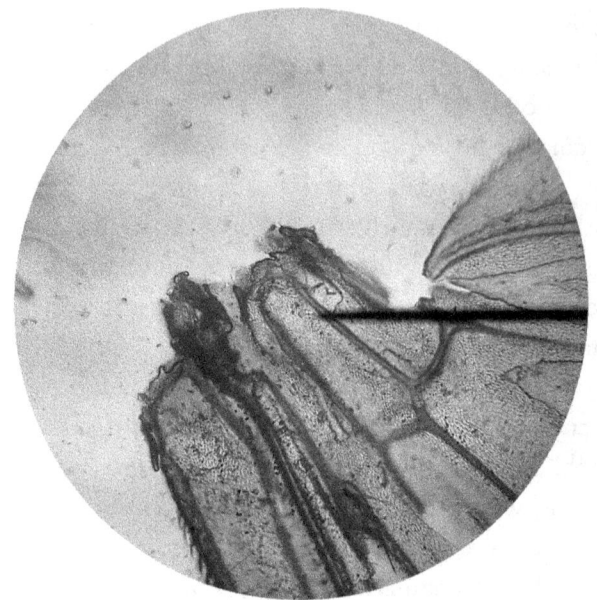

From p. 346 of the wonder book. Detail of the severed insect wing.

From p. 195 of the wonder book. The 'flat, furry splodge ... Crusted over the 'p' of 'prince'.

From the crest of the cliff above Mosman Bay is the river then the plain. And it all – that feeling which is hopeless ashamed, and sorry – is a difficult thing to think through.

When I walk along the bay towards where the pylons from the swimming baths are, I do not like to turn around and watch the houses that I pass. But there is always something in the feeling of them being there. It reminds me. It reminds me of the oddness of the place I came to as a petulant – my parents may have said 'truculent' – 15-year-old. Certainly I was a reluctant emigrant. I did not see the sense in upping sticks, and did not understand any of the reasons presented for doing so. I do now. But then, I had not yet felt the ridiculous pleasure of this sunshine place – the kind of place I kept finding whenever I looked for Winnie, and wherever I looked for her. The high skies and the silent river seem to mask some great and terrible contradiction.

On the first day I remember being in Australia – that day shopping myself and my brother to potential schools either side of the dividing line of the river – I felt a lot like Charles Fox in the opening pages of *The Young Desire It* by Kenneth Seaforth Mackenzie, rather than the children on that newspaper page. As Charles approaches the gates of the school which will change him entirely, he finds himself already in the process of that change – there is something about the age he is, perhaps, but also something about the place, too, which makes him feel both intensely alive and intensely distant. He belongs at the same time as he does not:

> In the late afternoon of a day in February, that hottest of Australian summer months, when a brutal sun stood bronze above the river flats ... Charles came to the School with his mother, walking from the railway station to the gates by a private path across a burnt, untidy field, overhung with Cape lilacs that still drooped, dusty and melancholy, in the late heat of afternoon.

They cross a road, and that 'burnt field', to where 'the dark old wood of the school gates' threaten, and Charles is afraid. That is what I remember of being 15: a fear of all that was new and contradictory inside me. Then, with no chance to turn anything around, Charles and his mother cross the threshold. They walk, 'across the blazing roadway', 'And the gates swallowed them, like the blind open jaws of a dead shark, sinister and smally cathedraline. They had passed through. Freedom and innocence were, for Charles, left outside.' This is a layered kind of feeling now: there are aspects of this threshold I did not realise I had crossed when I came to Australia. But coming here – to this sunshine place – makes one complicit all the same. I do not think I sensed it then – the fear that I am left with now – but I learned quickly to distrust the innocence and legerdemain which exists alongside the river here, and within a city like this. And while I do not like the way it feels the place is still somehow irresistible – and I am obsessed, too, with that idea of innocence. I long for it, perhaps because I am now somewhere which has consequences, and those consequences are not something I can avoid.

I first read those lines by Seaforth Mackenzie on one walk along the river from Mosman Bay to where the Claremont baths were. (This reading was, I admit, somewhat intentional: it felt like the kind of book I should only read by the river, and sometimes I find that kind of synchronicity impossible to resist. I had been reading David Whish-Wilson's *Perth*, in which he quotes Seaforth Mackenzie writing about the upper Swan, where the river was different and perhaps a little more like it was before: there, 'the air was warm and sweet with the rotting water-levels of winter floods. Snags thrust up above their brown reflections … drying and crusted with their own watery decay, but hard as iron beneath, and slippery to the swimmer's naked foot'.) Where I was while I was reading was pristine. The river shone. The place was silent and scentless. I felt an intruder – I always do when I walk along the river, especially so when armed with the flimsy excuse of paper history. But that is the best I can muster here.

From p. 250 of the wonder book, *Cadmus and the Dragon*, by Gustaf Tenggren.

Exile, Rivers and Design:
A Designer's Journey across Rivers

Qassim Saad

Home, dislocation, exile and the second 'home', these terms form the core of a personal narrative concerning different places, their geographies, topographical variations and their environmental foundations. They are combined to sustain human living conditions and construct deep maps of places. Harris argued that 'Deep maps reflect the complex interaction of the physical and human environments and their relations and behaviors that are nuanced, nonlinear, branching, and so very difficult to map'.[1] This personal narrative articulates the betweenness of locations around rivers and places that are accommodated temporarily and then permanently form the 'home' throughout the personal journey of exile from Iraq since 1991.

This narrative provides personal insights into my professional design contexts and practices as an Iraqi industrial designer and educator, consolidating and reflecting my creative practices in theorising design discourses and designing and making objects. The relationship with experienced rivers and places moves from being informed by a 'flat ontology' to attempts to deepen the inherently socio-cultural and political aspects of the living environment, which inform the practices in design, moving beyond unified discipline to include trans-disciplinary approaches, further broadening the contexts of exile, home and the ontological betweenness beyond their emotional scopes.

Introduction

Rivers structure the core of this personal narrative; they play an important role in shaping and modifying the behavioural and the socio-cultural practices of me as a human. They determine the betweenness of incompatible geographical locations during the last five decades, where the inhabitation at the banks of international rivers as well as the local ones during the previous years has stimulated this self-narration. A river as a notion was broadly contextualised by Cioc as 'a biological entity – that it has a "fife" and a "personality" and therefore a "biography" – is not altogether out of step with scientific or commonsense notions of rivers. Rivers seem alive to us – restless, temperamental, fickle, sometimes ranging, sometimes calm'.[2] Moreover, the association between these rivers and their geographical locations considers a contradictory socio-political rhetoric, which has broadly influenced and shaped the self-personality that this narrative aims to address. These rivers enhance the uniqueness of this personal biography by narrating the interconnected story of exile, betweenness, and profession. Cioc analysed the interrelationship between the rivers and the human, building on the context that 'river with human inhabitants is much more than just a physical and biological entity: it is also the site of political, economic, and cultural activity'.[3] In this context, betweenness as a personal experience keeps dominating the transformation of this biography and shaping its contexts from the perspective of the geographical location and its situatedness in the experience of exile; these concepts are then aligned with the profession of being a designer, a practice that locates betweenness, objective and subjective, relating to characteristics of object – the aesthetic, functional and the human sensual experience. It is concerned with the interactional relationship between the object and the human. Such context sharing implies the 'chorology ... as being located on an intellectual continuum between science and art, or as offering a form of understanding, that is between description and explanation'.[4] This trilogy module of experience – exile, river, and design – interlinks and develops the scope of the interdisciplinary knowledge of chronology and geography, of time and location. It reflects the 'uniqueness' of this experience, and stimulated Schönach's argument about the uniqueness of each river: 'each river is different; each region is distinctive and each period involves the uniqueness of both material and societal structures that influence human action and inaction'.[5]

This biographical narrative provides insights about self-transformation throughout different living places situated around rivers. While crossing a river involves both physical and mental transformation from one side of the river to the other, the living experience of the betweenness of these places depends on both home and exile. This was articulated by Said:

> Exile is strangely compelling to think about but terrible to experience. It is the unhealable rift forced between a human being and native place, between the self and its true home: its essential sadness can never be surmounted.[6]

Mesopotamia: perpetual story of chaos between river flood and rebirth

In Mesopotamia the land and the socio-cultural context of its location have influenced society since ancient times. In fact, '[t]he conflict over constructions of culture and place between the former residents and the eco-managerial agencies revolves around the contradictory constructions of place'.[7] Both Mesopotamian rivers, the Euphrates and Tigris, begin in Turkey, and are endowed with a large supply of water from rain and melted ice from the Taurus Mountains. To its north, the Euphrates rises and crosses the mountains of southern Turkey, and then crosses the borders of Turkey and Syria. It then creates an influx into Iraq from the north west on its way to the deep south. The Tigris descends from the mountains of eastern Turkey, crosses north-west Iran and then forms an inflow from the north of Iraq, crossing to the deep south. The Mesopotamian floodplain covers a majority of the river flows in Iraq. The topographical structure of the land is related to the amount of water that flows, keeping the flows of both rivers in the deep south of Iraq slow. They generate and sustain the oldest human agricultural settlement, the 'marshland'. Moving further, the two rivers join and flow together into the city of Qurnah as one big river, the Shatt al-Arab. They maintain their inflow to reach the Gulf, while simultaneously creating a natural borderline between the two countries of Iraq and Iran. Both ancient rivers of Mesopotamia are 'active agents that shape processes and outcomes as driving forces in history'.[8] They are regional rivers, crossing borders and creating a borderline. They are considered 'powerful examples of the multidimensional nature of rivers as both concrete and negotiated boundaries and connectors ... in modern terms, environmental diplomacy'.[9] Across the four countries that they pass, the two rivers bear the influences of both climate change and human interference through water-management infrastructure. These two factors have determined the increased discharge and expansion of the river in recent years. Mesopotamian rivers are political agents: 'the riverine waters are political, and the human–river interactions are political'.[10] This context is a response to the expansion of human populations and the use of water for agriculture, hydroelectricity and other industrial applications, which have led to a considerable shortage of water for human consumption, particularly in Iraq, and to the expansion of desertification. Furthermore, flood disasters have been comparatively few compared with those reported in the ancient history of the land.[11] The ancient *Epic of Gilgamesh* is kept alive by its account of the relationship between humans and the river, where human death is associated with the river flood. That this is such a powerful context is based on the fact that both rivers flood in spring, when most of the crops in Iraq are ready for harvesting. This ancient dilemma has shaped Iraqi socio-cultural practices, including music and songs, food, human relationships, and the broader political and economic dimensions associated with the chaos of the river flood. Flood was a major concern for Sumerians because of the associated human deaths. This fact was expressed in the *Epic of Gilgamesh* in 2000 BC: 'He meets with Utnapishtim who had earlier saved the world from a great flood. Gilgamesh eventually learns that no human can escape death'.[12]

Living between the two rivers: the root and the deduced characteristics

I was born and raised in a conservative working-class family, consisting of grandparents, parents and eight children, in the city of Fallujah on the banks of Euphrates, situated at the narrowest distance between both Mesopotamian rivers. By local standards, we were a normal-sized family. I was the third child following two older sisters. In a working-class family of a traditional society the first male child inherits the family business, which in my case was furniture making as my father had his own furniture-making workshop. The 1970s could be considered the best decade in the contemporary history of Iraq. On the surface there was political stability. Iraq underwent a rapid socio-cultural and economic transformation aimed at implementing the principles modernisation, particularly in the socio-economic sphere. This forced Iraq away from its traditional agricultural economy to an industrial one. The early results of this placed Iraq in the leading position among countries of the region, and United Nations economic development statistics indicated it as a model to be followed by other developing countries.

Decolonisation was a political concept that many developing countries promoted, and what was known as the non-aligned movement was implemented after the Bandung Conference in

Indonesia 1955. 'Decolonization is the horizon of thinking and being that originated as a response to the capitalist and communist imperial designs'.[13] Iraq was one of the nations in the non-aligned movement and became an active member during the 1970s. The principles of this movement justified the Iraqi national government's move to implement socialist ideology in its political rhetoric and practices. This was reflected in broader social policies supporting the country's position as a leader in the provision of modern social services related to health, education and social security. Furthermore, these policies were associated with broader urbanisation projects and the quality of the construction of the country's infrastructure in housing, transportation, energy and water management, and more. These projects relied only on state funding, which expanded because of sharply increased revenues resulting from the nationalisation of the oil industry in Iraq early in the 1970s. The term 'exploded development' was broadly promoted through government-controlled media channels. 'Development' referred to the improvement of core objectives and the transformation of Iraqi society away from its ancient rooted traditions and socio-cultural practices into a new arena represented and implemented by urbanisation and a 'modern' way of living. This was extensively demonstrated through material goods and the socio-political rhetoric. Such rapid moves imposed on conservative Iraqi society reflected the imitation and borrowing of practices and lifestyles from other societies in the region such as Egypt, Iraq and Syria since the post-military coups and establishment of republican states in the early 1950s. These societies promoted 'detraditionalisation', which was broadly enforced and demonstrated through the rising of the middle class. Moreover, it justified the harsh transformation of society to align with urbanisation, modernisation and the exceptional role of socialism, nationalism and autocratic political orders in these countries.

My academic journey began in the late 1960s, when I started primary school in a school named after the day of the Ba'ath party.[14] The school was in a brand-new building, situated close to my home and closer to the banks of the Euphrates River, in the second block to the left of the 'old' Al-Fallujah bridge. This was the only bridge in the city, and was built by the British in the 1930s during their mandated control of Iraq. This bridge was an iconic iron construction, with one road for cars and two paths for pedestrians. The bridge was maintained until the 1970s as a convenient option linking both banks of the Euphrates River in Fallujah. It was a much-needed path for agricultural communities on the other side of the river to access the city and exchange their agricultural products at the local market. Furthermore, the bridge was a strategic connection to the road from Baghdad to the western desert, linking Iraq with the international borders with Syria and Jordan. Later, in the 1960s, the 'new' bridge[15] was built close to the 'old' bridge. It is a modern cement construction with two roads for cars and two paths for pedestrians. While the 'old' bridge represented the colonial era, the 'new' bridge was broadly promoted in the post-colonial propaganda of the time as a representation of the close ties between the two nations of Iraq and the 'old' Yugoslavia, both of them adhering to the principles of decolonisation and the non-aligned movement. The 'new' bridge represented technical exchange and collaboration, promoting principles of self-reliance between the developing countries. The Al-Fallujah city centre and its old suburbs were situated on the left side of the Euphrates River toward the south, and both bridges existed as 'examples of human methods to eliminate the river as a natural barrier while existing at the same time as politicised constructions with spatial and social implications of their own'.[16] In contrast, on the right bank of the Euphrates River was agricultural land, with a large number of farms and orchards situated between the bank and the western desert. This land benefited from the rich soil of the river, which was fertilised during the flood season in spring.

On the bank of Euphrates, between the 'old' and the 'new' bridges, were my home, school and the family's furniture-making workshop. I studied at the public school, which followed a modern study curriculum with a scientific perspective. School study progressed in parallel with another learning experience – developing the craftsmanship of furniture making. This traditional system of skill development was directed by my father. I lived between these two learning systems and an urban modern lifestyle. Positioning my experience 'between' these three factors contextualised my relationship between self, materiality and both the 'old' and 'new' bridges – 'significant not because of their inherent value, but rather because we assign value to them in relation to our projects'.[17] However, considering the possibilities of an urban lifestyle alongside a river, my overall interaction with the Euphrates was limited. It included very simple practices such as sitting on the river bank socialising with friends and crossing the iron bridge to the other bank and returning. I did not have the opportunity to learn how to swim in the river, fish or develop other skills related to the water. I justify my inadequate river experience by my movement away from a traditional lifestyle, which would have offered many of these experiences, to a modern one.

The late 1970s saw the first major shift in my living experience. The era culminated the achievements of two milestones: my graduation from high school and my professional recognition as a craftsman in the furniture-making business. Both of these achievements supported and directed my personal and 'modern' professional preferences, which led to the selection of the first option out of a few of further studies at a university.

I enrolled at the University of Baghdad in the very late 1970s to study industrial design. Study requirements required me to live in Baghdad, the capital of Iraq, away from the Euphrates, and to live my life on the banks of the River Tigris. Baghdad, a big, crowded, lively city, exists on both sides of the Tigris. Each side of the city has its own historical name: Al-Karkh is situated on the western bank, and Al-Rusafa on the eastern bank. There were around eight bridges linking both sides of the city in the late 1970s[18]. Crossing the bridge via public transport from my place of living to my place of study became part of my daily routine. Furthermore, living in Baghdad, away from Fallujah, was the beginning of what became my predominant living situation – that of being away from home and questioning, physically and emotionally, the meaning of the notion and context of 'home', with my physical location implanting self with a web of factors including temporal, physical, spatial, cultural, socio-political and historical. These factors are interconnected and represent extensively complex relationships with the self. Entrikin argued that the natural context of space is 'associated with particular ways of life … include the symbolic context that we create as agents in the world'.[19] This articulation followed the French regional geographers' concept of *milieu*, a term defining place as context, and represented the natural quality of space. This natural context consists of both centric and peripheral elements, where we consider 'home' to be a centre, surrounded by multiple layers of other elements, such as streets, houses and the Euphrates. This central element of 'home' links with our fragmented memories, indicating a strong sense of specific spatial elements and acknowledging it as the home of birth and family, where we develop a sense of our cultural preferences, and as a space associated with learning and practices in life. These are the multiple layers of contexts, practices, and preferences associated with the term 'home' in our memories and emotions.

My reality of a 'modern' way of living guided engagement with the broader offerings of Baghdad, such as art exhibitions, cinema, music performances and other social activities. These things expanded my experience of self away from the lifestyle of and socio-cultural practices of Al-Fallujah. Moreover, they extended the gulf between the links to my 'place of living' in Baghdad and the place I considered 'home' in Fallujah. This self-journey was motivated by the desire for difference, moving me away from the traditional path of domesticity. Further, many circumstances forced me to align with the border between my previous path and the one I had created to accommodate my existence in Baghdad. This border was not linear, and my crossing between the two paths was based on my memory, sense of home and many other factors.

In any city with a river, crossing is a part of the daily routine of human movement in an urban landscape. It is necessary to cross the river is to go to home, work and venues of social activity. This routine action is guided by the geography of the land and location; when we move to a new place, we intentionally settle and confirm our sense of the settlement as home. Living in Baghdad meant opportunities to cross more than one bridge a day. I used to cross an old iron bridge called Al-Sarafiya. It was considerably bigger and wider than the 'old' bridge in Fallujah, with a train line beside the two roads for cars and the pedestrian paths. I usually crossed it in the morning on my way from Utafiyah, a quiet suburb in the Karkh, to the college of fine arts in Waziriyah, an old suburb in Rusafa. On my way back home I occasionally used another route, from Waziriyah to the Baghdad city centre, where more cultural activities took place. I visited art galleries, went to the cinema, socialised with friends and attended the monthly performance by the Iraqi National Symphony Orchestra. On my way back home I would cross the Al-Ahrar bridge, a bridge designed in a similar way to the 'new' bridge of Fallujah. My experience of this modern way of life was reflected in my cultural practices. For the duration of my study and work in Baghdad I developed specialised knowledge and expanded my professional network. A decade of living around the Tigris considerably enriched my experience as a maker, designer and design educator.

Jordan River: the invisible discrepancy

Place and culture play a dominant role in shaping our experience as humans; they are the core elements that shape our individuality and collective identity. This was articulated by Entrikin as 'place presents itself to us as a condition of human experience. As agents in the world, we are always "in place," much as we are always "in culture"'.[20] Moreover, we encounter rapid transformation in our contemporary lives as humans, which influences our perception of the contradiction between our core subjective views of being a part of a place and time and our peripheral objective view that goes beyond the elements of here and now – 'our awareness of the gap between the two perspectives is a part of the perceived crisis of modernity'.[21] The significance of place in the modern context is associated with *situatedness*. This objective value related to human beings in space is characterised by specific universal elements that aim to identify place in our current lives; space in this context includes elements of both identity and action. My journey since 1991 of moving *out of place*, combining both physical and emotional exile, responded to broader circumstances imposing on me the leaving of 'home' and Iraq – away from the excessive expansion of the autocratic political regime and the pressure to utilise specific professional experiences to serve ends that contradicted my personal beliefs and principles.

My first exile relocated me across the western Iraqi border, and I lived in Jordan for a decade from 1991 to 2001. The initial plan was a short stay that would allow me to later move to Europe in order to fulfil my desire to pursue higher education in my speciality, industrial design.

The journey from Baghdad to Amman in July 1991 was concurrent with the extensive political tension that led to another war between Iraq and the USA, shortly after the end of the Operation Desert Storm. It was an experience of spatial changes, along with the memory triggers of home, family and friends. These things, along with the many other aspects of the traveller's life, combined with a 'deep-felt sense of restlessness, alienation and displacement' in my 'escape from a dysfunctional home society'.[22] I was travelling without a map. In my experience, maps had always been associated with borders, and Iraqis had long been long banned by the government from travelling outside the country. In fact, my generation and others – before and after – never got the experience of travelling, particularly during the decade of the 1980s, that of the long war between Iraq and Iran. We grew up with extremely limited knowledge of maps, as they did not exist for civil use. Even for domestic travel people relied on asking others directions to their destination. We missed out on the knowledge and cultural practices associated with maps as elements in our 'stories, conversations, lives and songs lived out in a place ... inseparable from the political and cultural contexts in which they are used'.[23]

My short stay in Jordan extended longer than planned. It supported the expansion of my professional practice in academia.[24] At the same time, I awaited news relevant to my continuous attempts to move out of Jordan. Between 1991 and 2001, visiting Iraq was not an option due to political circumstances; this reinforced my increasing feeling of exile. I lived and worked in the capital of the northern province of Jordan, the city of Irbid, the second largest metropolitan city after the capital Amman. It is an ancient city and a centre of transit trade, close to the Decapolis city of Um Qais. It borders the Jordan Valley, and is situated close to the south Syrian border with Jordan. The fertile plateau of Irbid is a typical feature of Middle Eastern towns. There is a variety of natural scenery and the regional climate reflects both the mountains and the desert. The varied climate and natural scenery offered new experiences. The absence of a river, bridges and crowds added to my sense of dislocation, impatience and instability, heightening the experience of exile. As Said articulates:

> The exile knows that in a secular and contingent world, homes are always provisional. Borders and barriers, which enclose us within the safety of familiar territory, can also become prisons ... Exiles cross borders, break barriers of thought and experience'.[25]

Taieri River: immigration and the sense of second 'home'

A yellow vintage train departed Dunedin train station and slowly left the city suburbs, heading toward the centre of the island. Initially train lines ran within the green of surrounding nature, but as the train moved deeper into the Otago region, finally reaching the small town of Middlemarch, the green gradually transformed to brown, with rocks dominating the scenery. The train climbed up the rocks, traversing tunnels and crossing rusty iron bridges linking the mountains and the gorges. Then, suddenly, from the top of one of these gorges the first image of Taieri River appeared – powerful, rapid water flows, carving the gorge's hard rocks. This image combined with the sound of water dominates my first impression of this river made during that tourist's train trip from Dunedin.

The Taieri river keeps its flowing, and after a relatively short, wavy path, it reaches the ocean through the 'Taieri Mouth', where the it transforms into a wide, calm river, passing a forest-like area and then a short, wide bridge linking the river banks at the river's influx into the ocean. Taieri River has a complex topographic profile that reflects the river's interaction with the underlying basement structure'.[26] Reflecting on this visual impression of the Taieri and the experience of my immigration to New Zealand, I considered the transformation of my feeling of being in exile to that of being content and having a sense of being at 'home'. The associated image of the Taieri, the river, differed from those of my previous experiences of both Mesopotamian rivers, with their geographical and natural contradictions and the powerful impressions made by their flow.

Travelling on a one-way ticket was very exciting! I had never had that sense of finality – that of leaving the familiarity of the western Asian region behind. I left the landscapes, typographies and climate that had shaped my life, social and cultural, both while living in my home country of Iraq and my country of exile, Jordan. The destination of my one-way trip was far away on the edge of the south-western Pacific Ocean: New Zealand, a land of multiple islands that has no border with other countries. It is a unique location unfamiliar to a person from the Middle East and was unlike like anything I had previously experienced.

It takes longer than a full day to fly the distance between New Zealand and the Middle East. In 2001, the route was unfamiliar to travel agencies in my home region. The first flight departed Amman, Jordan, and linked with other flights through many stopovers. The

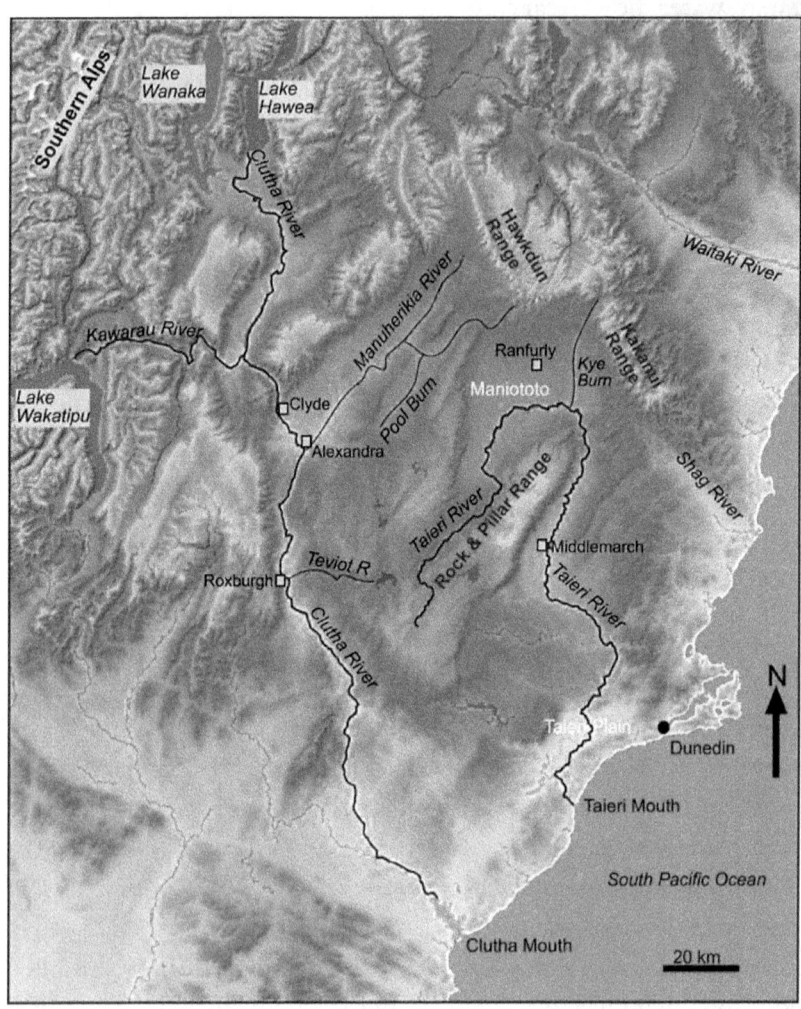

Topographical profile of Taeri River[27]

three-day journey ended in Auckland, which is the major destination for immigrants to New Zealand. Upon arrival in Auckland, I recall negotiating feelings of anxiety, helplessness and loneliness – of being very far away in a new world. In this mix of emotions was the hope of a new start and anxiety about the challenges of starting a new life in an isolated place very far from home. An 'exile is predicted on the existence of, love for, and bond with, one's native place; what is true of all exiles is not that home and love of home are lost, but that loss is inherent in the very existence of both'.[28] I did not experience these emotions and challenges during my journey of exile away from my home to Jordan. Living in this impermanent location just across the border from home for a decade-long 'stopover' was a harsh experience of exile, both physically and mentally, especially as I was so close to home, but unable to cross the border to it. Moreover, as an Iraqi national and passport holder, it was difficult to obtain the right to travel outside of Jordan.[29] This complication is articulated in the idea that '[t]he not-home is based on a desire for difference in the traveller's mind, and the experience of familiar aspects in the actual not-home triggers a mental movement towards the home'.[30]

I quickly felt settled, physically and mentally. I had a feeling of 'home' in this new country. A permanent full-time job in academia four months after my arrival greatly enhanced this feeling. This was associated with a move to the city of Dunedin, the principal city in the Otago Region, deep in the south island. Associated with this was a sentiment of being at home – a physical and mental departure from my sense of exile.

The Nile: ambiguous expatriation

Egypt is a considered a leading state in its region, and for Arabic people, Cairo is a major cosmopolitan and culturally influential capital. This is strengthened by Egypt's ancient history and its large population. The country was a leader in implementing modern social, cultural and economic practices, beginning with its modernisation in the late nineteenth century. In fact, for decades the only higher education institutions for students of Arabic and Islamic countries were in Egypt. Egypt adopted many other modern cultural practices. Furthermore, the spread of post-colonialist ideology was associated with the establishment of the modern the republican state in Egypt in 1952. This phenomenon was repeated later in Iraq and Syria, being influenced by Egyptian leadership in this socio-economic and political rhetoric. Egypt's geography, including topographical variation, also played a significant role in supporting its standing in the region. A well-known concept in Arabic is 'Egypt, the gift of the Nile', which confirms the Nile's extensive role in the sustenance of Egypt – of its people, economy and culture. The Nile has empowered Egypt since ancient times.

One of the world's largest rivers, the Nile originates from the highlands of east Africa, the higher mountains shaped by the rift zone at the upper Nile basin, which guides the flow of the river north, crossing many geographical and climatic regions to reach the Mediterranean. This fact strengthens the significance of the Nile as a natural resource, and contributed to the expansion of the political power of countries in this region of Africa.

'Vertical travel writing' was identified by Alison Calder and cited in Springett as an action considering the narrative interweaving of 'autobiography, archaeology, stories, memories, folklore, traces, reportage, weather, interviews, natural history, science, and intuition'.[31] I considered this context when articulating my experience of living in Cairo from 2013 to 2015.[32] I lived on the island of Gezira situated on the Nile in the west of Cairo. The el-Zamalek neighbourhood, where I lived, is a very wealthy and culturally influential part of the city. Its nineteenth-century apartment blocks and historic buildings are occupied mostly by non-Egyptians.

This part of my narrative is meant to 'go beyond description or simple communication, [but] rather ... an enaction of place'.[33] I wish to indicate my ambiguous sense of expatriation resulting from leaving Dunedin to live in Cairo, which due to my cultural background was familiar because of its language, food, and socio-cultural practices. Further, living close to the Nile evoked nostalgia for my previous lifestyle around the Tigris in Baghdad. However, we must consider the variables of this experience related to the river's geographical location, the el-Zamalek milieu and my living conditions. The Nile represented a 'domestic' site, as it was close to my apartment. I revisited previous practices of crossing a bridge on a daily basis, and this was exciting. Moreover, the Nile is considered a central point on the world map. It allows easy connections between broader locations, both locally and internationally. After a decade of living far away in the isolated deep south of New Zealand this centralness was also very exciting.

Cairo at that time was undergoing a volatile political transformation that resulted in the Arab Spring, a series of anti-government protests initiated in North Africa and the Middle East in late 2010. There were non-violent civil resistance, acts of civil disobedience and strikes against the then president, Hosni Mubarak. This protest, known as the 25 January revolution of 2011, forced President Mubarak to resign in February 2011. This was followed by the election of the next president, Mohamed Morsi, in June 2012. This was shortly followed by internal and external escalations that culminated in the army coup of July 2013, which removed the elected President Morsi. In June 2014, Abdel Fattah el-Sisi was elected as president of Egypt. These volatile actions re-established the use of 'democratic elections' by the authoritarian military regimes that have dominated the region since the 1950s. People living in el-Zamalek supported this and showed their loyalty to the regenerated military–political order. As a foreigner living in Cairo during these events, I was forced to abide by many restrictions on basic day-to-day activities, as well as safety regulations enforced by my university and the New Zealand government.

At an emotional level, living close to the Nile in Cairo, a major Arab capital with considerable cosmopolitan and cultural influences, was not much better than my previous experience of living in exile in Jordan. This was despite the presence of the Nile and its interesting urban features. In fact, my experience of Cairo was that of a life-consuming city that failed to offer a satisfactory life to an ambiguous expatriate.

The Swan and Canning rivers: walking, walking, and re-adaptation

Walking is a relatively new hobby in my daily routine. It has attracted a considerable amount of my attention. It can involve diverse epistemological approaches including the geography of place and its constructional elements. This interactional practice supports the generation of new knowledge. The nature of walking encourages topographical research of the land and geographical mapping. This new knowledge supports connectedness and initiates the conversation between people and the place. I remember the excitement of my very first long walk in Perth. Passing the big palm trees at the bank of Swan River in the CBD, I remembered my first visit to the city in mid-2014. Furthermore, since my relocation from Cairo to Perth in the early 2015,[34] my walking trips have guided me forwards and introduced me to new locations on the coasts of the Indian Ocean, the inner city and around the banks of both the Swan and the Canning Rivers. I have also explored many places to the south and the north of the rivers through walking.[35] This recalled memories and images of similar locations in Middle Eastern deserts and New Zealand's Pacific Ocean coast. Living close to both the Swan and the Canning rivers and my exploration and physical interaction with this place engendered self-discovery. This led to a desire for adaptation to and stability in place.

Many have searched beyond *flat ontology* with the aim of creating '[d]eep mapping ... to address ... hierarchies, which are specifically social and ecological in nature in a way that is inherently political'[36] in their future relationship with place. In my current 'permanent' situation to the south of the river, I made a definite move to achieve this desire of feeling at home. Recently, driving across the Riverton Bridge to Riverton Jetty Park while listening to classical music on the radio has become routine at the start and the end of each working day. This is a ritual reminiscent of earlier times: crossing the Tigress river daily on the way from home to the university and then going to the Iraqi National Symphony Orchestra Hall; or crossing the Nile on the way home from work and visiting Cairo's remarkable 'Opera House' on the bank of the Nile to enjoy listening to the Iraqi musician Naseer Shamma[37] performing on his oud at 'El Sawy Culturewheel'[38] in el-Zamalek.

Interpreting exile and rivers through design

This long journey across geographical and topographical entities was always associated with the rivers and the significance of their situatedness. They are the key elements identifying place and topography. This journey sustained and shaped the experience of 'situatedness and the closely related issues of identity and action'.[39] My own interaction with these rivers and their surrounding topographical entities has been reflected through diverse creative design practices, such as writing discourses on design and designing and making objects. I have theorised on some of my design work. I have selected as an example of these creative practices the design of a 'lighting unit'. These products got major attention from designers of all disciplines, and new designs representing them as social agents reflecting culture, emotional interaction and technological progression keep emerging. I will review two examples of lighting units I have designed and made. These designs were selected to articulate my interpretation of my experience living around the Taieri River in New Zealand and of living around the Swan and the Canning rivers in Perth.

Enarah-1[40]

Enarah-1 was created in Dunedin in 2007. The design addressed a process-based emotional inspiration, and the materials used in fabrication and techniques of production reflect my experience of furniture making in Iraq. I used native timber as the main material and used the traditional techniques of slip casting and glassing. The design reflects the interconnection between Fallujah and Dunedin, which are linked through the practice of my life as a designer in Dunedin and the nostalgic inspiration of my home in Fallujah. In this design I was inspired by the dynamic interplay of light, shadow, and darkness, and the ways they illuminate the complex relationship between the natural and the artificial. A part of this inspiration was drawn from my own visual memories of childhood and adolescence. I still enjoy remembering the image of harsh sunlight falling on the open courtyard of my family home in Fallujah, and how this defined the visual environment in which we lived, played and worked. All of the objects that we designed interacted with light in some way, and my memories of my family home's open courtyard are partly memories of the unique physical characteristics that the light took on when it existed within an open spatial environment that was nonetheless dominated by artificial objects. There are fascinating sensations that can be evoked when light emerges from its source to reveal the hidden shapes in an object. I have a tendency in my own design work to make light sources invisible parts of many of the lighting units that I create. Personal interpretation is actively encouraged for the viewer to identify the value of these aesthetic objects, their natural and artificial materials, and the relationship between the aesthetics and the nature that they imply. Composition in design involves the identification of the essential qualities in the domain and then addressing the unexpected relationships within the entire structure. *Enarah-1* was publicly exhibited twice in Dunedin in 2007 in the Salisbury House Gallery, and later in 2009, at the Dunedin School of Art at Otago Polytechnic.

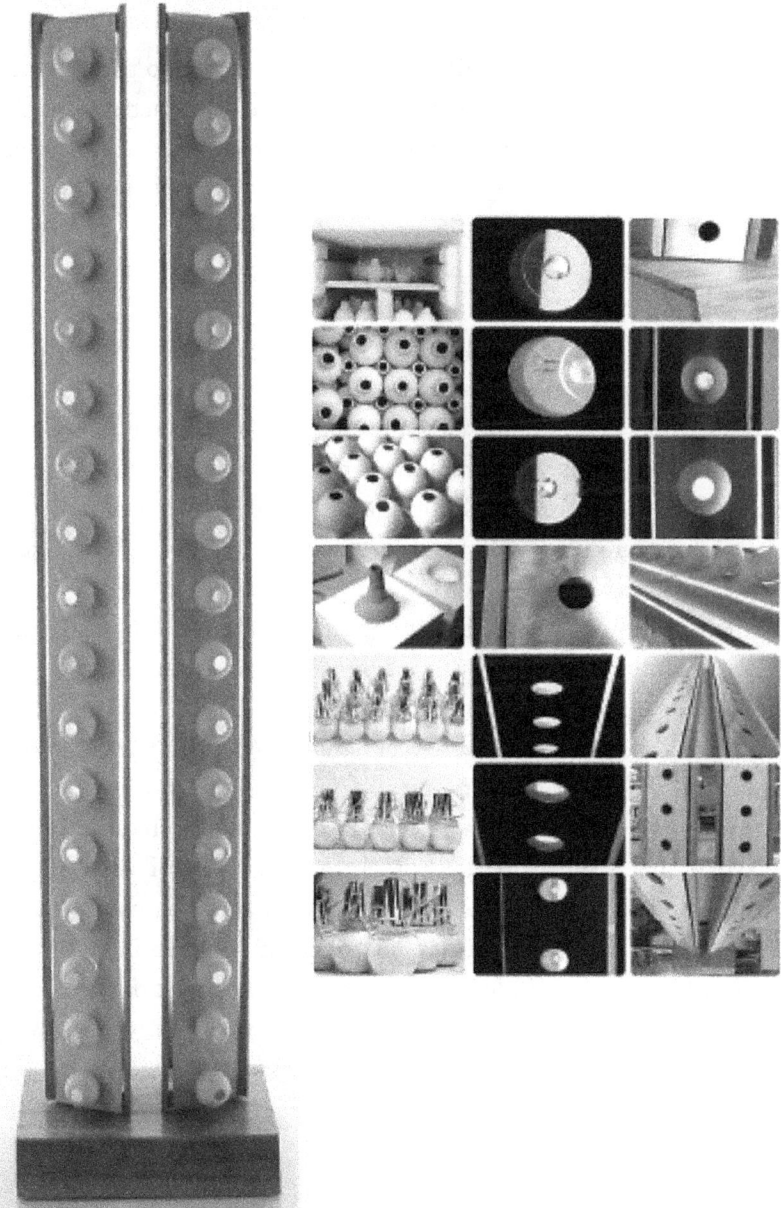

Enarah-1. Making process and the final working model. Rimu, New Zealand's native timber, ceramic slip casting, and LEDs, 300 × 400 × 1,800 millimetres, DLH.

Enarah-3

In this work I leave nostalgia behind and move beyond the influence of the movement and its changeable sequences – the actions shaping the way we live and interact with the surrounding environment. The reshaping of the self is affected by new knowledge, age and new inspirational experiences, along with the way we understand these variables and utilise them as the main resources in the process of creating a new design.

Enarah-3 was designed and produced in 2017. It reveals a geometric composition dominated by a structure of synthetic material over natural. The design elements reflect the direct influences of situatedness in a newly established milieu dominated by artificially created objects, high-tech buildings, streets and infrastructure. These are combined with a remarkable natural scene. The design represents two identical rectangular frames, each frame containing its lighting source and fully functioning as a separate lighting unit. This treatment addressed the personal visual articulation of the major elements of my new living experience since 2015, where both the Swan and the Canning Rivers are the dominant interactional elements. *Enarah-3* was structured from transparent acrylic plastic sheets, with the outer surfaces treated technically to show the frosty textural effects when the light is on. A thin frame of native Jarrah timber divided the mass between the two major transparent plastic frames. The influences of the surrounding environment on this design led to a flat understanding and a lack of depth in relation to the personal situatedness in Perth at this stage of my new living experience. My interpretation of this context was considerably influenced by my experience of ambiguous expatriation while living along the Nile River.

Conclusion: revisit 'home' again

'We often visit physical sites and landmarks to help remember the past. But when those identifiable markers have disappeared, what then?'[41] My preparations early in 2019 to revisit home in Fallujah and the

Enarah-3. Acrylic transparency sheets, jarrah native timber and LEDs, 55 × 170 × 300 millimetres, DLH.

Euphrates in response to repeated requests from my father and family were mainly driven by emotion. I was anxious not only about the preparation for a long trip home, but also the short stay. My anxiety was based on the anticipation of unknown entry requirements at Baghdad Airport for non-Iraqi passport holders. I had travelled through that airport only once since, on a previous trip home in 2005.[42] There were also extremely restrictive security regulations concerning the eligibility of entry by non-residents to my home city of Fallujah. These regulations have been in place since the liberation of the city after the third battle of Fallujah, which started in mid-2016, when the government forces and their allies' militias forced what they called the 'Islamic State' fighters to leave the city.

Following the advice of family and friends, during the trip I carried only an Iraqi official ID card with me. I had saved it as proof of my being an Iraqi citizen. At the airport arrivals gate, I was advised by the security personnel to join the non-Iraqi queue for the immigration check, and upon my turn, I presented both my Iraqi ID card and my non-Iraqi passport to the immigration officer. He looked at me and then at both the documents, and then checked the screen in front of him. Then, he asked another officer from outside the booth to check my documents. After the other officer checked all of my documents, my passport was stamped and I was allowed to enter 'home'.[43]

I left the airport to meet my two younger brothers who were awaiting my arrival in outside the airport. It was a one-hour trip by car from there to home in Fallujah. The road to Fallujah was full of many checkpoints controlled by government forces and other militia, and I was advised not to show my passport but use the Iraqi ID card. After two hours, we arrived home safely. I experienced the country's instability from the airplane's exit door to the family home. This was evident from the dilapidated airport building, and the war zone showed through the boomed roads, bridges, public buildings and houses, both inside the city and outside of it. Furthermore, both the Fallujah bridges across the Euphrates had been bombed, but until recently had kept being 'unsafely' used.[44]

The experience of my trip back to a drastically changed home is well articulated by Peter Read as a '[j]ourney to nothing ... where there is a seeming void, a nothing ... [that] demonstrates the vibrant memories and intense attachments to those places'.[45] This experience engendered a large number of personal statements about uncertainty and the future, relating to existence in a place and along its rivers. They recall Edward Said's statement:

> When I arrived in Cairo after graduation, I soon saw that my memory of it during my exile in the United States as a place of stability was no longer accurate. There was a new uncertainty: the placid paradise for foreigners was beginning to lose its durability.[46]

A Single Day's Riding

Susanna Castleden

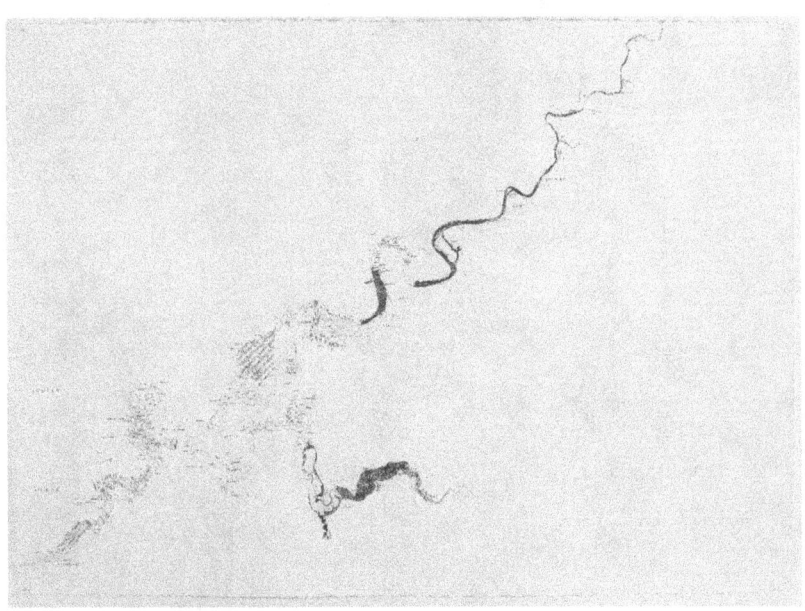

A Single Day's Riding. Gesso and screenprint on rag paper,
107 centimetres × 150 centimetres.
PHOTO BY ROBERT FRITH, 2021.

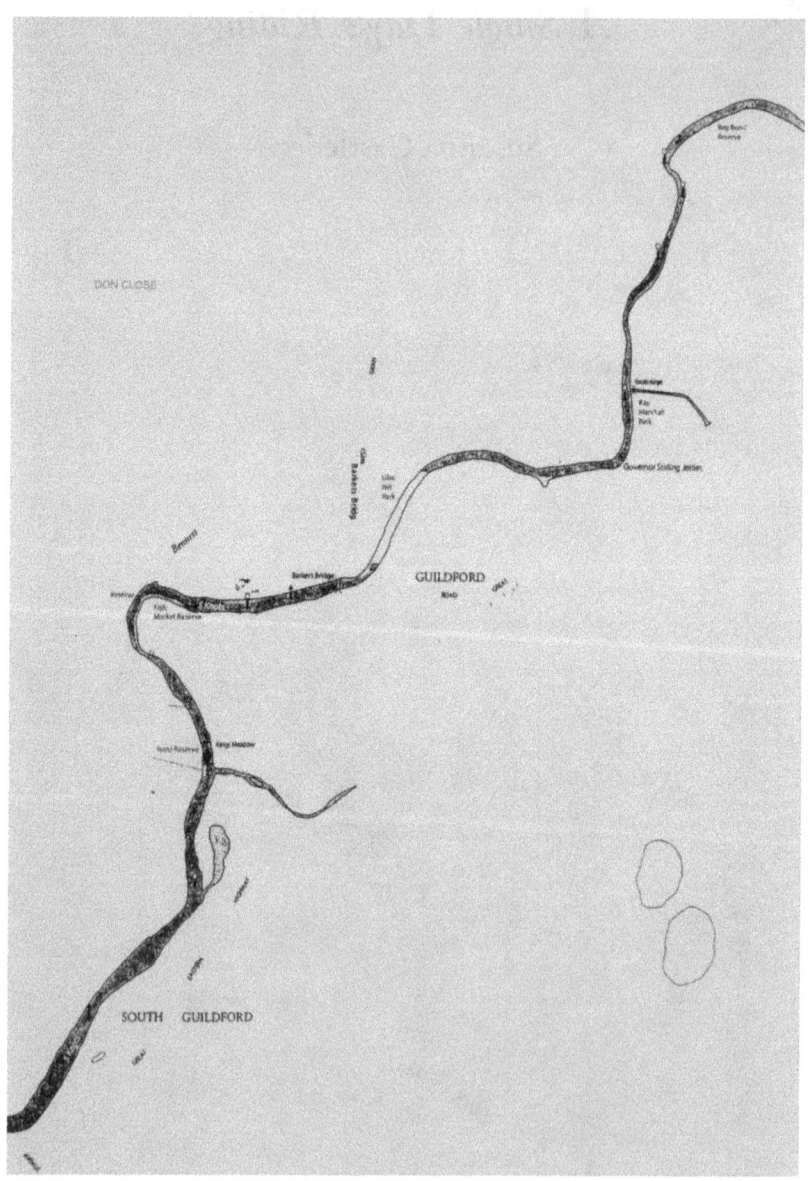

A Single Day's Riding. Detail.
PHOTO BY ROBERT FRITH, 2021.

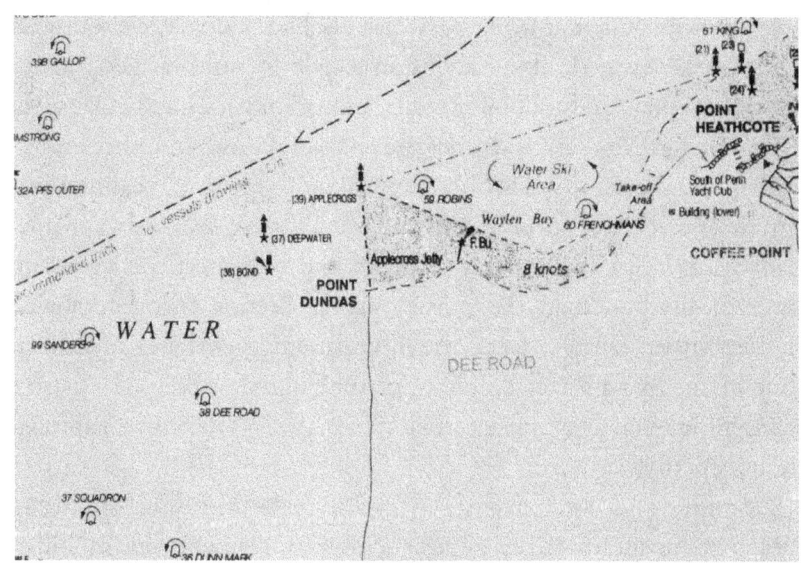

A Single Day's Riding. Detail.
PHOTO BY ROBERT FRITH, 2021.

This artwork emerges from, with and through a bicycle ride. The intertwining catalysts for this project were my entangled experiences of commuting to work via bike along the Swan and Canning Rivers, thinking about an article by cultural geographer Justin Spinney, and grappling with the complexities and curiosities of mapping. My daily ride, despite the ubiquitous and unrelenting Perth winds, is a space for physical and mental recalibration: rhythms of pedals, corners, hills and breath bring the landscape into close proximity to the body. Human and non-human encounters sporadically punctuate the journey via the fleeting encounters with unknown yet familiar faces, the intermittent appearance of Akuna, one of the Swan River dolphins, or the tangible sweep of a galah's wing momentarily alongside. The ride is always a lesson in ruptures to its repetition.

Spinney, an avid cyclist, in writing about riding up Mont Ventoux, posits that 'the experiences of movement and mobility can be seen as constitutive of the meaning and character of a place because of an ongoing dialectic between body and place'.[1] In focusing on the embodied sensation of movement, Spinney takes an ethnographic approach to the ascent of the 'Giant of Provence', considering the integral physical and conceptual interplay of bodily rhythms, suggesting that 'it is through rhythm that riding is inhabited'.[2] It was through reading Spinney's article (after I too had ascended Mont Ventoux) that the idea germinated to approach the *Four Rivers Deep* project through examining the sensation of circumnavigating the Canning, Swan, Dee and Don Rivers by bike. However, geographical thinking could not fix the problem of geographical distance. The Canning and Swan Rivers are present and sentient in my everyday Perth landscape, but for me, the Dee and Don were distant, unfamiliar and physically unreachable.

It was through the thinking time provided by my daily cycling commute, and triggered by a heightened sense of observation, that I eventually found a way to bring these distant places together. It was while riding home one day that I noticed the short downhill road that runs into the banks of the Swan River, a section I pass daily, was coincidentally named Dee Road. A Google map search revealed an apt pairing – Don Close, an unfamiliar road in an unfamiliar suburb, but one that, at a push, could possibly be travelled to by bike if I followed the edges of the Swan and Canning Rivers beyond the reach of my usual commute.

On a hot, humid and uncommonly windless day in February I embarked on the 125-kilometre ride around the Swan and Canning Rivers, via a road named Dee and a close named Don. Titled after cultural geographer John Wylie's seminal paper, A 'Single Day's Walking' (2005) the focus of the artwork was intended to be on the subjectivity and spatiality[3] of the day's ride. However, through the process of creative practice research – making, looking, reworking, erasing, reading, writing and thinking – it emerged that the methods of tracing and recounting the ride visually placed unwanted emphasis on the subjective. Thus, in this work the rivers are the focus. The surrounding Perth region is absent, replaced instead by a buffed blank gesso surface, leaving the rivers dominant, stretching diagonally across the page. The ride was ultimately dictated by the rivers, and here the track of the ride is represented by its absence. Rather, the experience of the day's ride is revealed in the grey and slippery surfaces, hinting at the misty atmosphere of the clammy and humid day. The artwork is essentially an accumulation of types of mapping – of a ride, a place and of a way of thinking about rivers on other sides of the world.

Moving Bodies along the Swan River

Tom Wilson

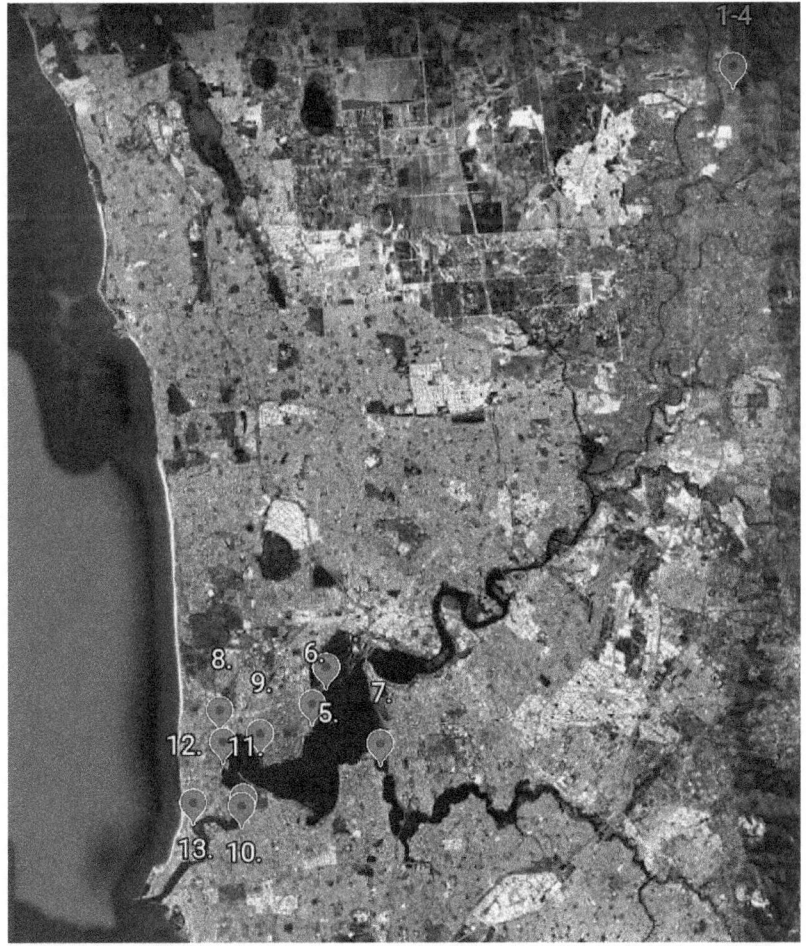

Stops on a decade-long journey down the Swan River. The numbers correspond with the sections of writing below.

IMAGE: GOOGLE DATA SIO, NOAA, U.S. NAVY, NGA, GEBCO CNES/AIRBUS.

1.

The rain kept coming in thin misty and mysterious sheets. Despite this, the air wasn't cold and the sun was never far away. Walking through a woodland of flooded gums along the river we heard a multitude of bird and frog songs. The birds were excited at the changing sky: rain, sun, more rain. Shell ducks flapped down their flight paths onto the river's surface. A mother kangaroo, or *yonga*, licked her daughter's wet grey coat and then stood tall and stared at us, the furless intruders. The earth sprang wet, fresh and green to our eyes. Angular suburbs were only a memory.

I kept looking around with a sense of surprise as I walked along the river banks, through Walyunga National Park. Used to living in a dry and crackling place, I couldn't get used to all this water. To this feeling of gurgling surfeit and softness that it gave to my experience of place. In winter the Noongar went inland to areas like this sheltered river valley. The rain has been falling frequently over the last few weeks in south-western Australia and the Swan River, known as the Avon where we walked along its banks, had swollen and flooded its edges. The water, brown from the soil it picked up on its flow through the wheatbelt, roared over the rapids, and chuckled in the feet of the melaleucas, then flowed with a quiet lapping sound in the broader stretches of the river's path. Most of the waterways coming out of the Darling Ranges were dammed for Perth's water use before this writer was born. But here a big winter flow was on.

2.

Another year, and it is summer. A friend and I camped beside the same river. It was the only place we could see that was flat enough, a grey, slightly muddy area. But we scooped up lots of sand from up on the hill and dropped it on the area, and we had a camping spot beside a big pool fringed by towering jarrah trees and vocal frogs. That night the frogs chorused in three dimensions through dark space, while fire flickered over her face on the sandy edge of the river. We sat on granite boulders I had carried there from a river bed nearby and drank a bottle of red wine and ate sandwiches. And talked. It was good to be there with Gilliane and the fire and the dark and the thumping on the other bank from roos in the wilderness and intimate conversations about our loves and losses, our hopes and fears. With the flat pan of the river before us and the trees and bushes sheltering us behind and to our sides and the fire there on the edge of the river, just as it would have been for the white explorers of this river like Dale and Roe in the 1830s. And our little *mia*, our little *cabane des naturels*, behind us, into which we would later crawl and relax and sleep. That night I slept covered by my *buka* (kangaroo cloak), with the soft downy press of kangaroo fur on my cheek.

3.

One of my favourite spots is near the summit of the tallest hill on the edge of the Darling Scarp where the Avon exits the hills. This time it was hot and we were tired from the very steep walk. Down, down, in a crook of the valley behind us, a wide and fast flowing Avon River glinted. With the heat baking us, it encouraged us backwards. But we trod forward nonetheless. Soon we reached the top, clapping our hands loudly as we waded through tall grass to scare off errant dugites. A large granite boulder crowned the bald head of the hill. That was it. We climbed on top of it and stood, finally, looking out on the table cloth of paddocks and trees stretching out beneath us to the west. It was a vista which, as the eye moved up towards the horizon, quickly became roads and houses, before ending with the flat blue rim of the sea. This urban settlement had been placed atop old sand hills and, despite all the changes, we could still see the same maker of the old sands, the Indian Ocean edging, in the distance. The pleasure of topping out and having a larger perspective on the world was ours.

Later we walked back down the red gravel track to the bottom of the valley. A big black monitor lizard shot off its basking place on a granite boulder and scurried out of danger. Soon we were unclothed and swimming in the cool and fast flowing Avon. My feet touched the bottom of a deep section in the bend of the river. Clinging to the edge of a rock while Gilliane enjoyed the sun on her skin. Feeling the bottom with my feet and seeing the slopes of the valley, full of granite boulders and balgas and jarrah and marri and not even a footprint or a memory of a tourist, feeling the fast-flowing water on my body ...

Go forth with your eyes wide open. Shadows sway. Surfaces are real. You are human. Go up into those hills. They are waiting, just out of view of the city.

4.
Another day I wondered shirtless and comfortable along the river, moving east downriver along the river bank, this time with another friend. The ground was open and occasionally granite boulders pushed up from the ground to our right, which rose upwards. Roos bounced out of our way. Less rain falls here than in the jarrah forests further south, and so there's less of a tangled understory to stop the wanderer. The freedom of movement that such openness allows is enjoyable. The air was like a warm perfumed liquid when we walked past blossoming shrubs. As we stepped over river-bed pebbles, the mud laced the air with a sweet scent. I drew the mix of flower and river mud perfume deep into my lungs with satisfaction. I feel a connection with this north and western area of the Darling Range forests, dry and open and wound around by this old river. It is a place – if privacy sometimes permits – for naked swimming and boulder clambering, looking higher for a vantage point over the plain to our west.

That night I stepped out the front of our four man dome tent, looked to the west through the silhouettes of branches and trunks and saw the orange glow of the ceaselessly metabolising city light up the sky to our west: Perth. A feeling of gladness to be away from that fiery halo, and bunkered down here in this valley along with a more ageless Australia.

5.

Most human lives in Western Australia are lived further down the Swan River, in the streets and buildings of the city. Very often, when I'm tired of being dutiful and productive in my life, I get up and walk to the Swan. When I'm perched desk-side at the University of Western Australia, I have a habit of regularly standing up and running downriver along the grass and amongst the trees. At one particular point upon reaching my old haunts in Dalkeith, I veer right and climb a slope and a tree – I stand there with the river below me and feel at peace again. Feel a moment of reprieve and exhilaration. In winter I have to go for these snack jogs where I run down along the river in lulls between rains. Like a shot of sanity into my main vein, these experiences make me feel alive, stable and engaged again after hours of reading and writing and literate, physical inactivity. Not moving one's body for too long can cause all kinds of mental strangeness. Being sedentary in the city usually comes with the territory, but it need not. Let the fools play at being solemn, revolving on their spinal columns. I hold with movement.

6.

Too much of the *vita sedentaria* is not a recipe for health and human flourishing. Being a writer and a reader means that you're often sitting down. Too much of the *vita sedentaria* is not a recipe for health and human flourishing and is an occupational risk. After reading in my apartment near the university I often walk to the river before sleep. Being down by the river in the night's air: quiet, empty of people, wet, winter, expanse of water, old place, real nature, real world. Blood moving again. A rallying of the spirit. My thought proceeds so much clearer after this little bit of motion.

7.

Once when sitting at the end of a wooden jetty on the Canning River with a friend we heard the noise of what sounded like a large fish jumping just out of sight in the dark. Distracted from our conversation, we looked left out into the dark to see what was making the noise. Soon a fin cruised in a steady line towards the jetty, and then another. It was a pod of small river dolphins herding and hunting a school of fish. They were making large circles around the school, breaching and sucking water in abrupt hisses before ducking down again to continue the hunt. They came within reaching distance of us in a maelstrom of powerful underwater movements, elegantly and silently sliding under the surface all around us.

To be so close to them as they moved around us, weaving through the jetty pylons below us, or doing a sharp right angle turn around the end of the jetty, we could see close up how large their bodies were and how fast they could move through the water. They are really large – much bigger than us humans. They move so fast that it lifts your spirits. You take in air with delight and surprise to see such big intelligent beings so mobile and intent and close in the night air. Just me and a friend and the pod of hunters circling and chasing in the dark mysterious water.

Robinson Jeffers wished for us all – humanity as a whole – to *uncenter ourselves a little*.[1] Dolphins in the Swan River help the people of Perth, at least those who are attentive enough, to uncenter ourselves, at least a little.

8.

Another evening, around 6.00 pm on a Thursday evening in spring conditions. Perfect temperature for a jog, and no wind. I was running along a gravel path 3 or 4 metres above the Swan River in Peppermint Grove, with the slope continuing up on my right hand side and the river on my left. Trees and shrubs and a verdant cover of fresh green grass covered the slope, which turned into a limestone cliff further up, cutting off any noise of traffic from the road above. Alone on the trail, and running barefoot. The water to my left was a smooth, grey sheen, with faint skin-colour tones and the odd cloud in the sky out over the water was tinged by the apricot glow of the sunset. I ran and felt the sweat on my skin. The world was silent, and the path wound forward around a tree-lined corner. Then the silence was broken.

A large bottlenose dolphin hissed out from the water's calm surface five metres to my left.

Then another.

Then another.

Seven dolphins broke the water surface, the youngest and smallest jumping right out and falling back with a splash. They were all going the same direction as me. While looking left, I didn't stop. I kept running.

I realised that a large family of wild dolphins was travelling the same speed as me, in the same direction. Actually they were travelling faster than me. Speed up. It's fine to know intellectually that these mammals can travel up to 35 kilometres an hour, but it's another thing to actually run with them at that speed, barefoot. To keep pace with the band I was not jogging, I was sprinting. I kept alongside them for around 1,000 metres – it was the best 1,000 metres I've ever run. I was a few metres away from a playful band of wild mammals more than five times the weight of me, moving forward with knife-like ease, moving through liquid with elegance and power. I could hear my breathing, pulling air down into my lungs in gasps. I could hear their breathing, drawing air down into their lungs and hissing it out when they surfaced. Feeling what it's like to travel at dolphin speed. They sliced the smooth water of my previously complacent mood like surgical implements. With every leap forward of my gait, matching their sinusoidal path up and down through the water, my spirit bounced up. It didn't come down again for hours afterwards.

The path where I was running goes past what was, for many years, my principal sanctuary in the natural world. I would regularly jog along the river near Freshwater Bay in Peppermint Grove, along a limestone cliff path that skirts the steep river bank there. In the late afternoon stillness between rainfall the native cypress that I loved stood out proudly and beautifully over the still sheen of the river's water. It was a little like a bonsai, projecting a wild angle out over scree, while remaining self-contained and symmetrical. It became a habit to regularly climb out on one of its horizontally projecting limbs and stand and think how good it is to connect with the natural world, so close to my home. Then I did the same another morning in the sunshine with the water rustling in limpid clarity along the limestone rocks and boulders and the shoreline, and the winter greenery looking cheerfully refreshed in the morning's light. My mood lifted each time I stood on the limbs of this *Callitris preissii* (what some call Rottnest Island pine – although its endemic to more than just that island off the coast).

And then, one day, the tree was gone. During my regular jog along the river, I came to my favourite tree, looking up expecting to see it projecting horizontally over the Swan, and found that it was not projecting outwards, but had fallen down during the night into the water below. The stump and some of its branches remained rooted, but the bulk of the tree had perished. The winds of a stormy winter's night must have been to blame. The friend I was walking with didn't understand why I suddenly stopped in front of this fallen tree and stared in disbelief. I wouldn't move for some time. I'm sure it seems overly dramatic to a casual passer-by, especially one for whom nature is 'scenery', but that tree had been an axis of stability around which many other parts of my life had changed. The river of time flows on. Only sometimes do we get intimations of the Niagara that lies up ahead.

Another day. I'm at Freshwater Bay again, and now it's a strangely warm and sunny mid-morning in July. The water is scintillating, a rolling table of fierce photon marbles. *Ficus macrophyla,* a Moreton

Bay fig, spreads its branches out over a narrow sand beach. Behind the tree and the beach, a flat patch of grass and then a street.

I jump up, grab hold of one of its overreaching horizontally extending branches.

Up, up, and then inch down the thick tree limb. Shuffling out over the shallow water with its sandy bottom. Then sitting there motionless, heart beat slowing.

Welcome to the mansion of waxy leaves, a decussating, billowing Whitman of a tree. Dark green multitudes, and lapped by the south-wester. I had found my own palace amongst the waterfront millionaires. It was a refuge and respite from the masonry of economic inequality on the other side of the road behind me. The view before me is tree branches and leaves, floored by shallow sloping river water below. Feet dangle down over the water. The human becomes an unspied epiphyte, observing passing pedestrians or motorists.

The wind sways my perch, and I remember John Muir up another tree on another West coast, in another hemisphere, more than a century ago. He stands astride rivers of air and creaking wood and waving branches and he has a big smile on his face. I look out over the water, and imagine I'm in an isolated corner of the Daintree Rainforest, or on a Reunionnais river bank, other pieces of earth to which *Ficus macrophylla* has journeyed flanked by wasp conspirators. I am contained and held by a mammoth. Sinews of wood fibre, flexing in tree-time, support my mammalian bones. Bones and branches, struts struck against the weight of gravity. A tangled root city communicating down below the grass, cellulose reaching up out through the air, suspended over river waters. The waters Heraclitus knew... I think, sitting and contemplating age and confusion. I'm supported by my sense that *Homo faber* is not the paragon of species, and I'm glad I've found a new place to meditate on slow flowing, many-storied Perth banks.

9.

Another day, and another run along the Swan. Afterwards, as is my habit, I climb a tree. Stop and look at the tannin coloured water. Again aloft in the elephantine limbs of a Moreton Bay fig, looking down in quiet and stillness. Soft sunshine on green grass below leading to sand shore. This is a tree from north-east Australia here on the Swan with its roots out in a deep woody tranquillity of residual at-homeness. Behind branches below me, the shimmering surface of the water. This is an image, a reality, which soothes me. Water clear at the edge, fading to dark. As I walked back to the campus, mind quiet, I think – perhaps I need to listen to fewer podcasts, read fewer books. Maybe I just need to be the protagonist in my life some more.

The next day walking and running along the river in the evening with the water pink and smelling burley on the warm gravel and being reminded of being a boy with my dad mucking about with a prawn net ... feeling adventure and no worry and the constant suck and surprise of the future drawing me on. The clear water and the still cool air. The white sails over the river's centre. No headphones on my head. No news. No social media. No podcasts. Just me in the centre. In my life, in my body. Living my life first hand, before I miss it. We metropolitans probably all need to do more of this: reject the era of proxy living by a pink sun-setting river beach, a calm shore, starting this evening.

Heed Blake's advice, ye of the *civitas*, now more than ever:

> Turn away no more: Why wilt thou turn away.
> The starry floor. The watry shore.
> Is giv'n thee till the break of day.[2]

10.

Another day, climbing the cliff at Mosman Park, further down river, and squatting in the shade of some high trees. Watching two sea eagles on branches beneath a massive nest of sticks and twigs, high up in a dead tree's boughs. Their talons gripped onto a ledge of precipitous tininess. They hold on to the edge of the world, on to a victorious empire of blue space. They dome the air. The breeze ruffled the white feathers on their proud chests, and high squeaky cries passed between the pair. They are beyond us, behind and above the suburbs of Perth and its domesticated dramas. The sun will set down there and their presence will remain a gust of wildness. The sun will set, and down at that patch of un-engineered terrain above the river the imperious elders will follow the orange creep of light on the water far below. They will watch it return in the morning, as their ancestors have done, without us here, for hundreds of thousands of years. Seeing this pair of masters of space from my cover of leaves, I was gifted with a shot in the arm. A shot of Hard, High Reality.

Perhaps Western Australian land and flora is hard to appreciate aesthetically if you're a member of *Homo sapiens* from high-nutrient lands with greater rainfall. Say Britain or Malaysia or China. That was at least the case for many early British settlers and some more recent migrants. The land that inspired Cowper, Wordsworth, Keats, Housman, and Thomas, or the land that inspired Thoreau, Emerson, Muir, Oliver and Rogers, had more biomass being turned over each year. However, if you understand how life in the south west of Australia is adapted to survive extremes – as for example Barbara York Main did and illustrated so well in her book *Between Wodjil and Tor* (1967) – that is, if you understand how nature works here, then that will put you ahead in your effort to appreciate the non-human world here. If you look at the micro-patterns of the flora here that will help. If you look at the birds that will help. And so on ... If you leave the pavement and open your eyes. And if you stop seeing nature here as something 'out there', hours car drive away, then you could ride your bike to a local park or river's edge and take it into your life.

I've done these things myself, and it has changed me. Made me more grounded, more appreciative of the world encountered every morning. If you do all these things you will no longer hold a Eurocentric outlook which sees this landscape as drab and ugly, but perhaps, after time, you will learn to love this place. This is where Australian society must go if its people are to heal their souls and not be just materialistic and lost and drifting urbanites. And until a few of these things progress, I'm going to have to keep watching people like Andy Goldsworthy and Prince Charles at work on the hills, and in their green fields, and doing so with a feeling of regret and wistfulness that such intimacy with the land does not regularly happen much in the Australia where I live.

11.
This morning I'm on the south side of the Swan. I walk along Blackwall Reach. Fingers of limestone pointing up on the edge of the cliff. The sound of the water rebounding in the crevices of the overhangs at water level below. The tide is high as it is the full moon tonight. Thoughts of what it must have been like here before whites came ...

A thousand years quickly vanish in my daydreaming. A wallaby thumps its way away on the lower side of the track, amongst bark and forest litter. I freeze. It freezes. I freeze longer. It starts to nibble and hesitantly hop, with me camouflaged on the track. Below us both comes the sound of the river flowing over stones. Above us both comes intermittent bird songs from the canopy. Looking down into the forest and thinking: 'Every day this wallaby sees the same trees and boulders in the same places. Hears the same bird songs. Hears the same river rolling. Can expect the sun to rise and the sun to set in the same way. Can expect the same food sources to be there.' I thought how comforting it was that there was an enduring bedrock of reality in the natural world.

Human-made civilisation may twirl and spin, but outside the houses and the cities and the farms and the screens and the noises, there persists a millennium-old fabric of cosmos, one which moves slowly in cycles and tides and seasons and growth and decay. This wallaby will find, if he looks, the same jarrah trees on this slope tomorrow that he finds today. The river will still grace us, if I join him, with its low babble. Waters will still slip and drip. Leaves will keep growing in the same places. This was so, with a few tree falls, when my parents were young men and women. When my society was undreamt of. When my species had not evolved in Africa. How can such towering endurance of reality fail to inspire reverence? How can knowledge of such an unfalteringly smooth stride of biological reality not bring calm? If I am an environmentalist it is because I am driven by this deep Real, and by the calm this ecosystem gives my soul. Being an environmentalist in my case can't be a passing fad. When I contemplate this patch of forest and its denizens, standing still and alone, I feel like I'm in the middle of some of the most meaningful stuff that human life may be consoled and guided by. Thirty minutes of Chronos-exempt dwelling with the earth. At the end my embers are stoked within to act in a way that will further conservation. No, these refuges by the Swan River are not escapist pastoral fantasies; they are redoubts. Redoubts where I reignite my passion for guarding what I love.

Today and tomorrow I will stand above the Swan river and see a patch of ground that was nature's: *le patrimoine matérial*. High above the water, under the sun, and the green grass and the trees standing sentinel-like around me. A feeling of outlook. A good place to be Western Australian.

I ride home along the river. As I ride, I pass through a section of the riverside lawn and trees area that is close to my house, yet away from suburbia, and shaded in lovely *Casuarinas*. Clumps of them with the ground a dead mat of their needles. Having these trees close to me is comforting: it reminds me of my biological links to the trees of Indian Ocean islands like *La Réunion*, across the other side of the salty sea. The winds whistle through the needles of these trees, as they whistle across the oceans to the needles of the trees of those tropical shores. All are dear to my heart. Winds sighing in the rigging. The winds bind us, our trees and our otherwise so dissimilar lands, side by side.

12.

What about under the surface of the Swan? My recommended travel kit includes: E. O. Wilson's great book *The Diversity of Life* (at least for pre-departure), a new silicon mask and some good diving fins. Good accoutrement if you live by the Swan River. Snorkelling under limestone cliffs with new fins and feeling exhilarated by sliding down into the undersea world of star fish on the river bottom and silver fish gliding along the rocky drop-offs. Summer weather had been swelteringly hot recently (30 degrees Celsius the other night in the kitchen at 11.00 pm) and the water had warmed up considerably (the only benefit of this weather). From the tannins of the Swan to a day trip to Rottnest and a dive in Fish Hook Bay ... The wild earth in a sequestered zone is always available.

To celebrate my last day of being 37 years old I skinny-dipped in the dark river. It was May and cool. Swirls of bioluminescent algae gave off a bright blue light as my body moved through the cool and dark translucent liquid – as if I was dancing in outer space with stars trailing off my arms and legs. The river was silent and the moon shone down on me. I felt glad I was alive, after a prolonged semi-boredom of waged life duties. I needed to dance and shout and dive out into the deeps.

13.

Another evening it was summer and friends had an unembarrassed *Dead Poets Society*-style meeting in a cave on the cliffs above the river in North Fremantle. My Swedish friend Ove placed candles everywhere in the cavern to illuminate the niches and far corners, and it gave a mysterious feeling of space. Swimming in the river before and after. I swam out into the river I saw back the soft illumination of the cave, just as it may have looked thousands of years ago when Aboriginal people were in there. I read a poem called 'Piute Creek' by Gary Snyder and a poem by Wendell Berry. Then we talked, drank and played drums and guitars in the hot evening air. Good to have a new experience in a place I've lived all my life. Home still has plenty of unknown up its sleeve.

I repeat myself now. It is good to end your days with a walk in the dark down to the banks of the Swan river. The last thing seen before going to bed is the quiet and still waters of the Swan shining under the moon. Sometimes a flock of dark shapes – the eponymous spirits of our river – are roosting out on the waters. Times like these I hear them call to each other in delicate, lilting cries. These are high and touching grace notes in the darkness. They rise and fall with gentle insistence, against a background of silence.

Stop walking and look out on to the dark and still waters. Listen.

This is not the River Lethe. This is the river of remembering. Remembering who we are. Remembering where I really am.

Watching

Susan Midalia

It's only with the jolt of memory that I see skinny legs teetering on a railing, feel the fear choking my throat, and then one brown body turning to me and *jump*, says the boy, *come on, jump, it's fun*. I stand behind him on Garratt Road Bridge, which spans the Swan River in Bayswater. Baysie, people called it, when we were kids. Maybe they still do.

It was 1962. I was eleven years old, the child of post-war migrants whose river was the Danube: picturesque, deep blue, romantic. My childhood river was murky brown, swarming with jellyfish, and littered with what I would come to know as *other testimonies of summer nights*. It was flanked by scratchy grass on one bank, and on the other a sprawling, messy rubbish tip that my brother would later scour to find parts for his first, proud car. A black FJ Holden.

I knew nothing then about the Indigenous history of that river. How prior to colonisation, the surrounds were inhabited by the Mooro people to the north and the Beeloo people to the south. I knew nothing, either, about the brown-limbed boy on the bridge. I'd encountered Aborigines before, but always from a distance: boys with excited, piping voices, kicking a football in the playground; girls who walked arm in arm, giggling and shy; men who swaggered down the street, and whose inky darkness made me grip my mother's hand. Natives, they were called back then, kids and adults alike. Or Abos. Boongs.

Years later, my brother became a teacher of Aboriginal children in wheatbelt towns that didn't see rain for months, sometimes years. At his funeral, several Indigenous people, all unknown to me, told me in different ways how much they had valued him, how much they would miss him. I too became a teacher, mostly of privileged white kids whose river was dotted with leisurely yachts under a clear blue sky. Matilda Bay, Crawley, near the University of Western Australia, where people used words like oppression, victimisation, marginalisation, and the deleterious effects of ongoing colonial power.

I snake back to the river of my childhood, and the ease of that smiling, carefree boy, eager to plunge into the river, so many terrifying feet below. I watch as he hurls himself into unbounded space, knees braced, a flash of brown against the immensity of sky, then plummeting like a rock, the shock of the spray as he hits water, and I wait, wait, until finally, blessedly, he is there, hollering with joy, arms raised to the sky, triumphant.

Did I ever jump? No. Not once. Did I say hello to that boy? I don't remember.

James Quinton

Dolphins

Cement bags shore
bulrushes
wooden sleepers
casurina obesa
limestone blocks
jarrah jetty
eucalyptus marginate
old car tyre
concrete slabs
a cormorant, still baking
its black feathers
moving in water reflection
caustic light.
Bamboo stands
fallen tree
banks quite high

fresh kills, land fill
a stratum of ripples
gravel blocks concreted
together, piles of palms
dirt bank
broken brick bank
deck chairs, a deck across branches
fence between houses
a movement underwater
makes ripples
eucalyptus rudis, a swing
the green leaves yellow in morning light
you can hear great eastern highway throb
violence; the wake
high tide algae
constant smashing of foamy water
a fish swallows a fish
the paddle breaking the surface
knock of metal on canoe wood.

Sand, cream grey orange
many footprints
a divet you can see the bottom in the water
but the sky, the shimmering trees
a twenty eight, rosellas ripping
tuarts to pieces
a rubbish truck, its dinosaur armature
great roots occasion the air
a tree re-rooted after fall.
The fall loud and raucous
when owls chase mice
smashing their skulls
single skulls, single rocks
a blue heron pulls up on a log
blue rocks, a moved quarry

a house worth of blue metal
looks quarry-like as a bank
the shore stabilised
by a inflated yellow balloon
a house worth of blue metal
dumped in the river.

Cyclist

We move into the cool dark,
the long line
the earth moved
two times a day
shadows mark an edge
of the channel
mulloway stalk prawns
mullet jump, sometimes
ten at once all around the canoe
half a dozen dolphins
in a feeding frenzy
a sudden feeling of excitement,
we move closer.
The dolphins roll, a dog, barking
swims out to eat them.
To play with brushmatressing,
parallel to waves, dolphins
settle, galahs fire up, squawking
sickly dorsal fins, their breathing
almost too often, thrashing
and violence in the arch of their back,
Ron Courtney Island in the background.

Walk on …

The Seer

if not I, who sees *The River* when inside four walls?
who sees the eyes glaze over, lacrimal glands

becoming bereft, bare and bone dry, like my knowledge
of Noongar river names, Noongar ways.

if not I, who sits below the causeway staircase
scraping together dried tobacco dregs

wearing a black jumper on a 35 degree day;
who follows the fledgling cormorant

coming up for riverair, as casual as a Coles shelf-stacker?
who follows the rhizomes into the chasmic hollow?

whoever sees, I long to surrender to their sight
I'm sick of trying to make a name for myself.

whoever sees the pandemic, the supermarket
shelves bereft of bog roll, of hand sanitiser,

the ruse is that the seeer never surrenders:
river-like, and androgynous, the seeer has figured

out the way to breathe without breath,
to discover direction in the dark mud-stirred murk.

Inferno Canto 3 Liszt's River Dante Opening Form to Antiphony [D minor]

for Tracy

John Kinsella

The search for beginnings to a river sets us off on a wrong course —
its beginnings are its catchment and its flow and the idea of it that runs
as a thread that binds what it generates together. Rivers run through

oceans and sky, and earth-rivers reach out beyond the gravitational
pull of the sun that spoke them. As I cross *this* river and get shaky feet,
I accumulate the wastes as grief, whether I want to or not. As I cross

Newcastle Bridge north of Toodyay — sometimes twice a day —
    thinned algal
water pixelates the reflection of an egret as something much more
    than *pointillist*,
a trick of the post-Enlightenment eye struggling for grip, ultimate hold.

I can't do this rivering, not really, this childhood swimming through
and not knowing how to see as I extract something attuned to *my*
    moment,
something *I* can draw into a system of self-affirmation in the face

of my own less-than-precise reflections, listening to Liszt's *Dante
Sonata*
in the music centre of memory where no string holds its note
perfectly.
This is no Acheron outside its agri-effluvia pumped-up depleted
waters,

its antimonies rafted over on 22-gallon drums roped together,
favouring
the waterholes like they are the answer to the *between* of school
finishing
and school starting again. Trained into oblivion, the ferryman speaks

bitter and you don't really try to understand what's being said, the
mozzies
irritating and gnats stuffing up future memories, as if they've got in
via the mouth
and started their journey through your circulatory systems, battling
antibodies

and lymph nodes. Who is this old codger so interested in damning us
to hell
in our summer messing-about, our making-do with what's to hand?
But that
wasn't *here*, but further up the river, a visit into the town of York

from *Wheatlands* farm — you know, out in the catchment, drawn
down to where
the water inevitably percolates. But it's taken decades to flow here
via Northam
for all the cascading the intermittent flooding the bare bones drought
the paperboats

reaching the seamouth the disrespect countered by the work of
    traditional owners.
But it's here now, forty-five and a half years later, and whether or
    not the egret
pursuing its quarry notices it as something out of the
    ordinary — which it doesn't —

I remake it in an *own image* I don't like, one that relies on the river
    swelling,
washing away the salt-stain lines of the failure my swimming
    engendered,
the taking the ferryman for granted, whoever he was, whatever he
    meant.

Tidal Tensions and Littoral Potential: Coming of Age and the Derbal Yerrigan

Claire Jones

There is something about the changeability of the Swan River that draws me in. Sometimes the river appears gem-like, a sparkling, sapphire expanse: that picture-postcard view of a summer city that is used in any news broadcast from Perth, whatever the weather. Other times the river is choppy and churning, with the banks closing in as the water slaps against bricked-in shorelines. Occasionally it is shrouded in fog and the space between water and air is indeterminable. These scenes of the river, and each variation in between, offer something picturesque. But every so often I see the river and sense a tension. The skin of the water is still and taut and the river looks fit to burst; the surface bulges to contain the competing tensions of the tides, the run off and the swell of groundwater as it enters the river system. On these days the river emits a sense of anticipation, a burgeoning potential, and this fullness has fascinated me since childhood.

The river, its moods and the potential that it contains, is not only part of my own my multi-sensory memory. This river is a literary site, and many writers, both locals and visitors, have captured how the river acts a place for interaction, discovery, revelation, transformation and, very often, as a location of coming of age. Whether we turn to works from Western Australia's contemporary writers or the traditional stories of Noongar culture, there is a recurring motif: the river is liminal, an in-between space, where personal liminality can be explored and transformation can result. This chapter will take personal recollections alongside literary works and map them against the shorelines and depths of the Swan River. It will consider the ways figures can navigate the cultural currents, within those of the river, and how literature mimics the littoral tensions of this body of water to understand the moments of initiation and transformation. This study will consider locations and scenes from Melville Waters to Bennett Spring near Guildford.

I grew up on a parcel of land with a creek running through it that is in itself a mini-tributary to the Swan, and I still return to it a couple of times a week for family visits and to simply be at home in this place. At certain times of the year the creek is dry and you can walk the bed through the pea gravel, with the banks at shoulder height and the littoral substrata exposed for all the read. In *Makuru* and *Djilba* seasons the runoff from the ranges cascades through the little gully. This flow brings renewal. The brittle grasses drained of colour from the long hot seasons grow new green tufts overnight, and tiny orchids and bright purple creepers appear as the old gums let out a breath they've been holding during months of searing sun. This flow is welcome relief and my familiarity with this cycle pulls me close to the water and its ways. During my childhood this creek was my escape. It was the scene for adventures, somewhere to test my independence and the planned location for running away where I would build a hut and live off the land. In time it became a place to test further boundaries – friendship dares and double-dares, physical challenges with the highest tree and farthest creek-jumps, as well as first kisses and first breakups. And as my world expanded so did my connection to the river's reaches. Early driving experiences, knowing how to navigate the few river crossings and university years tracing the river each day to arrive at

Matilda Bay, a new location where water would become a place to question and confide.

Like so many from this town my daily engagement with the river is now mainly in transit. While I'm always aware of my location in proximity to the river, my contact is governed by the few river crossings and the traffic bottlenecks that they create on the daily commute. But in my glimpses I always try to read my river-friend's expressions. Renewal and relief are easily observed. Big rains and storms bring flooding and excited electricity, while relaxation comes with sunny days and the morning easterly winds that make the city reaches a millpond. But when the river bulges, when it is taut, something about the familiarity of the river seems to disappear, our intimacy shifts and something is unreadable. I first realised this fullness of the river wasn't simply my own fancy when reading David Whish-Wilson's *Perth*. His chapter 'The River' begins by explaining the 'diurnal bulge of water' that causes the 'the skin of the Swan River' to rise as the 'tidal surge makes it way from the river mouth at Fremantle through Perth Water and up into the higher reaches of the river' and that in winter 'when a layer of brackish water runs off the scarp towards the ocean, the river flows in two directions, with the fresh water flowing seawards above the saline water flowing in beneath it'.[1] Some days this surge is a ripple, some days unnoticeable but when the competing tensions of fresh and salt water each exert enough force the river dilates, bulges and the river is in-between, on the verge of one state or another, liminal and littoral.

To stay with Whish-Wilson's work, his physical immersion in the river is recollected in brilliant detail in 'The River'. He explains that 'the river was a haven' and, though he moved to Perth as a child, it was through the river that he found a place to belong.[2] It is the tidal surges that drives his recollection, and diving and digging in the littoral zone enables him to inhabit the layers of this location and drift with the currents and jellyfish so that he might understand the spirit of the place. He writers that 'all of the sensual confusion of cold water and hot sun, and levitation and submersion, came together in a sudden recognition that I have never forgotten: the feeling of belonging to a place that did not belong to me, but only made an introverted kid feel more protective, even loving, of the river that carried him along on its soft skin'.[3] In Whish-Wilson's description of this sensation, which is both physical and emotional, he terms it 'a small epiphany', and it is this moment of revelation, as well as its potential for transformation, that can be found in other stories about the Swan River. What might be termed genius loci in European or settler language, and recreated through literary efforts, can be explained through Noongar culture through the story of the Waugul (Water Serpent), as well as specific rites and rituals.

While this water body has been shaped by colonial impact, and the relationship between the river and so many generations of Whadjuk Noongar people has been disrupted, this grouping of stories about the river and youth demonstrates a resilience and universality of the spirit of this place. The river and its banks are marked by various locations that have cultural significance to Indigenous people, many of which relate to coming-of-age rituals and initiations. One such location is Gooniniup and, the springs that rise up along side it, Gooniallup, which are at the base of Cooya or King's Park. This location was known as an important initiation site. The rocks and springs were formed by the Waugul as it struggled to the surface and laid eggs creating this series of springs. Noongar Elder Barry McGuire (cited in Whish-Wilson's *Perth*) explained that the location was used for 'the early stage of the male ceremonies coming into the Law', and that at this site 'young men were housed in a cave of great importance...until they'd learnt "how to be within their community"'.[4] This littoral location and its history of repeated rituals acts as a foundation for an experience which is timeless and specific simultaneously. If we consider the long history of the Derbal Yerrigan, or the human experience of the river in deep time, we hear the echo of a particular experience in the rhythms of the river.

This echo can be heard as Gooniniup later becomes a critical location within Tim Winton's family saga, *Cloudstreet*. Not only do we have a somewhat comical scene in the novel of pre-pubescent Red Lamb's time at the Crawley baths (adjacent to Gooniniup) but also Quick Lamb often travels the Mounts Bay Road that hugs the shore and the cliff face of King's Park, directly through Gooniniup. During the summer in which Red is made aware of the rituals associated with sexual curiosity, she develops her 'method' by which she pissed into the faces of boys swimming under the floor of the girls' change rooms with precision.[5] This act of rebellion sees Red respond to her feelings of violation, but it is also telling in the way in which her older sisters feign shock but appear resigned to this long-ago scripted gender drama. Gooniniup, and numerous river locations, become critical to Quick Lamb's coming-of-age journey, which is the central arc of the novel. So many of his moments of self-realisation or transformation in this novel occur on or in the water, with Mounts Bay Road figuring numerous times as Quick observes, analyses and comes to understand the way his community operates, as well as how he comes to sit within it. However, his gradual maturation reaches a point of finality with his retrieval of a young child's body from the river. Quick, a junior policeman by this point in the novel, is undone by the lifeless body of the child as it prompts connections to himself, his son and ultimately his brother and the way in which their story will continue to play and haunt them. In response to his situation he rides to Mounts Bay Road, through the Gooniniup location, reflecting on his past and feeling the sensation of liminality between the water, air and land, and trying to reconcile the space between life and death, guilt and innocence, crime and justice.

> Quick rode to Cloudstreet feeling useless as a twelve year old, reckless across the Narrows Bridge, ready to drive into the river at any second. He caned the BSA up Mounts Bay Road, leaning into curves with only wind holding him free, past the Crawley baths where he'd swum as a kid where jellyfish piled up like church camp food and the rotting stink of blowfish blew past.[6]

While Winton's river offers comfort and appears to pull Quick into it as he seeks to make sense of himself, Lucy Dougan's poem 'The Mice' (set a little way upriver) captures the tensions of youth with an adventurous spirit, where the littoral zone is soft and forgiving of the experiences lived. This work again echoes the genius loci of the river and its suitability as a location for coming of age. The persona recognises the primal pull to a littoral location. The poem is set on the river's edge, an area filled with samphire and the introduced pest bamboo. The place itself is swampy, neither water nor solid ground. This in-between location, neither river nor shore, replicates the liminal state of the adolescent. The poem begins:

> My mother took them to the river
> With a packet of weet-bix
> Their carousel – that scampering
> Roundabout of *Who am I?* –[7]

It then explores how the mice, and young person alike, are not set free but 'abandoned' to a 'wasteland', but return as 'feral colonies'. In this poem the mother 'unlatched the cage and said / Kids, you're on your own', addressing the mice and the child simultaneously. What transpires is an exploration of the primal, attraction to what is earthly and natural, which in turn exposes itself to be socially taboo.

> that stretch of land by the river
> it really was wild
> a wasteland then
> we lay in clumps of bamboo
> and smoked our first cigarettes
> bamboo bumsuckers
> the lost mice clambered inside
> my headspins[8]

The terms 'feral' and 'wild' play against each other in this context of colonial contestation and introduce a tone of regret that the child is unable to develop without, and the interplay of children and priests in this landscape provokes something more taboo than cigarettes and ankles. The final stanza of the poem reflects on how those who have experienced the river in youth might come to view it as an adult. A desire to 'reclaim a little rank whiff' is thwarted by progress and development. There is nostalgia for a sacred location, a littoral zone, now made into firm land. The place is recognisable, but also unrecognisable, as are we.

Further upstream the connections between the river and coming of age continue. One critical location is Guildford at the confluence of the Swan and Helena (Moort bidi) Rivers. A long established meeting place for different Noongar groups, it was later reshaped by colonial settlement as the first inland settlement of the Swan River Colony, with a river crossing and eventually a convict station. The river takes a sharp bend where Bennett Brook meets the river which the settlers named the Devil's Elbow. This stretch was originally known as Nanook, where fresh water enters the brackish river, and was known as a sacred place and one of the resting spots of the Waugul. Jean Boladeras explains '[t]hat's his nest for him there, where he stays, it's one of his resting places, so it's pretty important that place, to us, and always will be'. She also explains that children were cautious of this place because of the Waugul and there were rites of passage, as well as family lessons to be taught in the location. 'If he [referring to the person who shared this story with her] was to run past this spot here, the [Waugul] would be in there, so he had to throw sand on the surface of the river, to make the water all choppy, so the [Waugul] couldn't see him run past. And he wasn't allowed to go for a swim until his grandmother had talked to the [Waugul] and it was ok for him to go for a swim and so he was a little boy, right from early days he knew that'.

As the river rounds Nanook, the river's edge flattens out from carved cliffs into floodplains. Sitting above these floodplains is one of Perth's elite boarding schools, Guildford Grammar. Almost transplanted from England with its architecture, early staff and even its house-based culture, the school seems in stark contrast to Boladeras's story above. But writers Randolph Stowe and Kenneth Seaforth Mackenzie both spent time at the school as students, and their work looks to the environment, and particularly the river, as one of the influential educational forces at Guildford Grammar.

Mackenzie's bildungsroman *The Young Desire It* casts the river, and particularly the river flats, as a critical figure in the novel. The environment is the constant source for peace, support and self-knowledge, as well as a location for trauma, self-awareness and transformation. The central character, Charles Fox, first encounters the school '[i]n the late afternoon of a day in February, that hottest of Australian summer months, when a brutal sun stood bronze above the river flats'.[9] Charles' time at the school is tinged by brutality and loneliness, and his experience is continually paralleled by his environment. The problematic, but critical, relationship that he forms with his master, Penworth, begins in the school's grounds, and is characterised by their river walks. Charles' romantic encounters with Margaret also take place at the river, or by springs and streams. The sun, cloud, rain, wind, reflected light from trees, all reflect Charles' emotional state: pathetic fallacy is critical in the novel.

The pathetic fallacy employed by the novel connects the character Charles and his surroundings so much so that the river flats seem to nurture and nourish him, as well as enable his understanding of himself and his community. It also sets him apart from his fellow students who disrupt the stillness of nature. Charles realises his difference early in his school life where his 'defiance grew as he slowly became aware of everything about himself that was different to others. He knew, without understanding why, that there was this difference.'[10] This is emphasised in the novel by the passage directly following, when in a hot February the school boys descend on the river each afternoon, while Charles remains removed from the pack.

> The boys came noisily down, under the care of an excellent old athletics master ... and the place was shattered and outraged by

their shouts and laughter. They were the blessed of the earth; they were lords of this tarnished stretch of original creation that spread flatly and wearily in the brassy light.[11]

It is apparent that the protagonist is at odds with this notion of dominance held by those he has such opposition with. Instead Charles comes to 'trust in moods and intuitions of selfhood' and 'felt the growth of self in himself; it showed in his heightened and now consciously intensified reaction to ... beauty' and this provided confidence and sustained him in his study and his actions again the crowd and against authority.[12] Again we observe genius loci operating in crucial ways to sustain the experience of a young person seeking self-knowledge and understanding.

Recently I was walking along my childhood creek with my nephew, who now sleeps in my old bedroom. He is 12 and I have been lucky to watch him grow from the moment he was born. I know his moods and expressions, his fears and the things that make him burst into a wicked giggle. We reached the old galvanised steel tunnel that helps the creek to pass under a road. It's one of those 'I dare you' locations – dark and spidery – and I expected him to take the dirt path that takes you up to the road and back down to the creek. He didn't even hesitate but waded through the water and I watched his silhouette as he cleared the tunnel at the other end. I splashed through to catch up and asked, 'Is that the first time you've gone through the tunnel?' He shot me a narrow-lidded look and told me he and his friends always used the tunnel now they knew there were no snakes in it. I'm not convinced of the snake assessment, but something about the familiarity of my nephew's face seemed to disappear for a second, our intimacy shifted and something about him was now unreadable. I felt a tinge of sadness and the warmth of excitement.

The Gill Net

David Whish-Wilson

When a friend of mine, whose uncle owned a power launch, told us about the quantities of booze kept unlocked on the moored riverboats, we went out onto the dark river that same night.

After all, there was a party that weekend. There was surely another the weekend after, and the weekend after that, and on into eternity, or so we imagined.

Night-time foragers in the darkened suburban streets, sneaking out of bedroom windows at midnight to rendezvous in the local parks, we were used to being chased by the police. No policeman was ever going to catch a fourteen-year-old on foot, but knowing how important our bikes were to us (they would wait nearby), we parked our bicycles behind some ti-tree bushes where they couldn't be seen. We waited in the warm silence of the shoreline darkness, sand in our toes, stripped to our shorts, until we were ready. Water rats scurried across the limestone reefs, large and glistening, swimming where necessary to regain the shore.

The river stretched taut and flat before us, silvered by the moon. In the distance, behind the mask of a limestone bluff, the CBD glowed red and gold, but all around in the dormitory suburbs the good citizens were asleep. Cicadas buzzed in the lushly watered gardens of the nearby park. Wavelets lapped at the shore. Somewhere in the dark, a night heron bended her notes.

Beside us was a familiar patch of remnant bush, clinging to a tall limestone cliff, and I looked at it nervously. A few weeks ago I'd suffered the comic misfortune of being chased through the ti-tree and native cypress scrub by a swarm of angry bees. I had foolishly decided to spear their nest, glued to the side of a limestone boulder, with my homemade gidgee, hoping to prise out some honey. Ignoring my friend beside me, the bees chased me up and down the dunes and around the shoreline paperbarks until I dived into the river, where they swarmed as I watched them from beneath the surface, holding my breath while they searched for me. When the bees finally returned to their hive, and my friends had ceased their laughter, we counted that I'd been stung 24 times on my back and neck. The miracle was that the hive had chased me, the culprit, and ignored my friend beside; the innocent. We couldn't figure that out.

As was usual with our adventuring through the suburbs at night, there was no need for a signal, or for us to come to a decision. One among us stood, and we all waded into the inky river. Feeling with our toes along the sandy bottom, sea lettuce and algae catching on our ankles, we moved cautiously forward. Each of us had previously suffered the barb of the cobbler – the fish that we hunted with our gidgees and sold, filleted, to local fish and chip shops. Once we discovered where the nocturnal catfish gathered during the daylight hours (under reefs, inside sunken boats, among weed and rocks) we speared so many cobbler that killing them became a nauseating experience; their hateful eyes looking up at us while we sawed off their heads. It was while killing one large specimen, which I had speared beneath the hull of a sunken yacht, that my grip slipped and I caught the barb in the webbing of my knife hand. The pain from the toxin was incredible, and it endured, even as the familiar refrain of laughing friends signalled to me that yes, just like with the bees, there was justice in the situation – there was some form of conversation being had.

The sun-heated skim of warmth in the shallows cooled as the black water rose around our hips, waists, chests. The colder water flamed brightly against our sunburned shoulders as we slipped beneath the surface. It was at this depth that an ever-mysterious bioluminescence made the river currents glow like fireflies; agitated by our treading water and paddling hands. Giant translucent white and brown jellyfish bumped against us, their boiled egg skins brushing our chests, necks, faces. On my back was an empty knapsack, in my teeth a small torch. Our destination was a group of five luxury launches moored 50 metres out in the bay. We paddled without speaking, the dark depths increasing the volume of our fears, blending with the excitement of doing wrong. We split apart to take a boat each, drawing ourselves up onto transom decks and swimming platforms, sliding over onto the fibreglass lower decks, mirroring the sleek movements of the river rats we'd been watching only minutes before.

It was everything we'd hoped for. Tequila, gin, vodka and whisky, champagne and green ginger wine; a favourite among teenagers for its bite and cloying sweetness. We helped ourselves from the cabinets and cupboards before slipping into the black water, swimming sidestroke to the shore, clinking bottles tugged behind.

From then on, week after week, month after month, we repeated the raids up and down the length of the river, working our way through the river-moored boats before turning to the launches in the exclusive yacht clubs; a dripping sentry posted to warn of the security guards who did their rounds. The raids satisfied our need for party-booze and for excitement, too. The thefts weren't hard to justify. The boat-owners could afford it, we figured, and had given their vessels names like *Banker's Hours*, *Gravyboat* and *Cur'N'Sea*.

It was on one such ordinary raid that I found the gill-net, stuffed into a lidless plastic rubbish bin, on the back deck of a sixty-foot power launch called *Feelin Nauti*. I sniffed the net and it smelled of old bait. With a booze-filled knapsack on my back, I dragged the laden bin through the diesel-smelling waters of the yacht club, out into the deeper water, before turning longshore toward our rendezvous a hundred metres down the beach. I nearly didn't make it. The net began to unfurl in the water, catching my bare legs, tangling my feet, the floats bobbing around my head. I swam one-handed, self-rescuing to the pale line of beach, until the water was shallow enough for me to crawl, and drag myself free.

Because of my father's service in the armed forces, according to my mother, our family of five moved some twenty times before I reached the age of seven. This upbringing probably explains why the town where we finally stopped – after my dad took a job with a salt company up in the Pilbara – is the place that made the most enduring impression upon me, and has shaped my identity more than any other.

We lived in a company house on the edge of Karratha; a town with a population of a couple of thousand. Over our back fence stretched the spinifex scrub that carpeted the nearby hills, broken by deep gullies lined with rivergum. After school, my friends and I disappeared into the bush, returning only for dinner. We explored among the caves and secret valleys. We fought mock battles against one another, learning how to be stealthy and elusive, how to vanish in plain sight. These battles were undertaken with 'boondie' and 'ging', or stone and slingshot, and made the bush ring out with shouts of pain and triumph.

We had no sense of history, back then, and therefore irony was lost on us. One of my best friends, an Aboriginal boy called Danny (who was called, in those days, a 'half-caste'), was a welcome participant in our warfare due to his accuracy with a ging, and his ever-quiet ways. It never occurred to us, even in Danny's company, that we were re-enacting the historically recent dispossession of his people from the area. We played footy against Aboriginal kids from Roeburne; my mother took us out onto the Dampier Archipelago to look at the million-odd petroglyphs that date back some fifty-thousand years; we stalked the tidal mudflats of the mangrove swamps looking for mud crabs, as people had done for millennia, but none of this longer history registered with us – ours was a 'new' country.

The powerful atmosphere, or *genius loci* of the spinifex hills, however, was another matter, which in its silence sometimes hinted at this greater absence. It wasn't uncommon for me to spend whole days up in the hills by myself, following the giant bungarra, or goanna, as they searched for carrion, or other reptiles, to eat. Large pythons inhabited the riverine gum trees, perfectly camouflaged and preternaturally still. I followed mobs of skittish kangaroo from valley to valley, and climbed the sheer red cliffs looking for the nests of wedge-tailed eagle.

I was a solitary child, perhaps, but in truth I was never really alone – I had for a long time an imaginary friend who I described to my mother as 'short, black, hairy and old' who accompanied me everywhere. My younger brother also claimed to be able to see him, although he was scared of my friend, and his allegedly belligerent ways. My brother barricaded his door at night, so that my 'black' friend wouldn't come and take him away – another irony that never breached the consciousness of us kids, or our parents. This was a time, of course, when it was routine for black children to be taken by white officers, as part of the Western Australian government's long-standing policy of assimilation that resulted in the 'stolen generations'.

It's hard to imagine a more alien species of human in that harsh, hot, semi-desert, than barefoot, shirtless and hatless me. The light was fierce year-round, and the sky bore sharply down upon my scalp and pale freckled shoulders, in the days before wearing sunscreen was considered necessary for a young boy. Genetically engineered for northern European climes, able to draw vitamin D from the most lacklustre of light – the northern Australian sun scorched, scored and tattooed my skin to the point that it has never really recovered, even as my bare feet toughened and became leather-like (we mostly wore bare feet to school) from all the running through the bush. School and town were fine, but I was in truth most comfortable away from the dusty streets, together with my friends or alone, tracking animals or quietly observing the birds and reptiles that populated the plains and ranges that stretched inland, broken only by dirt tracks, for thousands of kilometres.

It was a shock, therefore, to come home from school one day to learn that we were moving to the city. The five of us packed into my mother's Volkswagen for the 1,500 kilometre drive, arriving in the city on a cool winter's afternoon. So alien was the new experience of being cold, that my kindy-aged sister didn't have the words to describe the odd sensation of cold air against her tanned skin.

We moved to a suburb where there was little remnant bush, but where the river could be reached after a bike ride. Unable to find the roaming and reflective space that I was accustomed to in the northern semi-desert, I soon found its equivalent beneath the surface of the river, where I quickly learnt to skindive and spearfish, but more importantly, to occupy the depths in much the same way as I had the bush a few months earlier. The sun beating down on my head, I learned to float on the river's currents, watching the dozens of species of fish and the cormorants that hunted them. Just as I had spent hours watching and following the bungarra in the hills outside Karratha, on the river I became obsessed with the skilful and wily cormorant, a bird that appeared comfortable in three realms — on land, in the air and underwater. Hunting alone or in groups, their webbed feet cycling powerfully, they made arrows of themselves and inevitably found a mark in the schools of trumpeter, mullet or juvenile tailor that thronged to the estuarine waters of the lower reaches of the Swan.

A balm against the fierce light above water, the sepia depths of the river were also cool and silky — there was gracefulness to be found for a gangly boy in my arcing, curling and unfurling through the water, lungs empty of air, sinking deeper and deeper into the darkness.

Where my parents and grandparents harvested prawns and mussels from the shoreline, with a spear-gun bought from a church fete I sought instead to emulate the hunting strategies of the cormorant. I tracked the giant black bream who lurked around the pylons in the deeper water, or I drifted across the submerged sand banks at high tide, silent and still, ready to ambush school fish moving across the current, a skinny pale silhouette above the flathead who watched me as intently as I watched them.

If the Swan River had an Aboriginal history, I wasn't aware of it. Unlike up north, where the cave paintings and petroglyphs were a living reminder of the deeper origins of the people who had never left the area, there were no such atavistic traces in the city landscape, at least that I was aware of. There were plenty of Aboriginal people living in Perth, but it seemed like the suburbs stretched from horizon to horizon, blanketing the earlier history with repetitive forms carried from the homelands of Europe. Along the coastline, too, this absence of trace endured as the product of the ocean's eternal movement, and of the constant erasure of wind and wave.

It was only down on the river, late at night, where that longer history emerged as a constant and haunting presence – the sense of a deeper time than the one I inhabited. It is a river, after all, that has run the same course for some sixty million years, articulating itself to the people who came to inhabit its shores in the form of a shared language of currents, depths, moods and tides. This river-language naturally cohered, over time, into narratives of place that I wasn't able to apprehend, despite the laying down, like sediment, of my own literal and metaphorical experiences of immersion in the river; a multi-dimensional space that I grew to respect, and deeply love.

Over subsequent years I have learnt a lot about the river, from the textbooks and articles I've read about its geology, geomorphology, flora and fauna. More important, however, have long been the quiet impressions formed as a child, many of which were made underwater, carried along on the gentle currents upriver, or more vigorously, and dangerously, in the turbulent deeper water down near the harbour mouth.

The gill net had a medium gauge and was made of strong nylon. We took it down to the nearest footy oval and stretched it out. It ran for 50 metres, weighted at the bottom with lead sinkers and topped with painted wooden floats, giving it a span of 2 metres from base to bridge. I could tell from the algae that had dried on the net that it had been previously set in the river. This was illegal, because gill nets kill many more species than are edible. Despite this, and because we were eager to sell more fish to our local fish and chip shop, my friends and I decided to set the net that evening, in the deepest part of the river, in the channel between Point Walter and the rough limestone headland of Chidley Point.

We waited until after midnight, and rendezvoused as usual in the local park. The net was heavy at the back of my bike, and we took turns carrying it on the hour ride to the riverbank. It was a hot, still evening, and the river stretched flat and wide. Channel markers winked out there, but there were no boats on the water, or people on the shore. We carried the net along the shoreline to a point where I knew the water became very deep, very quickly, and where I hoped that there wasn't any limestone on the muddy bottom to catch the net when we wanted to bring it in.

I stripped down to my shorts, and my friend began to feed the net out to me. Another friend would carry the middle portion out into the water. I was immediately out of my depth, and could feel the current tugging at my legs. The water in this part of the river was 20 metres deep – I knew this from having consulted charts and maps. The weight of the net made it difficult to swim, but I paddled gamely, watching the glistening face of my friend doing the same behind me, his head bobbing between kicks.

When the net became taut, I watched my friend on shore wade out with the end of the net, until he was neck deep. He dropped his end, and making sure (this time) that I wasn't tangled in the mesh, I too let go.

It was always eerie swimming in the river at night, but on this occasion I was more than usually eager to get to shore. The bush on either side of the river was dark and silent. There was no sound at all from the city around us, or light from the port further downriver – we could have been thousands of kilometres away, thousands of years ago – a spatial and temporal lacuna that I usually enjoyed, but not on this occasion.

We drank vodka to keep warm. None of us had brought a towel, or a change of clothes. We thought about leaving the net out in the river for the next twenty-four hours, so that we could get home with sufficient time to get ready for school, but something about that disturbed me.

I made no mention of it to my friends, but I began to think about the gill net, and how it might snag a beloved cormorant, or even worse, one of the juvenile dolphins we saw from time to time, carousing with their mothers. Both of my friends fell asleep, heads rested on their hands in the moon-shade of a gnarled old paperbark. I couldn't stop thinking about the net, watching the first float bobble on the tide, the rest of it concealed and stretching down into the gloomy depths. I became increasingly agitated, and the vodka didn't help.

It wasn't the fact that gill-netting in the river was illegal. It was, I realised too late, also somehow shameful and underhanded – emotionally distant compared to the taking of an animal on the end of a fishing line or a barbed spear.

While my friends slept peacefully, I began to draw in the net. It was heavy, and I soon began to see why – the gauge was laden with algae caught on the current. I shook it off as I passed it back into the plastic bin, the silver droplets waking my friends. We drew the net in together, shaking off the water and seaweed. When we reached the halfway point, marked by a red float, we stopped and stared at the perfectly round hole in the netting, a perfect metre in diameter. None of us said anything, although I felt my stomach tumble. While I held up the net, my friend climbed through the hole, then back through the way he came. He did it another time, as though he couldn't believe what he was seeing.

We knew that there were sharks in the river. Big bull sharks, with blunt, hard-charging heads. Creatures who had swum with dinosaurs. We knew that, but it had never bothered us. We dived at the back end of Rottnest Island, after all, where the white sharks cruised the continental shelf. Living with the fear of sharks was part of growing up; part of being a surfer and diver, but this was something else.

I felt like dropping the net and running, as though it were a line, or a link to something deeper than the riverbed, larger than the shark that had chewed its way through. But we continued to gather it in, silently hoping that there was nothing captured, nothing caught to mark our time there. The net was empty. We packed it in the plastic bin. On the way home we tossed it into the skip at the back of a supermarket, then buried it with boxes.

Back at home, I wasn't able to sleep. I watched the sky lighten outside my bedroom window. It was going to be a long day at school, but I didn't yet feel tired. I examined the agitation that I'd experienced at the river, thinking about the gill net. I couldn't put it into words then, and I can't now, except to say that I knew that the midnight raids out into the river, and so much else, would soon cease. Not because of the shark, but because of something that the shark had articulated, demonstrated, warned against, without needing to make itself seen. It was a warning that I understood had been building up within me, spoken in the language of the river.

LOSS:
Dyarlgarro Beeliar/Canning River

Anna Haebich

1. Introduction

I'm usually a sea person. Rivers were never my passion. Of course, being in Perth you can't escape the Derbarl Yerrigan/Swan River, the city's major water way, front yard of the rich and famous, tourist eye candy. It's beautiful, commanding. Then there's the Dyarlgarro Beeliar/Canning River, the modest river that merges silently with the Swan near Applecross. Dyarlgarro Beeliar has been the river of life and spirit for its Wadjuk Beeliar custodians for over 60,000 years yet for centuries visiting European crews who noted and mapped the Swan overlooked this stretch of water. Even Captain James Stirling's expedition in 1827 to assess the establishment of a British colony ventured no further along the river than Point Heathcote, despite the enthusiasm of the crew's botanist Charles Fraser:

> The botany ... is splendid ... [with] magnificent *Banksias* and *Dryandras*, a remarkable species of *Hakea*, two species of *Grevillia*, a species of *Leptospermum*, and a beautiful dwarf species of *Calystris*. Here we came to great abundance of fresh water on the beach, by

scratching the sand with our fingers, within two inches of low-water mark.¹

Sailing back down the short stretch to the Swan, Fraser was obstructed by shallow river flats of alluvial mud deposits with 'extensive beds of oyster shells', and he was overawed by the 'truly astonishing' sight of black swans 'at least 500 ris[ing] at once'.²

The Dyarlgarro Beeliar riverscape of wide stretches and narrowing curves snaking 100 kilometres from the Darling scarp remains obscure to this day. Little has been written about the matrix of sustaining Nyungar custodial *Kartijin* (knowledge) and care and the rituals and ceremonies that maintained the river and its living species for millennia. Nor has settler colonial responsibility for degrading of the river environment and dispossession of its custodians been adequately documented. The Dyarlgarro Beeliar epitomises the claim that 'rivers reveal and conceal and do not give up secrets easily'.³ This 'less spectacular'⁴ shadowy riverscape triggered in me that haunting sense of 'when disturbed feelings cannot be put away, when something else, something different from before, seems like it must be done'.⁵ Hence this personal excursion to name and render visible the loss and 'ruination'⁶ that continues, not exactly a history of the river but snapshots, stories of people, time and place, approached through deep mapping processes of 'observing, listening, walking, conversing, writing and exchanging … of selecting, reflecting, naming, and generating.⁷ I was inspired by Nandi Chinna's research and poetry in her book *Swamp*. How she sought out Perth's 'phantom water bodies … just visible beneath the surveyor's lines and grids' by walking and using 'body and imagination' and sitting and 'engaging deep listening' to intuit emotions and knowledge from her surrounds. This revealed the now-dry city of year-round water restrictions to have been a 'seasonally wet place with an abundance of fresh water' and 'complex chains and suites of wetlands, fed by fresh springs and underwater aquifers'.⁸

I also found inspiration in Paul Carter's imagining of stories from Victoria's Mallee region as 'criss-crossing tracks' littered with fragments, repetitions, multiple perspectives, peeling back the accretions of history and memory. He used the name 'ichnography', the writing of tracks.[9] Federica Goffi provided a definition from architecture:

> From the Greek iknos, (track footprint) and graphia (writing), making the passage of time visible. The ichnography is the chosen instrument providing memory traces on the 'drawing site', acting like a veil and bearing the traces of the building's presence within time.[10]

To write in this way required potent sources and three fell fortuitously into my lap: an archive of colonial survey maps of the left bank upstream of the Dyarlgarro Beeliar/Canning River with field notebooks created in 1841 by German botanical collector Johann August Ludwig Preiss; a recent set of interpretative heritage plaques along the river foreshore; and a new Nyungar Wadjuk performance at Galup (Lake Monger) across Perth from Dyarlgarro Beeliar but closely linked to the river through mythology, history and geology. Each source provided a different engagement with the river: the original fertile timbered riverscape of wetlands and lakes mapped for settler land grants; the sacrifice of wildlife and sustaining river mudflats and bush to make way for farms and suburbs; and the catastrophe of colonisation for the Dyarlgarro Beeliar and the river system's Nyungar Wadjuk custodians and the healing spirit of performance. Walking was an element of each iteration. The theoretical analyses of settler colonialism, Patrick Wolfe[11] and Glen Coulthard,[12] provided framing constructs of dispossession, destruction and displacement and of the resilience to survive through the powerful relationships of Indigenous cultures, families and Country. I also drew on historian and anthropologist Ann Stoler's nuanced concept of 'ruination' that brings the genealogies of colonial dispossession, destruction and displacement together with psychological disablements, and also, her analyses of neglected and forgotten elements of ongoing colonial processes that reveal the 'corrosions ... and violent accruals of colonial aftermaths, as well as their durable traces on the material environment and people's bodies and minds'.[13]

2. Loss I

Ludwig Preiss's archive came as a surprise. I had been researching his visit to the Swan River Colony but missed this treasury of beautifully rendered maps and two field notebooks packed with surveying details and drawings.[14] Preiss arrived in the colony in December 1838 and immediately began walking through the bush collecting specimens of plants (he claimed at least 200,000) as well as birds and other wildlife, and made copious notes, now lost. Coming three years later the commission to survey the left bank of the Dyarlgarro Beeliar would have been a welcome addition to his dwindling funds. The survey was also important for the colony. Historian Ann Moyal explains that surveyors' fastidious work maintaining records of expanding frontiers and measuring and fixing boundaries of land grants was crucial for 'the identification of the country's landscape and its evolving settlement'.[15] For this they were well rewarded with land and government posts, but not Preiss. Most came from surveying, naval, military, scientific or university backgrounds. Preiss was educated in Germany and had connections with botanists at the University of Göettingen and Hamburg Botanical Gardens. He was sometimes addressed as Dr Preiss. After three years of extensive botanical collecting he also knew the bush.

Preiss's commission came from Governor John Hutt (1795–1880), who arrived from London in 1839 with instructions to make the colony productive. Good land and water were 'central pillars' of colonial settlement but both were in short supply.[16] Large areas of useful land along the Derbarl Yerrigan and the foothills were held by officials, military officers and some absentee speculators. Small conditional grants with narrow river frontages petered out into ribbons of sandy soil. The Dyarlgarro Beeliar needed further mapping. The few large grants were largely unimproved. Kelmscott town site declared in 1829 was only a small barracks. Captain Churchman's vast adjoining grant of 5,666 acres (this included the future sites of Roleystone and Bedfordale) remained undeveloped after he died suddenly in 1833.[17] Preiss and his assistants, soldiers from the 57th Regiment, began work in April 1841. They were to survey the left bank of the Canning upstream, the few alienated blocks marked by boundary trees, piled stones, stakes and trenches and draw the first boundary lines and record new sites for settlement with good soil, streams, lakes and timber.

As a European scientist, Preiss was an outsider in the small British colony. His 'mental landscape'[18] was shaped by a culture of forest 'Wandern' from his village in the Harz Mountains and his studies in natural history dominated during the nineteenth century by biogeographer Alexander von Humboldt and his logical vision of the world's landscapes as the 'totality of all aspects of a region, as perceived by man ... landscape as the sum of all aspects, natural, cultural, geographic, geologic, biologic, artistic'.[19] The colony's botanist, John Drummond, reaped the benefits of his British origins in land grants, appointments and botanical connections in London, but he lacked Preiss's botanical training and focused collecting. He rode on horseback with his kangaroo dogs while Preiss reportedly walked, probably along Nyungar pathways. The intimacy of his 'body-centred perspective' of walking as a way of coming to know,[20] his proximity to plants and the earth and the stop–start movements to peer closer, sharpened his eye for shapes and colours of the bush and his capacity to interpret tracks already made. There was a fit with the role of surveyor in the complicity of both in furthering the colonial project. However, surveying went further as an act of possession, as Preiss calculated and measured with his compass and chains, assessed the value of what he saw for colony and empire and translated the natural forms around him into lines, numbers, measurements and writing.[21]

Tim Ingold explains that maps 'make the unknown known by assembling data collected from multiple locations into a comprehensive survey'.[22] Read carefully as historical sources

Preiss's maps delivered a wealth of information beyond the arts of photography, not yet available in the colony. Read from today they also trace 'the future history they inaugurate of colonization, territorialisation, and the authorization of new political and social orders'.[23] Visually compelling in his field notebooks were the stands of trees everywhere, drawn, described, botanically named and classified, and some measured. Also, the river's long line of fresh water, and the fertile swamps and lakes, were suggestive of fruitful plants, plump birds and animals, and well-nourished Nyungar families with surplus foods for large seasonal gatherings of ceremony, feasts and trade. It was no surprise that these colonial survey maps were devoid of signs of the original people and flora and fauna. Geographer J. B. Harley reminds us that maps are 'instruments of discourse', with culturally determined signs, symbols and annotations constructed by mappers who 'select, leave out, simplify, classify, make hierarches'.[24] For the colonial project Preiss's maps documented 'the significance of the earth ... as a space to be occupied'.[25]

Nyungar names of waterways and landscapes were absent, along with ecosystems, spatial territories and narratives. Some were already known to colonists in the early 1830s. Territories of the coastal plain were narrated by Yagan to Robert Manli Lyon, a sympathetic colonist from Inverness in the Scottish Highlands, who published details in the *Perth Gazette*:

> Beeloo, the district of Munday, is bounded by the Canning on the south; by Melville water, on the West; by the Swan and Ellen's brook, on the North, the Eastern boundary of this district I cannot accurately define.

> Beeliar, the district of Midjegoorong, is bounded by the Melville water and the Canning, on the North; by the mountains on the East; by the sea on the West; and by a line due East, from Mangles Bay, on the South.[26]

Incidents of colonial conflict were ignored: the site of revenge killings of colonists on the Fremantle road near the tributary Gabbiljee (Bull Creek)[27] followed by the vengeful killings of Midgegeroo and Yagan; and at Kelmscott barracks a soldier and Weeip's kinsman killed and his son jailed.[28] Preiss's maps created a *tabula rasa* for colonists to inscribe their dreams of prosperity. Today they are historic documents of the possession of Dyarlgarro Beeliar as a site for British colonisation.

Could Preiss be held accountable for his role in these outcomes? What were his responsibilities? What choices did the 'paradox of humane colonisation' allow in the early colony where acts of violent frontier dispossession mingled with the language of Christian humanity?[29] In the early 1830s, Scottish colonist Robert Menli Lyon was unique in choosing personal responsibility when he publicly opposed punitive raids and demanded justice for Yagan, who he accompanied into exile, and documented his language and culture for posterity. For Lyon, Nyungar dispossession must have recalled the Highland clearances. He saw his Scottish bardic heritage reflected in the Wadjuk 'bards' seated around their fires 'chanting their poetic compositions. I have reason to believe that their history and geography are handed down from generation to generation orally in verse'.[30] Lyon's stance drew hostility and threats from other colonists and in 1834 he left the colony but continued speaking and publishing about Aboriginal rights well into his old age.

Preiss cannot be easily absolved. He could be held responsible for his failure to act like Lyon to mitigate the impact of colonisation around him and accountable for his less-knowing contributions to the long-term consequences of the colonial project, these being instances of Hannah Arendt's 'ethical trespass', those 'actions without evil intent that can cause unforeseeable damage'.[31] Collecting specimens to further science and his career made Preiss complicit in the global north–south exploitation of Indigenous resources and knowledge. Collections were acquired by European institutes, assimilated into universal science classifications, theories, laws and publications and returned to the colony couched in polices of land possession and usage.³² Indeed, Preiss's collections were central to the first reference volumes on Western Australian flora, *Plantae preissianae sive enumeratio plantarum quas in Australasia,* which stimulated intense interest in the region's botanical biodiversity.³³ We have seen how Preiss was further compromised by his role as a surveyor. He was also seduced by the miasma of colonial privilege and wealth, and began plans to become a British colonist with extensive land holdings. In 1839 he applied to become a British subject (granted in 1841) and he offered to sell his collections to the British government for £3,000 but was rejected. He also promised to bring 50 German farming families to the colony in return for land. Had these plans gone ahead, Preiss would have contributed directly to the multi-species biological colonisation of the colony. This meant the destruction of ancient Indigenous ecological accommodations, which were replaced by adaptations of northern hemisphere species and methods, with catastrophic results. It took less than 200 years for these practices to transform the unique biodiversity of the south west that Preiss had heralded into a designated global biodiversity hotspot, with catastrophic loss of plant species. Mazstnak et al argue that biological colonisation practised over many centuries has been a major casual factor of the Anthropocene.³⁴

Preiss's dreams of landed wealth in the colony were dashed by misfortune on his return to Germany in January 1842. He could not fulfil his renewed promise to return with German families and funds, and was forced to sell his collections to survive. Deprived of his chance to benefit financially from the colonial project he now advised that 'with few exceptions [the] land is not suitable for agriculture'.³⁵ Preiss never returned to the Swan River Colony.

Almost 180 years after Preiss completed his survey of the Dyarlgarro Beeliar, surveying students at Curtin University have created a framework for transforming his original location survey data and the 14 historical maps into today's geodetic referencing system. Preiss's data, collected using primitive equipment, proved to be remarkably precise. The students also produced visualisation techniques to analyse and share their results with non-experts in accessible formats. Applying their results to the field notebooks where Preiss drew and named botanical and natural features, it may now be possible to reimagine and map the original plant biodiversity, freshwater lakes and fertile wetlands of this millennia-old riverscape.[36]

3. **Loss II**

We now leap forward from colonial mapping to Perth in 2019 and the contemporary source of the heritage walk along the Wadjuk foreshore between Mount Henry and Shelley Bridges. This time I was walking to learn, observing the riverscape and reading the interpretation signage. Distinguishing features of stands of trees, the river, wetlands and lakes in Preiss's maps were notably absent from this tamed riverscape, now populated with stories of loss of birds and other wildlife, plants and the sustaining alluvial river mud. Overall, the information plaques were surprisingly straightforward about how and why this happened. Local resident and interpretive historian Susan Harris played a pivotal role in their creation as the consultant engaged by the City of Canning council to develop the walk design installation and in their maintenance through the local community group, Wadjup-Gabbilju.[37]

The walk was part of the Canning River Regional Park of 266 hectares, extending along both sides of the river for 6 kilometres, created as a suburban conservation and recreation reserve and listed on the Register of the National Estate.[38] This was one of several initiatives recouping the river heritage of the Swan coastal plain. The 2011 *Statement of Significance for the Swan and Canning Rivers* recognised their 'natural and cultural heritage significance'.[39] In 2014 the ambitious Marli Riverpark interpretation study acknowledged the 'waterways and surrounds of the Swan, Canning, Helena and Southern Rivers ... [as] a distinctive geological formation with an evolved ecosystem ... used intensively by humans for millennia ... [and] characterised by a diverse range of heritage values'.[40] The significance of the 2006 Nyungar native title claim was also recognised. It had led to the state government's 2013 native title settlement package, offering self-governance agreements, land, funds, housing, services and formal recognition of Nyungar custodianship for Perth and the entire south west. A Nyungar advisory panel of elders and custodians representing nine families was appointed to advise on heritage matters and protocols.[41] The knowledge they shared, cited in the study, demonstrated their continuing spiritual custodial responsibilities and their intention to 'make something new' from the enduring entanglements of colonial formations that had denied them a public role in its restoration.[42] The study report recommended interpretation strategies to promote 'effective management of heritage values of the river park while ensuring those values are accessible to a broad range of audiences.'[43] The approach was 'not instruction, but provocation. The place should be presented as a space for public discourse ... to share the excitement of thinking about the past, the present and the future'.[44] The river walk fulfilled some of these aims.

We set out on a warm, sunny day from near Mount Henry bridge. The river was broad at this point, but the walk reserve was a narrow strip of lawn with a concrete path between the road and sandy river edge. Clumps of rocks and trees on the opposite bank suggested a more challenging walk. Our side was distinctly suburban. Homes of the well-to-do vied for picture-postcard views looking down the river to the Perth skyline. Behind them, suburbs stretched away to Leach Highway and beyond. Our guides for the walk were 26 strategically placed engraved metal plaques, 'elegant, simple and permanent', requiring minimum maintenance.[45] Their interpretation role was to 'increase awareness of the local heritage and stimulate an interest in conservation; promote the area's history to visitors; publicly acknowledge significant conservation activity; and provide a ready-made recreational or educational excursion'.[46] They offered information and short explanations with a range of creatively placed illustrative material, maps, photographs, drawings and memories, and directions to identify sites in the river, which provided a beautiful background for the activities of walking, reading, looking, locating sites and taking photographs. There was a sense of discovery.

The signage began with a skeletal account of the Nyungar Waugal creation myth of the river system with some Nyungar language. Maps and information about the river and its connections with Gabbiljee and the Derbarl Yerrigan, tides, weather and winds followed, then came details about trees and plants endemic to the river banks and swamps. We were directed to a *Melaleuca preissiana* paperbark tree growing in the front yard of a private home. Birds were next – ospreys, migratory flocks, cormorants, swans, pelicans – all decreasing in numbers along with the marine life they fed on. History intervened with sightings of debris in the river, the remains of fences and dredging using convict labour and barges to remove river mud obstructing transport of people and timber from upstream. Further plaques explained changes to the river banks and suburbanisation and then, in quick succession, came warnings and rules about swimming, fishing, boating, river water pollution, foreshore erosion, and diving into muddy shallows. My tally of topics for the twenty-six plaques was: Nyungar, one (with brief mention in three others); nature, 10; history and progress, six; and warnings, nine. Of these 19 directly or indirectly mentioned loss relating to the river, its wildlife and environs.

Two features of the plaques stood out for me. First, that Nyungar people were as ghostly figures and their custodial and spiritual responsibilities for the river stretching back over 60,000 years were largely ignored at a time when Nyungar custodianship of the river was beginning to be recognised. The Marli Riverpark plan in 2014 documented that custodians still had special sites on the river of 'ancestral birthing, burial, camping and fishing sites' that they visited, as Albert Corunna explained:

> I see it important for us to help in the projecting of these river sites. When we go to the rivers one of the customs is to throw sand in the to let the Waugyl know we are here. This is a sign of respect which or ancestors can see we are doing the right thing.[47]

The second feature was the plaque text's surprising acknowledgement of the extent of damage to the riverscape and the causes, along with didactic warnings about the dangers, as demonstrated in the following excerpts from the plaques.

> **Still a bird retreat?** Before suburban development along the Lower Canning, there were wide uninhabited wetlands and nesting spots for water fowl … If the fresh-water creeks were still here, black swans would be more likely to nest nearby.
>
> **Spread of shells** This was originally a large wetland … to get ashore here at Shelley Cove, you had to push through thick stretches of rushes and sedges for a long way inland. There were freshwater springs along the foreshore. The boggy creeks are these days mourned as long-gone environmental treasures. Why are there sometimes no shells on Shelley Beach? Eroding beaches along the foreshore are occasionally topped up. The sand trucked in for that maintenance does not contain shells.
>
> **Displacing wetness** What a boggy place this was! But this wetland came to an end in the 1960s when the foreshore was "reclaimed". During the reclamation the wide wetland edge of the bay was covered with thick shelly slurry from the river bottom.
>
> **Convict fence** 200 to 300 convicts were there at different times reclaiming and dredging the river. Timber was used for damming back the mud and silt dredged from the channel.
>
> **Who's to blame?** Strong winds can lead to erosion … but people do their share. Random paths on the riverbank can erode: water moves along the paths like the ladders in a stocking, weakening the sides so they collapse. With time, Nature fills all estuaries. But the infilling is gradual, taking thousands of years … not a generation!
>
> **Fishing** Fishermen could net a thousand mullet a night. Nowadays one would be lucky to catch more than a dozen … there are hardly any river prawns … fish bait is harder to find … estuary cobbler is now rare. In the 1940s they caught blue manna crabs at the rate of 65 an hour, now you might see a few.

Wadjup Point Before, the mudflats attracted much wildlife. Residents want to save it from further pollution, but how? The river is the endpoint for groundwater flowing this way. It takes over a thousand years to get here from Jandakot Groundwater Mound. Unless we keep a dedicated watch over all the seepage into the deep sands generations along the river could be on the receiving end of pollution for at least the next thousand years.

Dirty river? Residents remember the Canning having crystal clear water up until the 1960s ... by the 1970s the river often became murky and uninviting ... Modern Mud ... polluted sediment collecting on the mudflats.

My walking companion added further river damage to the list. How Canning Dam had created 'Modern Mud' by stopping the natural flooding that cleansed river sludge sediment. The toxicity to water and soils from extensive dumping of sanitary waste and rubbish into river banks and wetlands. How algae growing naturally in the river water was exacerbated to dangerous levels by flow-off from gardens, parks and farms. The dangers of lowered ground water levels caused by agricultural, industrial and residential overuse. Already in 1972 environmentalist George Seddon penned the following chilling summary of cumulative damage to Perth's once seasonal wetness:

> Of all the resources of the coastal plain, the rivers, estuaries, lakes and swamps have been the most affected ... They are also the most biologically productive areas ... and support most of its wildlife. More than half a million acres of wetland have been drained for agriculture ... and reclamation has claimed 1501 acres along the shores of Swan and Canning River estuaries. This area was once a valuable waterfowl habitat ... from Yanchep to Rockingham 49 per cent (13,154 acres) of all wetlands had been drained by 1966 ... the point has been made repeatedly ... that the most productive part of most water bodies is the shallow water ... with dredging production of the estuary drops substantially ... [and] disturbs organic material ... so the water supports much less fish and

bird life There are no remedies. The decline is an irreversible consequence of European occupation.[48]

Ruth Morgan added a broader context from the 1970s of the drying of the Swan coastal plain, south west region and entire state and of water salinity from land clearing and degradation that created the 'largest proportion of surface water classified as marginal, brackish and saline in the country'.[49] There are also the effects of climate change, with recognition in the 1990s that water crises were no longer simply bad droughts but 'a new regional climate equilibrium: a state of lower rainfall'.[50]

The sacrifice of the Dyarlgarro Beeliar riverscape and Nyungar ecologies for the bland suburban landscape and the impact of climate change left me with a visceral feeling of 'solastagia', the concept coined by environmental philosopher Glen Albrecht, now a global catchword to express the distress and desolation caused by the realisation of negative environmental change in a treasured home place. This was 'the homesickness you have when you are still at home'.[51] In an interview in 2019 Aldrich explained how his understanding of the importance of place came from his own 'eco-biography.' He described the impact of coal mining on wetlands and birdlife at his then home in the Hunter Valley and residents' expressions of physical and mental distress at 'the collapse of what they call home'.[52] He also reminisced about his boyhood growing up on Dyarlgarro Beeliar and recalled long hours wandering in the bush, his love of birds, joining the WA Naturalists' Club and seeking solace alone in nature. The rapid suburbanisation of the riverscape in the 1960s and 1970s must have deeply impacted his youthful sensitivities. Today we are all prey to feelings of solastalgia as environmental damage becomes the 'new abnormal' with the worsening 'pandemic of earth-related distress'.[53] How much deeper and all-encompassing must be the anguish of the Nyungar custodians.

3. **Loss III**

My final source is the 2020 Perth Festival's Nyungar Wadjuk performance *Galup*, a mix of storytelling, memory and history recounted in Nyungar language, song and dance, with audience promenade and participation and a strong sense of place on site at Galup (Lake Monger). This cross-generational and cross-cultural work was the co-creation of Wadjuk Nyungar performer, writer and director Ian Wilkes and director and producer Poppy van Oorde-Grainger, working with storyteller, performer and author, Elder Aunty Doolann-Leisha Eatts. Ian's father had always told him that 'something bad happened there, never forget it. Always remember what really happened'. It was Aunty Doolann-Leisha Eatts' telling to Ian and Poppy of her great grandmothers' eye-witness account of the massacre at Galup that inspired the performance.[54] The performance restored the forgotten massacre to public memory. Embedded in the Perth Festival theme of *Bilya* (river) the performance also reunited Galup and Dyarlgarro Beeliar with the mythical narratives of the vast system of waterways created by the Waugul above and below ground.[55]

This local performance came from Nyungar family memories and personal passions. Aunty Doolan-Leisha Eatts had 'lived [her] whole life dreaming that this story would be told'.[56] It was also part of the burst of national and international Indigenous cultural activism this century, responding to what Ines Hernandez-Avila has called a 'post-apocalyptic stage of cultural political and spiritual revitalization and recovery'.[57] It also responds to the continuing reality of settler colonial environmental destruction and repeating cycles of colonial injustice. Tensions generated by these challenges of change and continuity have contributed to the impetus to reanimate Indigenous cultures and environments through performances that release and heal communities and provoke 'radical unsettledness' amongst general audiences.[58] Nicolas Rothwell describes the powers of Aboriginal dance performance as 'libraries of the Indigenous realm, where knowledge is crystallised ... hospitals where wellbeing is maintained ... banks where culture is stored [and] ... as a kind of lifeline into the future'.[59]

The environmental degradation of the system of waterways of the Swan coastal plain and the Wadjuk Nyungar custodians' performative healing also resonate with Indigenous global south activist agendas like that of environmentalist Adolfo Maldonado, who appropriates solastalgia for Indigenous psychological disorders from environmental damage to their lands. He describes the power and beauty of lost places where:

> ... memories are in the texture of the trees, in a horizon whose vision welcomes and integrates them, in the nightly music of the forests, in the smells of its seasons, in the flavours of its seasonal fruit, in its harvests, in the tasks of care of nature from which they obtain not only food but also dreams and aspirations for the future.[60]

He identifies the state's strategies of destruction of Indigenous 'defenders of nature' and places and the humiliation and illness caused: 'health is dignity and behind each illness there is always a cause of humiliation'.[61] He warns that 'we cannot afford the luxury of pessimism'.[62] He urges action to restore health and wellbeing through Julio Montalvo's concept of 'alegremia' or 'joy in the blood',[63] the quest of life from joy through performance:

> Welcome all those puppeteers, artists, animators, healers, shamans and herbalists, artists and singers, theatre makers of alegremia, crusaders in defence of life, firebreathers, fortune tellers and jugglers, clowns, storytellers and humourists, guardians of places and defenders of nature, because you more than anyone are needed to construct health. We cannot permit it to be trapped, confined in the hands of doctors. Let them cure disease, but among us all let's construct that health which is founded on joy.[64]

This agenda is mirrored in the Nyungar context. Nyungar people have survived the catastrophe of settler colonialism to become Australia's largest Aboriginal nation. But the legacies continue. With the slow pace of the Nyungar settlement process access to Country and the means to heal environmental damage are frustrated. Chronic illness, suicide and early death still devastate families. Survival comes from ancient family lineages with shared language, lore and laws and relationships that bind people and their places, as Elder Dr. Noel Nannup explained:

> And when we talk about the importance of flora and fauna as Aboriginal people, particularly here in Nyungar country, they're all part of the story and that's what connects you to country, they're part of the totemic system, they're part of you, you're part of them.[65]

Healing comes from myths and stories of courage and passion through cultural performances that are creative, passionate, innovative, courageous, political and hopeful and that pursue the 'quest of life from joy'. These are all features of the performance *Galup*.

Galup is grounded in Nyungar culture and history. Galup, the Wadjuk Nyungar performance place, is full of significant myths, stories and memories. It is the site of a lake with fertile wetlands that nourished Nyungar people for millennia. Dyarlgarro Beeliar and Galup are two powerful bodies of water unified through the creative actions of the Waugul merging and linking rivers, swamps, lakes, underground waters and tunnels. Galup is one site where the Waugul emerged from the ground and then rested after creating Dyarlgarro Beeliar and Derbarl Yerrigan. The myth of the Waugul is foundational to Nyungar culture and lands:

> Noongar people believe that the *Waugal* dominates the earth and the sky and makes the *koondarnangor* (thunder), *babanginy* (lightning) and *boroong* (rain). During the *Nyitting*, it created the fresh waterways such as the *bilya/beelier* (river), *pinjar* (swamps, lakes) and *ngamma* (waterhole). The Darling Scarp represents the body of the *Waugal*, which created the curves and contours of the hills and gullies. As the *Waugal* slithered over the land, its track

shaped the sand dunes, its body scoured out the course of the rivers, where it occasionally stopped for a rest, and created bays and lakes.

The *Waugal* rose up from *Ga-ra-katta* (Mt. Eliza at the foot of Kings Park), and formed the *Derbarl Yerrigan* and the *Djarlgarro Beelier* (the Swan and Canning rivers). It also created other waterways and landforms around Perth and the south-west of Western Australia. The *Waugal* also joins up with wetlands such as Herdsman Lake and Lake Monger, and resides deep beneath underground springs.

When the great *Waugal* created the *boodja*, he ensured that there was *wirrin* or spirits to look after the land and all that it encompassed. Some places such as the *karda* (hills) and *ngamar* (waterholes), *boya* (rocks), *bilya/beelier* (rivers) and *boorn* (trees) were created as sacred sites and hold *wirn* (spirits), both *wara/mambaritj* (bad) and *kwop* (good).[66]

Dyarlgarro Beeliar and Galup also share a history of loss and degradation that is encapsulated in the headings and final verse of Chinna's poem 'Cut and Paste Lake – Lake Monger – Galup': 'Galup' 'Drain' 'Into produce' 'Into park' 'Chironmids' 'No boating / no swimming' 'Landfill' 'Mitchell Freeway' 'Grave' 'Parkland' and its final verse:

Parkland
All night drains have been feeding up from the east, the north, bringing road wash buried creek line, compensation basin run off. In the early morning the lake is spat out onto periphery lawns; subsiding beneath the day's picnics.[67]

For millennia Galup has been an important meeting place located, as Yagan explained to Lyon, in 'the district of Yellowgonga (sic), [which] is bounded by the sea to the West; by Melville water and the Swan on the South; by Ellen's brook, on the East; and by the Gyngoorda, on the North. Galup is the capital'.[68] Lyon reported how Yellagonga retreated there for safety from colonists' attacks:

> The tribe of the quiet and inoffensive Yellowgonga (sic), was lately fired upon [by colonists] while fishing on the river, driven into the bush and plundered of their fish. The cry of this deeply injured race must be heard by the judge of all the earth; and their blood will assuredly call for vengeance.[69]

When Menang men visited Perth in 1833, Yellagonga and Yagan held welcome ceremonies at Galup with ritual exchanges of buka cloaks and displays of kidji throwing. Nyungar families continued camping there during last century.[70]

The performance *Galup* is dedicated to keeping Nyungar history and culture alive for the future. The on-site walking, observing and participating are imbedded in Nyungar practice but they also resonate with contemporary forms of promenade and site-specific and immersive theatre. The performance begins as we spiral down the footbridge from the Mitchell Freeway to the world of Galup below and our hosts welcome us with a smoking ceremony. Wilkes is brilliant. As the sole performer of the stories, dances and songs he leads our small group of spectators and impromptu performers around the lake, as we walk in silence, listening to his stories in Nyungar language. When we stop, he performs dances and songs and invites us to join in. Participating in this way and seeing Nyungar performance in place and up close (a first for most of our group) activates a powerful sense of living culture and place. At the same time our senses are energised by the sights and sounds and smells around us, of wildlife, lapping water and cooling air on our skin and in the background joggers and families and the rush of traffic on the freeway. As the light changes from dusk to darkness, we see a welcoming fire ahead at the lake's edge. Aunty Leisha is waiting for us. Once we are seated on the grass, with our backs to the cityscape, freeway and lake, she begins the story of the massacre. Her cultural authority and dignity create a performance space of respectful listening and learning for a beginning of healing for the catastrophic event at this site.

4. Conclusion

This study brings new layers of insights to the colonial history of Dyarlgarro Beeliar and, although not providing a deep mapping in time, it enriches our understanding of the river's past, present and, perhaps, future. However, the information that the criss-crossing tracks of the maps and heritage plaques reveals only goes so far. Arts theorist Owen Kelly writes that 'information' is like 'a window for which there is no door. We ignore what is going on around us, and stand with our noses pressed up against the window trying to peer into this other world to find out what is really going on'.[71] This window was opened by the experience of walking, participating and listening on site to the Nyungar wisdom and knowledge performed in *Galup*. The performance's embodied reveal of the pervasive power of settler colonialism to invade and restructure activated a determination to 'refract its efforts and assert something liberatory in its place'.[72] Following on from Montalvo's agenda for 'joy in the blood' this 'something liberatory' could be restoration of the whole matrix of Nyungar care for land, water and living species, rituals, ceremonies and corroborees, songlines and totemic relationships. Custodians fulfilled their responsibilities to the Waugul in this way for millennia to sustain the ancient waters and energies pulsing through the hidden tunnels and waterways.[73] Today Nyungar Elders are already restoring *Kartijin* to heal the land, often collaborating with scientists. Nyungar language, song and dance and welcome rituals are also reanimating the healing powers of performances and ceremonies.[74] Communities of supporters are being created through Nyungar performances like *Galup*. Local residents who value the life of the river are contributing their resources and skills. Could this be the way to heal the scars on the environment and people's bodies and minds and to restore the power and presence of Dyarlgarro Beeliar?

Eagle Warrior

Vanessa Corunna

This painting is inspired from the yarning by Elder Richard Wilkes about the eagle coming after the burial of Yagan's *kaat* (head).[1] The painting is about Yagan turning into the eagle and travelling over his Swan River People's country before returning to the Swan River spirit grounds. An eagle is a very spiritual creature in many cultures and in this painting it symbolises a form of peace that occurs because of the burial of Yagan's kaat.

Vanessa Corunna, *Eagle Warrior.*[2]
WATERCOLOUR, 2013

Notes

Prelude
1. This essay was previously published in *Westerly*, vol. 66, no. 1, 2021.
2. C. Lynch, 'Five Haiku', *Westerly*, vol. 64, no. 1, 2019, pp. 21–23.
3. R. Deakin, 'Introduction' in *The River's Voice*, Common Ground, Toller Porcurum, 2000.
4. Chen et al, *Thinking with Water*, McGill-Queen's University Press, Montreal, 2013, p. 8.
5. L. Collard, 'The Cosmology' in M. Leybourne and A. Gaynor (eds), *Water: History, Culture, Ecologies*, UWAP, Crawley, 2006, pp. 121–130.
6. O. Laing, *To the River*, Canongate Books, 2012, p. 14.
7. Chen et al, *Thinking with Water*, p. 9.
8. MacGillivray, *The Nine of Diamonds*, Bloodaxe Books, Hexham, Northumberland, 2016, p. 13.
9. 'Spirituality', Kaartdijin Noongar – Noongar Knowledge, South-West Aboriginal Land and Sea Council, https://noongarculture.org.au/spirituality/. Viewed 4 January 2022.
10. A. Neimanis, *Bodies of Water: Posthuman Feminist Phenomenology*, Bloomsbury Publishing, Sydney, 2017, pp. 1–4, and V. Strang, 'Fluid Consistencies: material relationality in human engagements with water', *Archaeological Dialogues*, vol. 21, no. 2, 2014, pp. 133–50.

Introduction: Deep Maps
1. In 2018, Curtin and Aberdeen University initiated a program designed for the purpose of cross-institution work, the Curtin–Aberdeen Alliance. Where, perhaps, the intended outputs for the alliances were projects in fossil fuel processing, the project sprang up out of a shared desire for alternative intellectual and creative aims.
2. M. Pearson and M. Shanks, *Theatre/Archaelogy*, Routledge, New York, 2005, p. 54.
3. I. Biggs, 'Deep mapping as an essaying of place' [illustrated talk], Bartlett School of Architecture, University College London, London, 9 July 2010.
4. T. Ingold, *Being Alive: Essays on Movement, Knowledge and Description*, Routledge, London, 2011.
5. Pearson and Shanks, *Theatre/Archaelogy*, pp. 64–65.
6. http://www.iainbiggs.co.uk/text-deep-mapping-as-an-essaying-of-place/, viewed 1 February 2022.
7. Chen et al, *Thinking with Water*, McGill-Queen's University Press, Montreal, 2013, p. 8; A. Neimanis, *Bodies of Water: Posthuman Feminist Phenomenology*,

Bloomsbury Publishing, Sydney, 2017, pp. 1–4; V. Strang, 'Fluid Consistencies: material relationality in human engagements with water', *Archaeological Dialogues*, vol. 21, no. 2, 2014, pp. 133–50; V. Strang, *Water: Nature and Culture*, Reaktion Books, London 2015; V. Strang, 'Re-imagining the River: New Environmental Ethics in Human Engagements with Water', *One Earth*, vol. 2, no. 3, 2020, pp. 204–206; and V. Strang, *The Meaning of Water*, Routledge, London, 2020.

8   B. Latour, *Reassembling the Social: An Introduction to Actor-Network Theory*, Oxford University Press, Oxford and New York 2005.
9   P. A. Coates, *A Story of Six Rivers: History Culture and Ecology*, Reaktion Books, 2013; and Strang, *The Meaning of Water*.
10 O. Laing, *To the River*, Canongate Books, Edinburgh, 2012; and Strang, *The Meaning of Water*.
11 J. Wylie, 'A Single Day's Walking: Narrating Self and Landscape on the South West Coast Path', *Transactions of the Institute of British Geographers*, vol. 30, no. 2, 2005, pp. 234–47.

Neil Curtis and Jo Jones – Introduction: The Dee and the Don

1   N. Shepherd, *The Living Mountain: A Celebration of the Cairngorm Mountains of Scotland*. Canongate Books, Edinburgh, 2008, pp. 27–28.
2   H. Smart, 'The Don' in A. Spence and H. Hutchinson (eds), *Silver: An Aberdeen Anthology*, Polygon, Edinburgh, 2009, p. 5.
3   L. Roberts, 'Introduction', *Humanities* (deep mapping special issue), 5 (1), 2016, p. 3.
4   https://www.arcgis.com/, viewed 7 December 2021.
5   https://www.arcgis.com/, viewed 7 December 2021.
6   G. Bachelard, *Water and Dreams: An Essay on the Imagination of Matter*, Pegasus Foundation, Dallas, 1983, p. 29.
7   W. F. H. Nicolaisen, *The Picts and their Placenames*, Groam House Museum Trust, Rosemarkie, Inverness, Scotland, 1996, p. 21.

Meredi Ortega – The Lower Dee: Swimming Upstream/Nowhere

1   N. Shepherd, *The Living Mountain*, 1977, Canongate Books, Edinburgh, 2011, p. 106.
2   A. Oswald, 'Severed Head Floating Downriver', *Falling Awake*, Jonathan Cape, London, 2016, p. 10
3   Juvenal, 'The Satires of Juvenal, Satire 6', *Juvenal and Persius*, (trans) S. M. Braund, Loeb Classical Library, Harvard University Press, Cambridge, Massachusetts, 2004, p. 249.
4   R. Duncan, 'Mute Swan nesting on the River Dee at Aberdeen; first breeding record for the Dee', *North-East Scotland Bird Report 1995*, North-East Scotland Bird Club, 1995, p. 65.
5   C. Main, 'Swans found shot and "missing flesh" in plastic bags on River Dee in Aberdeen', *Evening Express*, 13 March 2019, https://www.eveningexpress.co.uk/fp/news/local/swans-found-shot-and-missing-flesh-in-plastic-bags-on-river-dee-in-aberdeen, viewed 17 May 2019.

6   J. A. Henderson, *History of the Parish of Banchory-Devenick*, D. Wyllie & Son, Aberdeen, 1890, p. 255.
7   Henderson, *History of the Parish*, pp. 262–63.
8   'Aberdeen Town Council: Proposed Bridge at Maryculter', *The Aberdeen Journal*, 5 September 1893, p. 6, in *British Library Newspapers, Part I 1800–1900*, Gale Document Number: BB3205815903.
9   D. Jamieson and W. S. Wilson, *Old Lower Deeside*, Stenlake Publishing, Catrine, Ayrshire, 2003, p. 21.
10   Shepherd, *The Living Mountain*, p. 61.
11   Shepherd, *The Living Mountain*, p. 28.
12   V. Strang, *Water: Nature and Culture*, Reaktion Books, London, 2015, p. 49.
13   Strang, *Water: Nature and Culture*, p. 31.
14   W. James, *The Principles of Psychology, Vol.1*, 1890, Henry Holt and Company, New York, 1918, p. 239.
15   H. Pulaczewska, *Aspects of Metaphor in Physics*, 1999, De Gruyter, Berlin, 2011, p. 104.
16   P. Yaeger, 'Towards a Female Sublime', in L. Kauffman (ed.), *Gender & Theory: Dialogues on Feminist Criticism*, Basil Blackwell, Oxford, 1989, p. 191.
17   Shepherd, *The Living Mountain*, p. 2.
18   Shepherd, *The Living Mountain*, p. 79.
19   C. Main, 'Inspirational messages found hidden along Aberdeen walking route', *Evening Express*, 24 May 2018, https://www.eveningexpress.co.uk/fp/news/local/inspirational-messages-found-hidden-along-aberdeen-walking-route, viewed 24 April 2019.
20   G. G. Byron, 'When I Roved a Young Highlander', *The Poetical Works of Lord Byron: Complete in One Volume*, John Murray, London, 1844 p. 417.
21   C. Peacock, *Into the Mountain: A Life of Nan Shepherd*, Galileo Publishers, Cambridge, 2017, Kindle edition, note 54.
22   Shepherd, *The Living Mountain*, p. 24.
23   P. Marren, *A Natural History of Aberdeen*, Robin Callander, Haughend, Finzean, Aberdeenshire, 1982, p. 73.
24   N. Shepherd, 'The Lupin Island' in *The Deeside Field*, The Deeside Field Club, Aberdeen, 1966, p. 42.
25   J. Glenday, 'Two Ravens' in *The Golden Mean*, Picador, London, 2015, p. 10.
26   K. Jamie, 'Five Tay Sonnets,' in *The Overhaul*, Picador, London, 2012, p. 6.
27   D. Grant, *The Muckle Spate O' Twenty-nine*, 1884, The Bon-Accord Press, Aberdeen, 1934, p. 24.
28   R. Macfarlane in Shepherd, *The Living Mountain*, p. xiii.

Ian Grosz – The Don: A Sacred River

1   Jorge Manrique was a Castilian poet (c. 1440–April 1479). This quote is taken from *Coplas por la Muerte de su Padre* – *'Stanzas about the Death of his Father'* from F. A Domínguez, *Love and Remembrance: The Poetry of Jorge* Manrique, The University Press of Kentucky, Lexington 1989.

2   M. Certeau, *The Practice of Everyday Life*, (trans) S. Rendall, University of California Press, Berkley, 1984, p. 108.
3   M. Couto, *Woman of the Ashes*, (trans) D. Brookshaw, Farrar, Straus and Giroux, New York, 2018, p. 41.
4   W. F. H. Nicolaisen, *The Picts and Their Place Names*, Groam House Museum, Rosemarkie, 1996, p. 17
5   Aberfeldy in Highland Perthshire, for example, and Aberystwyth in Wales.
6   Nicolaisen, *The Picts and Their Place Names*, p. 21.
7   Nicolaisen, *The Picts and Their Place Names*, p. 21.
8   See J. D. Galbraith, *St Machar's Cathedral: the Celtic Antecedents*, Friends of St Machar's Cathedral, 1982.
9   E. Stock, *The Folk Lore Journal, VII*, London, The Folk Lore Society, 1889, sourced from http://www.glenbuchatheritage.com, viewed 1 February, 2022.
10 https://canmore.org.uk/event/560598, viewed 1 February, 2022.
11 Stock, *The Folk Lore Journal*.
12 https://canmore.org.uk/site/128563/corriehoul-cemetery, viewed 2019
13 http://www.glenbuchatheritage.com/picture/number921.asp, viewed 2019
14 Stock, *The Folk Lore Journal*.
15 See Noble, Greig, Millican in *Proceedings of the Prehistoric Society 78*, 2011, pp. 135–171.
16 Alexander Ogg was a land surveyor born in the nearby village of Kemnay on the banks of the Don in 1811. He mapped the estate grounds of the area and made a very detailed map of New and Old Aberdeen from earlier work carried out by architect John Smith. After going bankrupt in 1847, Ogg emigrated to New Zealand where he died in 1865 after making a living as a surveyor, teacher and gold prospector. His family remained in Aberdeenshire.
17 See https://www.undiscoveredscotland.co.uk/usbiography/f/saintfergus.html.
18 *In the Shadow of Bennachie: A Field Archeology of Donside, Aberdeenshire*, second edition, 2008, (2007, Edinburgh, Society of Antiquarians of Scotland in association with The Royal Commission on the Ancient and Historical Monuments of Scotland), p. 128.
19 *In the Shadow of Bennachie*, p. 128.
20 *In the Shadow of Bennachie*, p. 128.
21 *In the Shadow of Bennachie*, p. 126.
22 *In the Shadow of Bennachie*, p. 122.
23 *In the Shadow of Bennachie*, p. 119.

Ashleigh Angus – The Cucking of a Scold: River Dee, Aberdeen, Scotland

1   Adapted from J. Ashton, *Chap-books of the Eighteenth Century*, Chatto and Windus, London, 1882 p. 272. Retrieved from https://archive.org/details/chapbooksofeight00ashtuoft/page/272, viewed 27 January 2022.
2   As cited in H. E. Rollins (ed) (1922), *A Pepysian Garland: Black-letter Broadside Ballads of the Years 1595–1639*, 1971, p. 76. Retrieved from https://quod.lib.umich.edu/g/genpub/1438791.0001.001/104?view=image&size=100, viewed 27 January 2002.

NOTES

Jo Jones – The Derbarl Yarrigan (Swan River) and Dyarlgarro Beeliar (Canning River)

1. From J. Kinsella, 'Polysituated Ode with Occasional Demi-boustrophedon', in *Polysituatedness: A Poetics of Displacement*, Manchester University Press, Manchester, 2017.
2. From C. Lynch, 'Riverland', in *Five Short Blasts: I am Unsure of your Intentions and I Fear We May Collide*, performed at Perth Festival, 2019
3. https://www.arcgis.com/, retrieved 7 December, 2021.
4. The British settler of island state of Tasmania enacted a horrific genocide in the years after settlement. The infamous 'Black Line' was part of these actions, where a human chain stretched across parts of the island in order to murder or capture Indigenous groups.
5. See for instance, Kim Scott's novel about the King George Sound settlement 400 kilometres to the south of Perth, *That Deadman Dance*, Picador, Sydney, 2010.
6. In this introduction I draw in a general sense on the previous work of western Australian geographers, anthropologists and historians such Alexandra Hasluck, James Battye, Geoffrey Bolton, Tom Stannage, Sylvia Hallam, George Seddon, Ian Crawford, Frank Crowley, Jenny Gregory, Tony Hughes-D'Aeth and Andrea Gaynor.
7. Archaeological evidence exists of a Noongar presence for at least 45,000 years. Further information is available through the Noongar-run Land and Sea Council Website, Kaartdijin Noongar (Noongar knowledge), Noongar | Kaartdijin Noongar, noongarculture.org.au.
8. Songlines are trails or routes. The stories and histories of specific places are 'sung' while they are traversed and are at the centre of Noongar spirituality, culture and the seasonal movement of Noongar groups.
9. 'Populate or perish' is a phrase coined by immigration minister Arthur Calwell and has come to stand for Australia's post-war migration program. A key defining aspect of the program was White Australia Policy (1949–73), by which people of non-European descent were excluded from participating, although these restrictions were relaxed somewhat in later years.
10. G. Albrecht, 'The age of solastalgia', *The Conversation*, 7 August 2012, theconversation.com/the-age-of-solastalgia-8337, viewed 4 May 2019. Quoted By Anna Haebich in her contribution.

Chris Fremantle – *The Diaries of Fremantle (an Ancestor) Burnt into Map*

1. C. H. Fremantle, *Diary & Letters of Admiral Sir C. H. Fremantle G. C. B. Relating to the Founding of the Colony of Western Australia 1829*, London: Hazell, Watson & Viney, 1928.
2. D. B. Rose, 'Decolonising the discourse of environmental knowledge in settler societies', in G. Hawkins and S. Muecke (eds), *Culture and Waste: The Creation and Destruction of Value*, Rowman & Littlefield, Lanham 2003, p. 53.

3   V. Klinkenborg, 'The Voice of the Landscape' (review of 'Horizon' by Barry Lopez), *New York Review of Books*, Vol. LXVI, No. 14, 2019, p. 57.

Samantha Owen – A Tale of Black Beaks: *Naturaliste* Explorers Encounter the Derbarl Yerrigan

1   C. Alexandre Lesueur and N. M. Petit, *Atlas historique du Voyage aux Terres Australes*, Pt. 1, Paris: De L'Imprimerie Impériale, 1807.
2   A. J. Brown, *Ill-starred captains: Flinders and Baudin* (revised edition), Fremantle Arts Centre Press, Fremantle, 2004, pp. 34–35.
3   J. P. Faivre, 'Foreword', in N. Baudin, *The journal of post Captain Nicolas Baudin, Commander-in-Chief of the corvettes Geographe and Naturaliste, assigned by order of the Government to a voyage of discovery.* [1800-1803], (trans) C. Cornell, Christine. Libraries Board of S. Aust, Adelaide, 1974, pp. x–xii.
4   Brown, *Ill-starred captains*, p. 45.
5   N. Baudin, *The journal of post Captain Nicolas Baudin, Commander-in-Chief of the corvettes Geographe and Naturaliste, assigned by order of the Government to a voyage of discovery*, [1800–1803], (trans) C. Cornell, Christine. Libraries Board of South Australia, Adelaide, 1974, p. x.
6   Comte de Fleurieu, 'Plan of Itinerary for Citizen Baudin', in Baudin, *The journal of post Captain Nicolas Baudin*, p. 3.
7   First published in C. A. Lesueur and N. M. Petit, *Atlas historique du Voyage aux Terres Australes*, Pt. 2, Paris: De L'Imprimerie Impériale, 1811.
8   D. Looser, 'Viewing Time and the Other: Visualizing Cross-Cultural and Trans-Temporal Encounters in Lisa Reihana's in Pursuit of Venus [infected]', *Theatre Journal*, vol. 69, no. 4, 2017, pp. 449–475.
9   Looser, 'Viewing Time and the Other', p. 457.
10 M. Blaise, 'Becoming-with Merri Merri: Experimental Multispecies Storytelling as an Ethical Practice', Keynote Address, Western Australian Institute for Educational Research, 34th Annual Research Forum, 3 August 2019.
11 Chart of the Swan River, by Francois-Antoine Boniface Heirisson, 1801. Freycinet Collection, MN 2146/slwa_b2112066_30
12 W. E. H. Stanner, *After the Dreaming: Black and White Australians: An Anthropologist's View*, Australian Broadcasting Commission, Sydney, 1969.
13 A. Curthoys, 'WEH Stanner and the Historians' in Hinkson and Beckett, *An Appreciation of Difference: WEH Stanner and Aboriginal Australia*, Aboriginal Studies Press, ACT, 2008.
14 C. Rowley, *The Destruction of Aboriginal Society,* Australian National University Press, ACT, 1970; H. Reynolds, *Aborigines and Settlers: the Australian Experience, 1788–1939*, Cassell Australia Limited, Melbourne, 1972.
15 L. Ryan, *The Aboriginal Tasmanians*, UQ Press, QLD, 1981; L. Ryan et al, *Colonial Frontier Massacres in Eastern Australia 1788–1930, v2.1* Newcastle: University of Newcastle, 2018, http://hdl.handle.net/1959.13/1340762 , viewed 30 July 2019. This project has been funded by the Australian Research Council.

16 R. White, *Inventing Australia: Images and Identity 1688–1980*, Allen & Unwin, Sydney, 1981, p. ix.
17 White, *Inventing Australia*, pp. 1–16.
18 H. Reynolds, *With the White People: The Crucial Role of Aborigines in the Exploration and Development of Australia*, Penguin, Ringwood, 1990.
19 H. Reynolds, *Why Weren't We told?: A Personal Search for the Truth About our History*, Penguin, Ringwood, 1999, p. 188.
20 T. Banivanua Mar and P. Edmunds (eds), *Making Settler Colonial Space Perspectives on Race, Place and Identity*, Palgrave Macmillan, Hampshire, 2010 p. 1.
21 I. McCalman, *The Reef: The Great Barrier Reef in Twelve Extraordinary Tales*, Penguin Random House, Melbourne, 2013, p. 23.
22 B. Pascoe, *Dark Emu,* Magabala Books, Broome, p. 12.
23 Pascoe, *Dark Emu*, p. 17.
24 White, *Inventing Australia*.
25 S. Khatun, *Australianama: The South Asian Odyssey in Australia*, Oxford University Press, New York, 2018, p. 5.
26 Khatun, *Australianama*, p. 9.
27 Khatun, *Australianama*, p. 93.
28 Khatun, *Australianama*, p. 19.
29 Looser, 'Viewing Time and the Other', p. 171.
30 Comte de Fleurieu, 'Plan of Itinerary for Citizen Baudin, p. 1.
31 Comte de Fleurieu, 'Plan of Itinerary for Citizen Baudin', p. 3.
32 Fornasiero et al, 'Old Quarrels and New Approaches: Matthew Flinders and Nicolas Baudin', in *South Australian Geographical Journal*, 106, 2007, p. 12.
33 Brown, *Ill-starred* captains, p. 279.
34 P. A. L. Forfait, 'The Minister of Marine and Colonies to Citizen Baudin, Post-Captain, Commander-in-Chief of the Corvettes *Géographe* and *Naturaliste*', in Baudin, *The journal of post Captain Nicolas Baudin*, p. 8.
35 Forfait, 'The Minister of Marine and Colonies', p. 8.
36 Forfait, 'The Minister of Marine and Colonies', p. 9.
37 Baudin, *The journal of post Captain Nicolas Baudin*, p. 193.
38 Baudin, *The journal of post Captain Nicolas Baudin*, p. 195.
39 F. Péron, (continued by Louis de Freycinet), *A voyage of discovery to the southern lands, Vol I. second edition 1824. Books I to III, comprising chapters I to XXI*, (trans) C, Cornell, Friends of the State Library South Australia Inc., Adelaide, 2016, p. 146.
40 Bureau of Meteorology, Nyoongar Calendar, http://www.bom.gov.au/iwk/calendars/nyoongar.shtml, viewed 20 July 2019.
41 Baudin, *The journal of post Captain Nicolas Baudin*, p. 159.
42 Baudin, *The journal of post Captain Nicolas Baudin*, p. 179.
43 Baudin, *The journal of post Captain Nicolas Baudin*, pp. 180–181.
44 Baudin, *The journal of post Captain Nicolas Baudin*, pp. 181–183.
45 Baudin, *The journal of post Captain Nicolas Baudin*, pp. 184.
46 Horner, *The French reconnaissance*, p. 140.

47 Baudin, *The journal of post Captain Nicolas Baudin*, p. 192.
48 Baudin, *The journal of post Captain Nicolas Baudin*, p. 196.
49 J. F. E. Hamelin, *Journal de Mer, dealing with the time which this ship spent on the WA coast, 22 May–21 Sept 1801*, Freycinet Collection, Battye Library, MN 584, Baudin papers, ACC 282A, 407A. [translations my own], p. 118.
50 Hamelin, *Journal de Mer*, pp. 105–106.
51 Hamelin, *Journal de Mer*, p. 108.
52 F. Heirisson, 'Enseigne on the Naturaliste Report of an Expedition Up the Swan River with Heirisson, 17–22 June 1801', *Freycinet Collection*, Battye Library, MN 584, Baudin papers, ACC 282A, 407A [translation by M. Claude Giradin of Boya WA], p. 1.
53 F. Collas, 'Report of an Expedition Up the Swan River with Heirisson, 17–22 June 1801', *Freycinet Collection*, Battye Library, MN 584, Baudin papers, ACC 282A, 407A [translations my own], p. 1.
54 D. Hughes-Hallett, *Indigenous History of the Swan and Canning Rivers*, Swan River Trust, 2010. https://parks.dpaw.wa.gov.au/sites/default/files/downloads/parks/Indigenous%20history%20of%20the%20Swan%20and%20Canning%20rivers.pdf, viewed 20 July 2019, p. 20.
55 C. Bailley, 'Report on the Mineralogy and Geology of Swan River after the expedition with Heirisson, 17-22 June 1801' *Freycinet Collection*, Battye Library, MN 584, Baudin papers, ACC 282A, 407A. [translations my own], p. 1.
56 Heirisson, 'Enseigne on the Naturaliste Report', p. 1.
57 Bailley, 'Report on the Mineralogy and Geology of Swan River', p. 1.
58 Collas, 'Report of an Expedition Up the Swan River'.
59 Hughes-Hallett, *Indigenous history of the Swan and Canning rivers*, p. 6.
60 Hughes-Hallett, *Indigenous history of the Swan and Canning rivers*, p. 32.
61 Hughes-Hallett, *Indigenous history of the Swan and Canning rivers*, p. 32.
62 Bailley, 'Report on the Mineralogy and Geology of Swan River'.
63 Hughes-Hallett, *Indigenous history of the Swan and Canning rivers*, p. 32.
64 Péron, *A voyage of discovery to the southern lands*, p. 144.
65 Hughes-Hallett, *Indigenous history of the Swan and Canning rivers*, p. 51.
66 Collas, 'Report of an Expedition Up the Swan River'.
67 Pascoe, *Dark Emu*, pp. 27, 24.
68 Bailley, 'Report on the Mineralogy and Geology of Swan River', p. 3.
69 Hughes-Hallett, *Indigenous history of the Swan and Canning rivers*, p. 9.
70 Heirisson, 'Enseigne on the Naturaliste Report', p. 3.
71 Hughes-Hallett, *Indigenous history of the Swan and Canning rivers*, p. 60.
72 Hughes-Hallett, *Indigenous history of the Swan and Canning rivers*, p. 68.
73 Hughes-Hallett, *Indigenous history of the Swan and Canning rivers*, p. 68.
74 Péron, *A voyage of discovery to the southern lands*, p. 145.
75 Hughes-Hallett, *Indigenous history of the Swan and Canning rivers*, p. 32.

76 F. Horner, *The French reconnaissance : Baudin in Australia 1801–1803*, Melbourne University Press, Vic, 1987, p. 172; L. R. Marchant, *France Australe*, Editions France-Empire, Paris, 1998, p. 165.
77 Hamelin, *Journal de Mer*, p. 119.
78 Péron, *A voyage of discovery to the southern lands*, p. 151.
79 Péron, *A voyage of discovery to the southern lands*, p. 142.
80 Horner, *The French reconnaissance*, p. 4.
81 M. Sankey, 'Writing the Voyage of Scientific Exploration: the Logbooks, Journals and Notes of the Baudin Expedition (1800–1804)', *Intellectual History Review*, vol. 20, no. 3, 2010, p. 401.
82 D. S. Jones, 'The Baudin Expedition in Australian waters (1801-1803): the faunal legacy', Western Australian Museum, http://museum.wa.gov.au/fc/aos/dj, viewed 20 July 2019.
83 F. Péron. *A voyage of discovery to the southern hemisphere, performed by order of the Emperor Napoleon during the years 1801, 1802, 1803, and 1804 avec un Atlas*. Printed for Richard Phillips ... by B. McMillan, London, 1809. (Viewed: SLNSW, FL3989228)
84 C. A. Lesueur and N. M. Petit, *Atlas historique du Voyage aux Terres Australes*, Pt. 1, Paris: De L'Imprimerie Impériale, 1807; Lesueur and Petit, *Atlas historique du Voyage aux Terres Australes*, Pt. 2.
85 Lesueur and N. M. Petit, *Atlas historique du Voyage aux Terres Australes*, Pt.1, Paris: De L'Imprimerie Impériale, 1807; S. Pfennigwerth, 'New Creatures Made Known: Some Animal Histories of the Baudin Expedition.' *Discovery and Empire: the French in the South Seas*, edited by J. West-Sooby (ed), University of Adelaide Press, South Australia, 2013, pp. 172–174.
86 Péron. *A voyage of discovery to the southern hemisphere*. p. viii.
87 J. Fornasiero, Jean et. al. *Encountering Terra Australis: the Australian voyages of Nicolas Baudin and Matthew Flinders*. Wakefield Press, Adelaide, 2010, p. vii.
88 Horner, *The French reconnaissance*, p. 10; Marchant, *France Australe*, p. 115.
89 M. Sankey et al, 'The Baudin Expedition in Review: Old Quarrels and New Approaches', *Australian Journal of French Studies*, vol. 41, no. 2, 2004, pp. 4–5.
90 Lesueur and Petit, *Atlas historique du Voyage aux Terres Australes*, Pt. 2.
91 Marchant, *France Australe*, p. 163.

Nandi Chinna
1 A. Middleton, 'First video: Australian deep sea canyon', *Australian Geographic*, July 10, 2010, https://www.australiangeographic.com.au/news/2010/06/first-video-australian-deep-sea-canyon/, viewed 25 January 2022.

Cass Lynch – Haiku
1 These three haiku were previously published as part of 'Five Haiku' in *Westerly*, vol. 64, no. 1, 2019, pp. 21–23. Cass Lynch uses the Marribank orthography when writing in the Noongar language.

Carol Millner

1. Inspired by the now well-known words of Fanny Balbuk (Wahdjuk Noongar) who put up steadfast resistance to the Swan Plain colonists until her death in 1907. Here I have imagined the directions that Fanny might have given me if she were alive today. I have relied in particular on the words of Fanny Balbuk recorded by Daisy Bates and made most recently and publically available in David Whish-Wilson's *Perth*, NewSouth Books, Sydney, 2013).

Qassim Saad – Exile, Rivers and Design: A Designer's Journey across Rivers

1. T. M. Harris, 'Deep Geography – Deep Mapping; Spatial Storytelling and a Sense of Place', in D. Bodenhamer, C. John and M. Trevor (eds) *Deep Maps and Spatial Narratives*, Indiana University Press, Bloomington, 2015, p. 33.
2. M. Cioc, and W. Cronon, *The Rhine: An Eco-Biography, 1815–2000*, University of Washington Press, Seattle, 2002, p 5.
3. Cioc, and Cronon, *The Rhine*, p. 6.
4. J. N. Entrikin, *The Betweenness of Place*, The Johns Hopkins University Press, Baltimore, 1991, p. 15.
5. P. Schönach, 'River Histories: A Thematic Review', in *Water History*, vol. 9, 2017, p. 239.
6. E. W. Said, *Out of Place: A Memoir*, Vintage Books, New York, 2000, p. 173
7. D. Banerjee, 'Narrating Place, Negotiating History: The Politics of Place in Land Between the Rivers', *Local Environment*, vol. 17, no. 10, 2012, pp. 1079–1088.
8. C. Mauch and T. Zeller, 'Rivers in History and Historiography: An Introduction' in *Rivers in History: Perspectives on Waterways in Europe and North America*, C. Mauch and T. Zeller (eds), University of Pittsburgh Press, 2008, p. 7.
9. Schönach, 'River histories', pp. 241–242.
10. Schönach, 'River histories', p. 244.
11. J. H. A. Jotheri, 'Holocene Avulsion History of the Euphrates and Tigris Rivers in the Mesopotamian Floodplain', *Durham e-Theses*, Durham University, 2016, http://etheses.dur.ac.uk/11752.
12. P. W. Pruyser and J. Tracy Luke, 'The Epic of Gilgamesh', in *American Imago*, vol. 39, no. 2, 1981, pp. 73–93.
13. W. D. Mignolo, *The Darker Side of Western Modernity; Global Futures, Decolonial Options*, Duke University Press, Durham, 2011, P. xiii.
14. The school was called '17th July Primary School for Boys', representing the date when the Arab Socialist Ba'ath Party in Iraq initiated a coup on the national government in 1968, which allowed this political party to govern the country until the American invasion in 2003.
15. Locally known as the 'new' Bridge, after 1968, it was officially named the 'Al-Wihda' (unit) bridge; this term indicated one of the Ba'ath Party's core ideological principles, which promoted the concept of one 'Arabic Nation' over that of multiple countries in the region.
16. Schönach, 'River Histories', p. 241.

17 J. N. Entrikin, *The Betweenness of Place*, p. 16.
18 Currently, there are around 14 bridges linking both sides of Baghdad, all previous and current bridges were built before 2003.
19 J. N. Entrikin, *The Betweenness of Place*, p. 7.
20 J. N. Entrikin, *The Betweenness of Place*, p. 1.
21 J. N. Entrikin, *The Betweenness of Place*, p. 1.
22 K. Dannatt, 'Life on a Border: The Psychological Journey', in G. Greene's *Journey Without Maps* and *The Lawless Roads*, master's thesis, Department of British and American Studies, University of Oslo, 2004, p. 4.
23 Harris, 'Deep Geography', p. 18.
24 Driving factor supported travelling outside Iraq was based on a full-time annual contract job offered as a lecturer of industrial design at Yarmouk University in Irbid, I kept working in this role until I resigned in 2001.
25 E. W. Said, *Reflections on Exile: And Other Literary and Cultural Essays*, Granta Books, London, 2001, p. 185.
26 Craw et al., 'Evolution of the Taieri River catchment', p. 261.
27 http://www.otago.ac.nz, viewed 28 June 2019.
28 Said, *Reflections on Exile*, p. 185.
29 Reflected influences on Iraqis during the harsh UN economic sanction on the country during the 1990s.
30 K. Dannatt, 'Life on a Border: The Psychological Journey', p. 24.
31 S. Springett, 'Going Deeper or Flatter: Connecting Deep Mapping, Flat Ontologies and the Democratizing of Knowledge', in *Humanities,* vol. 4, no. 4, 2015, p. 625.
32 Invited by the German University in Cairo in 2012 to establish a Master's program in design, at the faculty of applied sciences and arts in Cairo. Shortly after my arrival, the university kindly requested me to lead the school and assigned me the role of acting dean from 2012 to 2015, managing the faculty on both campuses in Cairo and Berlin.
33 S. Springett, 'Going Deeper or Flatter', p. 624.
34 Offered a permanent full-time academic job at Curtin University in 2015.
35 According to the data that the Pacer pedometer app has provided since I started collecting information on 18 November 2017, the reading showed the lifetime total of 600 days and 3,791,535 steps in 977 hours, and a distance of 2,263 km, based on the reading on 10 July 2019.
36 S. Springett, 'Going Deeper or Flatter', p. 634.
37 https://www.shammamusic.com, viewed 18 January 2021.
38 https://www.culturewheel.com/en, viewed 18 January 2021.
39 J. N. Entrikin, *The Betweenness of Place*, p. 3.
40 *Enarah* is the Arabic word for a lighting unit.
41 C. Lee, 'Home Is Where the Hearth Was: Remembering and Place-Making a Vanished Town', in C. Lee (ed), *Spectral Spaces and Hauntings: The Affects of Absence*, Routledge, New York, 2017, p. 52.

42   Furthermore, I visited my family three times later during my stay in Egypt and Perth between 2012 and 2016; however, all of these trips occurred when the family relocated to the north of Iraq, to the capital of Kurdistan, Erbil, between 2014 and 2017.
43   Same scenario repeated concerning the passport and the Iraqi ID card checking in the process of departure Iraq.
44   The Old bridge rebuilt with assistance from the UNDP, https://www.iq.undp.org.
45   Lee, 'Home Is Where the Hearth Was', p. 52.
46   Said, *Out of Place*, p. 272.

Susanna Castleden – *A Single Day's Riding*

1   J. Spinney, 'A Place of Sense: A Kinaesthetic Ethnography of Cyclists on Mont Ventoux', *Environment and Planning D: Society and Space*, vol. 24, no. 5, 2006, p. 713. https://doi.org/10.1068/d66j, viewed 31 January 2022.
2   Spinney, 'Sense of Place', p. 718.
3   J. Wylie, 'A Single Day's Walking: Narrating Self and Landscape on the South West Coast Path', *Transactions of the Institute of British Geographers*, vol. 30, no.2, pp. 234–247. http://www.jstor.org/stable/3804521, viewed 31 January 2022.

Tom Wilson – Moving Bodies along the Swan River

1   R. Jeffers, 'Carmel Point', from *Selected Poems of Robinson Jeffers*, Tim Hunt (ed), Stanford University Press, Stanford, 2001, p. 676.
2   W. Blake, 'Introduction to the Songs of Experience', from *William Blake: Selected Poetry*, Oxford University Press, Oxford, 1998, p. 261.

Claire Jones – Tidal Tensions and Littoral Potential: Coming of Age and the Derbal Yerrigan

1   Whish-Wilson, *Perth*, New South Publishing, Sydney, 2013, p. 21.
2   Whish-Wilson, *Perth*, p. 21.
3   Whish-Wilson, *Perth*, pp. 32–3.
4   Whish-Wilson, *Perth*, p. 87.
5   T. Winton, *Cloudstreet*, Penguin, p. 255.
6   Winton, *Cloudstreet*, p. 806.
7   L. Dougan, 'The Mice' in *The Guardians*, Giramondo, Artarmon, 2015, p. 9.
8   Dougan, 'The Mice'.
9   K. Mackenzie, *The Young Desire It*, Angus and Robertson, Sydney, 1963, p. 9.
10 Mackenzie, *The Young Desire It*, p. 57.
11 Mackenzie, *The Young Desire It*, p. 58.
12 Mackenzie, *The Young Desire It*, p. 124.

Anna Haebich – LOSS: Dyarlgarro Beeliar/Canning River

1   G. Seddon, *Sense of Place: A Response to an Environment: The Coastal Plain, Western Australia*, University of Western Australia Press, Crawley, 1972, p. 180.

2   Quoted in Seddon, *Sense of Place*, pp. 181, 180, 182).
3   National Trust of Australia (WA), *Marli Riverpark: An Interpretation Plan for the Swan and Canning Riverpark: The Final Report, April 2014*, p. 9.
4   A. L. Stoler (ed), 'Introduction: "The Rot Remains" From Ruins to Ruination', *Imperial Debris: On Ruins and Ruination*. Duke University Press, 2013, p. x.
5   A. F. Gordon, *Ghostly Matters: Haunting and the Sociological Imagination*, second edition, University of Minnesota Press, 2008, p. xvi.
6   Stoler, "The Rot Remains", p. 11.
7   J. Bailey, and I. Biggs, '"Either Side of Delphy Bridge": A Deep Mapping Project Evoking and Engaging the Lives of Older Adults in Rural North Cornwall', *Journal of Rural Studies*, 28, 2012, p. 326.
8   N. Chinna, *Swamp Walking the Wet Lands of the Swan Coastal Plain Poems by Nandi Chinna*. Fremantle Press, Fremantle, 2014, pp. 9, 10.
9   P. Carter, *Ground Truthing: Explorations in a Creative Region*, University of Western Australia Publishing, Crawley, 2010, p. 37.
10 F. Goffi, *Time Matter(s): Invention and Re-Imagination in Built Conservation: The Unfinished Drawing and Building of St Peters, the Vatican*, Routledge, New York, 2013.
11 P. Wolfe, *Settler Colonialism and the Transformation of Anthropology: the Politics and Poetics of an Ethnographic Event*, Casell, London, 1999.
12 G. Coulthard. *Red Skin, White Masks: Rejecting the Colonial Politics of Recognition*, University of Minnesota Press, Minneapolis, 2014.
13 Stoler, "The Rot Remains", p. 2.
14 L. Preiss, Field Books, State Records Office of Western Australia 1841, https://archive.sro.wa.gov.au/index.php/informationobject/browse?topLod=0&query=preiss, viewed, 31 January 2022.
15 A. Moyal, 'Surveyors: Mapping the Distance, Early Surveying in Australia', *Australian Dictionary of Biography*, National Centre of Biography.
16 R. Morgan, *Running Out? Water in Western Australia*, University of Western Australia Publishing, Crawley, 2015.
17 "Roleystone, Western Australia", *Wikipedia*, https://en.wikipedia.org/wiki/Roleystone,_Western_Australia, viewed 14 June 2020.
18 P. Carter, *Dark Writing Geography, Performance, Design*, University of Hawai'i Press, Honolulu, 2009.
19 G. Ermischer, 'Mental landscape. Landscape as idea and concept', *Proceedings of the Second Meeting of the Workshop for the Implementation of the European Landscape Convention*, 27–28 November, 2003, p. 1. www.pcl-eu.de/project/agenda/mental.php. Accessed online 2 July 2019.
20 T. Ingold and J. L. Vergunst (eds) 'Introduction', *Ways of Walking: Ethnography and Practice on Foot*, Ashgate, Farnham, 2008, p. 14.
21 See images of surveying equipment used and a surveying party in action.
22 P. Carter, *Dark Writing*, p. 4.
23 Quoted in P. Carter, *Dark Writing*, p. 17.
24 Ingold and Vergunst, 'Introduction', p. 6.

25 R. M. Lyon, *Perth Gazette,* 23 March 1833, p. 64.
26 *Lost Whadjuk Names,* typescript, p. 2. File:///Users/178876g/Downloads/lost-whadjuk-names.pdf. Viewed online 18 April 2021.
27 P. Carter, *Dark Writing.*
28 G. Ermischer, 'Mental landscape. Landscape as idea and concept', *Proceedings of the Second Meeting of the Workshop for the Implementation of the European Landscape Convention,* 27–28 November, 2003, p.1. www.pcl-eu.de/project/agenda/mental.php, viewed 2 July 2019.
29 T. Ingold and J. L. Vergunst (eds) 'Introduction', p. 14.
30 A. Haebich, *Dancing in Shadows. Histories of Nyungar Performance,* University of Western Australia Publishing, Crawley, 2018, p. 17
31 P. Carter, *Dark Writing,* p. 4.
32 Quoted in P. Carter, *Dark Writing,* p. 17.
33 J. Lehmann, *Plantae Preissianae Sive Enumeratio Plantarum Quas in Australasia,* Sumptibus Meissneri,1844–1847 [1848].
34 T. Mazstnak et al, 'Botanical Decolonization: Rethinking Native Plants', *Environment and Planning D: Society and Space* 32, 2014, p. 363.
35 Quoted in K. Wilson and A. Wilson, 'Preiss's Account of his Western Australian Travels'. *Australasian Systemic Botany Society Newsletter* 171, June 2017, p. 24.
36 P. Helmholz et al, 'Geo-Locating Historical Survey Data and Images – A Case Study for the Canning River, Perth, Western Australia', *The International Archives of the Photogrammetry, Remote Sensing and Spatial Information Sciences,* XLIII-B4-2020, pp. 575–582. https://doi.org/10.5194/isprs-archives-XLIII-B4-2020-575-2020, 2020.
37 G. Moore, heritage officer, City of Canning council, personal communication, 28 October, 2020.
38 National Trust of Australia (WA), *Marli Riverpark,* pp. 60–61.
39 National Trust of Australia (WA), *Marli Riverpark,* p. 15.
40 National Trust of Australia (WA), *Marli Riverpark,* p. 16.
41 National Trust of Australia (WA), *Marli Riverpark,* p. 46.
42 Stoler, "The Rot Remains", p. 18.
43 National Trust of Australia (WA), *Marli Riverpark,* p. 13.
44 National Trust of Australia (WA), *Marli Riverpark,* p. 4.
45 S. Galt, *Guidelines for Heritage Trails, Heritage Information Series,* NSW Heritage Office Sydney, 1995, p. 7.
46 Galt, *Guidelines for Heritage Trails,* p. 2.
47 Albert Corunna cited in National Trust of Australia (WA), *Marli Riverpark,* p, 65.
48 Seddon, *Sense of Place,* pp. 226, 229.
49 Seddon, *Sense of Place,* p. 141.
50 Seddon, *Sense of Place,* p. 164.
51 G. Albrecht, 'The age of solastalgia', *The Conversation,* 7 August 2012, theconversation.com/the-age-of-solastalgia-8337, viewed 4 May 2019.
52 Albrecht, 'The age of solastalgia'.
53 Albrecht, 'The age of solastalgia'.

54 P. von Oorde-Grainger and I. Wilkes, 'Galup Know Your Neighbours', http://three.spaced.org.au/know-thy-neighbour-galup, viewed 9 July 2019.
55 *History Comes to Life on Lake Monger's Shores Galup Ian Wilkes and Poppy van Oorde-Grainger With an Oral History From Doolann Leisha Eatts Co-produced by Same Drum and Performing Lines WA*, Same Drum Perth Festival media release, Wednesday, 18 November 2020 https://www.samedrum.com/press.
56 Quoted in Same Drum media release.
57 I. Hernandez-Avila, 'Performing Ri(gh)t(e)s: (W)riting the Native (In and Out) of Ceremony', *Theatre Research International*, vol. 35 no. 2, 2010, p. 140.
58 Grehan, H. 2009 *Performance, Ethics and Spectatorship in a Global Age*, New York: Palgrave Macmillan, p. 20.
59 N. Rothwell, 'Rhythm Sticks', *The Australian*, 25–26 October 2008. http://www.theaustralian.com.au/arts/ rhythm-sticks/story-e6frg8n6-1111117814465. Viewed April 2015.
60 A. Maldonado, 'From "Solastalgia" to "Alegremia"', *WRM Bulletin 225,* World Rainforest Movement, July/August 2016, p. 9.
61 Maldonado, 'From "Solastalgia" to "Alegremia"', p. 9.
62 Maldonado, 'From "Solastalgia" to "Alegremia"', p. 11.
63 Maldonado, 'From "Solastalgia" to "Alegremia"', p. 10.
64 Quoted in Maldonado, 'From "Solastalgia" to "Alegremia"', p. 11.
65 N. Nannup, *Synergies: Walking Together –Belonging to Country (Djena Kooliny Danjoo Boodjar-an)*, directed by Glen Stasiuk, Black Russian Productions, 2015.
66 South West Land and Sea Council, *Nyitting – Dreaming*. https://www.noongarculture.org.au/spirituality. Viewed June 30 2019.
67 N. Chinna, *Swamp Walking*, pp. 70–72.
68 Lyon, *Perth Gazette*, p. 64.
69 Lyon, *Perth Gazette* p. 2.
70 Haebich, *Dancing in Shadow*, p. 32.
71 Quoted in K. Schaefer, 'Place, Identity, Belonging and Performance: Marrukeu's Burning Daylight', in R. Dennis (ed), *Burning Daylight Place History and Community*, Marrugeku, 2009, p. 84.
72 Z. Todd, 'A Commentary on Part 1 of Our Engagement Thematic Series, Lie on the Frontier', *Settler Colonialism, Part 1*, https://aesengagement.wordpress.com/2017/04/11/commentary-the-environmental-anthropology-of-settler-colonialism-part-i/, viewed 4 June 2021.
73 E. McDonald et al, *Study of Groundwater-related Aboriginal Cultural Values on the Gnangara Mound, Western Australia*, Department of Environment, Perth, 2005.
74 Haebich, *Dancing in Shadow*, pp. 5–6.

Vanessa Corunna – *Eagle Warrior*

1 The Nyoongar warrior, Yagan, was killed by colonising forces in 1933. His head was smoked and sent to England.
2 This image was previously published by the ABC Radio National website, abc.net.au/radionational/programs/awaye/the-spirit-of-yagan/5340718.

List of Contributors

Ashleigh Angus recently completed a collaborative PhD in creative writing at Curtin University and University of Aberdeen. Her PhD project consisted of an exegesis and work of historiographic metafiction exploring the history of an accused witch from seventeenth-century Orkney, Scotland. Her writing has been published in *Axon, Causeway/Cabhsair* and *Westerly*.

Sheena Blackhall is a writer, illustrator, traditional ballad singer and storyteller in north-east Scotland. From 1998 to 2003 she was Creative Writing Fellow in Scots at the Elphinstone Institute. She has published four Scots novellas, fifteen short story collections and over 170 poetry collections. In 2009 she became Makar (poet laureate) for Aberdeen and the North East, and Makar for the Doric Board in 2019.

Susanna Castleden is an artist and associate professor at Curtin University, Western Australia where she supervises PhD, masters and honours projects, usually based in printmaking, drawing and photography. She completed a PhD at RMIT University in 2014 and continues to explore ideas of mobility, mapping, distance and proximity in her creative practice. Susanna has received several awards including the Linden Prize in 2015; runner up in the Fremantle Print Award 2014; the Burnie Print Prize in 2013 and the Bankwest Art Prize also in 2013.

Vanessa Corunna is a Noongar woman from Perth with connections to Ballardong and Palyukl. She holds a bachelor of arts in archaeology and anthropology from the University of Western Australia, a bachelor of arts in Aboriginal and community management and development from Curtin University and an honours of research and traditional Noongar women's healing. Her research centres around Aboriginal traditional and contemporary housing issues in urban and rural Western Australia, Queensland and Northern Territory.

Neil Curtis was born in Glasgow in 1964, and came to Aberdeen in 1988 where he is now head of museums and special collections. He studied archaeology (Glasgow, 1986), museum studies (Leicester, 1988) and education (Aberdeen, 1995). He is a member of the Museums Associations' ethics committee and the Museums Gallery Scotland recognition committee. He was formerly convenor of University Museums in Scotland, vice president of the Society of Antiquaries of Scotland and vice chair of the Scottish Archaeological Finds Allocation Panel.

Chris Fremantle is a researcher and producer working across environment and health. Projects he has worked on have won Saltire and CIWEM art and environment awards. He has chaired the Ramsar Culture Network's art focus group, and is on the board of Arts Culture Health Wellbeing Scotland and the advisory board of the Centre for Creative Health. His personal practice is focused on drawing and he has exhibited internationally.

He lectures at Gray's School of Art, Aberdeen. He established ecoartscotland in 2010 and is involved in various ecoart networks. He has written in collaboration with Anne Douglas on the practice of pioneering ecoartists Helen Mayer Harrison (1927–2018) and Newton Harrison (b. 1932), known as 'the Harrisons'. He has also worked with them on projects in the UK, acting as producer for *Greenhouse Britain: losing ground, gaining wisdom* (2006–08), and associate producer for *On the Deep Wealth of this Nation, Scotland* (2017–ongoing).

He thanks Michael Agnew and Neil Cobban, for the idea and the doing of the laser cutting, and Fergus Connor, for the photography.

Maureen Gibbons has a doctor of creative arts from Curtin University. Her poetry is published in *Rabbit*, *Westerly* and *Cordite*. Her verse novel, *The Butter Lady: A Silhouette Biography in Verse*, is published by Rabbit.

Ian Grosz is a writer based in the north east of Scotland. With a first degree in environmental geography, he has long held a deep interest in landscape and place. In 2018 he completed a post-graduate certificate in social anthropology followed by a master of letters in creative writing, graduating with distinction from the University of Aberdeen in 2019. His work has featured in a range of publications both in print and online, including the Aberdeen–Curtin Alliance anthology *Pause*. In 2020 he was awarded a University of Aberdeen New Kings Studentship for a PhD in creative writing, further exploring the themes of time and memory, landscape and identity.

Paolo Gruppuso is an environmental anthropologist interested in urban ecologies, nature conservation, and the environmental and social history of wetlands and land reclamation in the Global North. He holds a PhD in social anthropology from the University of Aberdeen, and has carried out research and teaching appointments at the Max Planck Institute for the History of Science in Berlin, at the University of Gastronomic Sciences in Italy and at the Rachel Carson Center in Munich (in 2022).

Anna Haebich is an award-winning author with a passion for pushing history into new territories. She is best known for her challenging Aboriginal histories *For Their Own Good* and *Broken Circles*, classics in the field, and *Spinning the Dream*. *Dancing in Shadows: Histories of Nyungar Performance* was shortlisted for the 2019 Prime Minister's Literary Awards. Judges described her as 'one of our nation's great interpreters of our collective Indigenous and Australian settler histories. She personifies the spirit of reconciliation, ethical research, commitment, and generosity'. Anna also writes about women and crime, popular culture, visual arts and the environment. Anna is a John Curtin Distinguished Professor at Curtin University in Western Australia.

Claire Jones is a researcher and educator across secondary and tertiary English and literary studies. She is currently the chief investigator on The Big Picture Project: Subject English across secondary and tertiary education in WA, a joint project between the University of Western Australia and the English Teachers Association of Western Australia, and has a specialisation in curriculum history and text selection. She is also an active researcher in Australian literature and global literature, with a particular interest in littoral spaces.

Daniel Juckes is a writer from Perth, Western Australia. He is a lecturer in creative writing at UWA, associate editor at *Westerly* magazine and holds a PhD in creative writing from Curtin University. His creative and critical work has been published in journals such as *Axon*, *Life Writing*, *M/C Journal*, *TEXT*, and *Westerly*, and he was highly commended in the 2021 Fogarty Literary Award.

Adam Kealley is a teacher and PhD candidate within the Curtin–Aberdeen Alliance, a collaboration between Curtin University and the University of Aberdeen. His research interests include the Australian gothic, spectrality, queer theory and their intersections with young adult literature. He has published in this field in *Children's Literature in Education*, *Axon: Creative Explorations* and has edited two collections on children's literature.

John Kinsella has written over 20 books of poetry, as well as plays and fiction; he also maintains an active literary career as a teacher and editor. Kinsella's poetry is both experimental and pastoral, featuring the landscape of Western Australia. Kinsella's recent books of poetry include *Firebreaks* (2016), *Drowning in Wheat: Selected Poems* (2016) and *Insomnia* (2019). He supports worldwide Indigenous rights and is a vegan anarchist pacifist. Kinsella has received many awards for his poetry, including the Western Australian Premier's Book Award and the John Bray Poetry Award from the Adelaide Festival; he has won fellowships from the Literature Board of the Australia Council.

Cass Lynch is a writer and researcher living in Boorloo/Perth. She has recently completed a creative writing PhD that explores deep memory features of the Noongar oral storytelling tradition; in particular stories that reference the last ice age and the rise in sea level that followed it. She is a descendant of the Noongar people and belongs to the beaches on the south coast of Western Australia.

LIST OF CONTRIBUTORS

Susan Midalia is the award-winning author of three short story collections and two novels. Her latest book, a collection of flash fiction, will be published in 2022 by Night Parrot Press. She has a PhD in contemporary Australian women's fiction and has published on the subject in national and international literary journals. Susan is also the prose editor for *Westerly* magazine, the chair of the Australian Short Story Festival and a peer assessor for the Australia Council.

Carol Millner is a New Zealand poet and short story writer based in Boorloo (Perth). In 2018 she was awarded the Jillian Bradshaw Scholarship in the Humanities by the Graduate Women of WA. Her poetry has been shortlisted for the Whitmore Manuscript Prize and the Dorothy Hewett Award. Her first chapbook *Poems About the House* was published by Mulla Press in 2019. Carol is a Varuna alumna and is completing a PhD in migrant short fiction at Curtin University, where she also teaches. You can find Carol on LinkedIn.

Meredi Ortega is from WA and lives in Aberdeen. Her writing has appeared in *The Poetry Review*, *The Best Australian Science Writing*, *The Best Australian Poems*, *The Best Australian Stories*, *Contemporary Australian Feminist Poetry*, *The Rialto* and *Westerly*. She placed third in the Resurgence Poetry Prize with a poem about the Dee. She is currently finalising her first poetry collection.

Samantha Owen is a social and cultural historian who researches communities, education and contested histories. She is the co-lead of the Curtin University Gender Research Network and a senior lecturer in humanities and social sciences education at Curtin University.

James Quinton is preoccupied with rivers as a living literary metaphor. He grew up in Bassendean playing and grieving on the banks of the Swan River. He believes strongly that rivers display the symptoms of global health. He has written numerous poetry books, each one with the word 'river' in the title.

LIST OF CONTRIBUTORS

Gerard Rochford (1932–2019) was originally from Worcestershire but lived most of his life in Aberdeen, Scotland, where he was a distinguished professor, psychotherapist and poet. Widely published in his lifetime in literary magazines, newspapers and collections, as Makar for the *Scottish Review*, Gerard submitted a poem every month for over five years. His poem 'My Father's Hand' was chosen by the Scottish Poetry Library as one of the best poems of the year. Highly regarded for the quality and delicate lyricism of his work, Gerard wrote mostly about intimate human relationships, wildlife and politics. The inaugural Gerard Rochford Poetry Prize, established in his memory in 2021, attracted over 730 entries from more than 40 countries.

David Whish-Wilson is the author of eight novels and three non-fiction books. Two of his crime novels have been shortlisted for Ned Kelly Awards, and his creative non-fiction book, *Perth*, was shortlisted for the WA Premier's Book Award. David's next novel is *The Sawdust House*, out with Fremantle Press in April 2022. He lives in Fremantle with his wife and three kids and coordinates the creative writing program at Curtin University.

Simona Trozzi is a visual artist and illustrator interested in life drawing, landscape, grotesque imaginaries and fantastic art. In her practice she has explored varied techniques – for example, pencils, oil, airbrush, screen printing, digital art – across many fields such as advertising, design, painting and editorial illustration.

Thomas M. Wilson has spent his life writing about the human relationship with our home: the natural world. He has a PhD in literature and the environment, and is an honorary research fellow at the University of Western Australia. As well as being the author of *The Recurrent Green Universe of John Fowles* (Rodopi, 2006), Wilson has made numerous contributions to environmental journalism.

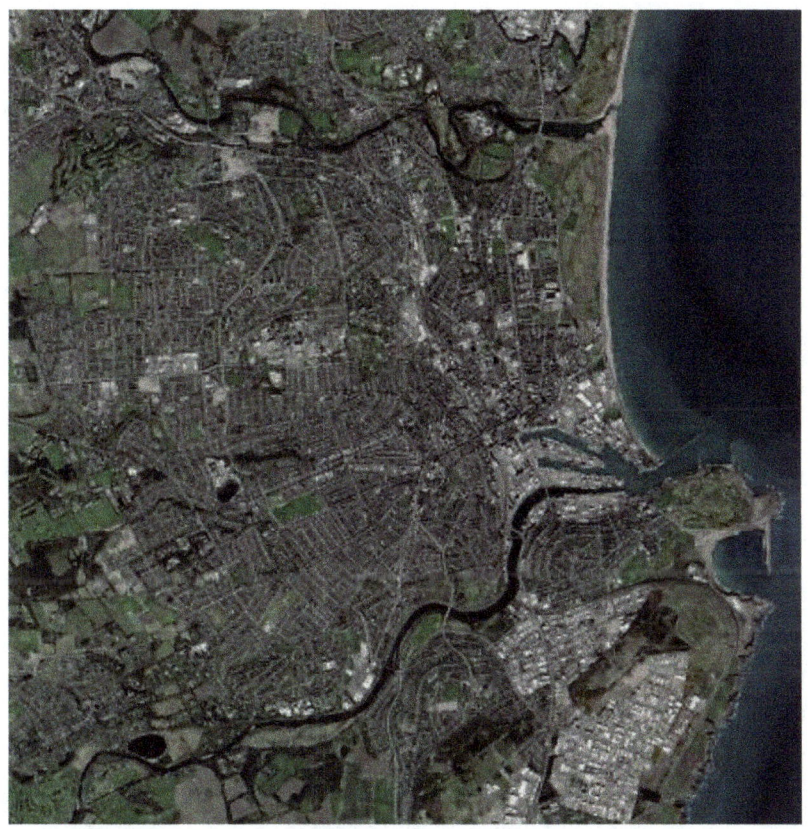

The mouths of the Don (north) and Dee (south) Aberdeen.

Scotland's north east, terrain of the Don and Dee.

View of Bennachie looking northwards along the Don, taken from Pitfichie.
PHOTO BY IAN GROSZ, 2019.

Corriehoul Burn.
PHOTO BY IAN GROSZ, 2019.

Deer Park Circle.
PHOTO BY IAN GROSZ, 2019.

Deer Park Circle.
PHOTO BY IAN GROSZ, 2019.

An Imaginative Map of Water in Seaton Park, front.

An Imaginative Map of Water in Seaton Park, back.

Swan coastal plain and Darling escarpment.

The Diaries of Fremantle (an Ancestor) Burnt into Map.
TEXT BURNT ON NAUTICAL MAP.

The Diaries of Fremantle (an Ancestor) Burnt into Map. Detail, top left.

The Diaries of Fremantle (an Ancestor) Burnt into Map. Detail, top right.

The Diaries of Fremantle (an Ancestor) Burnt into Map. Detail, bottom left.

The Diaries of Fremantle (an Ancestor) Burnt into Map. Detail, bottom right.

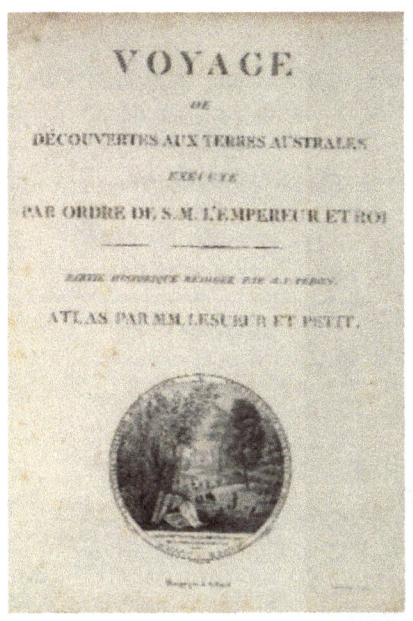

Cover of *Atlas historique du Voyage aux Terres Australes*.

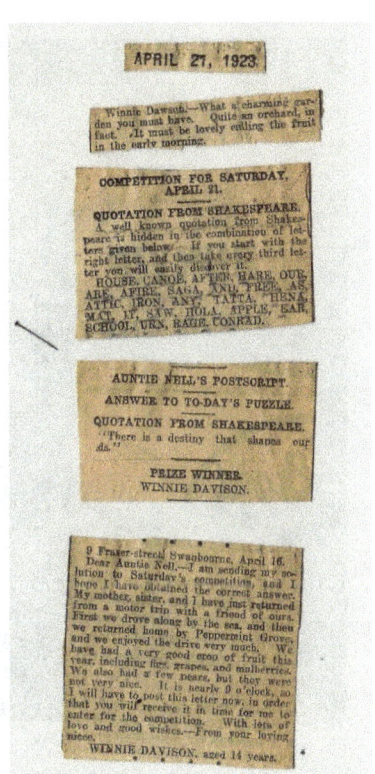

Clippings from *The Daily News*, taken from inside the wonder book.

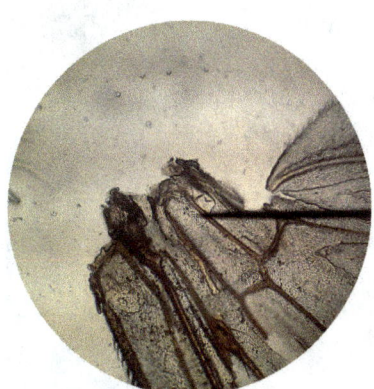

From p. 346 of the wonder book. Detail of the severed insect wing.

From p. 195 of the wonder book. The 'flat, furry splodge … Crusted over the 'p' of 'prince'.

From p. 250 of the wonder book, *Cadmus and the Dragon*, by Gustaf Tenggren.

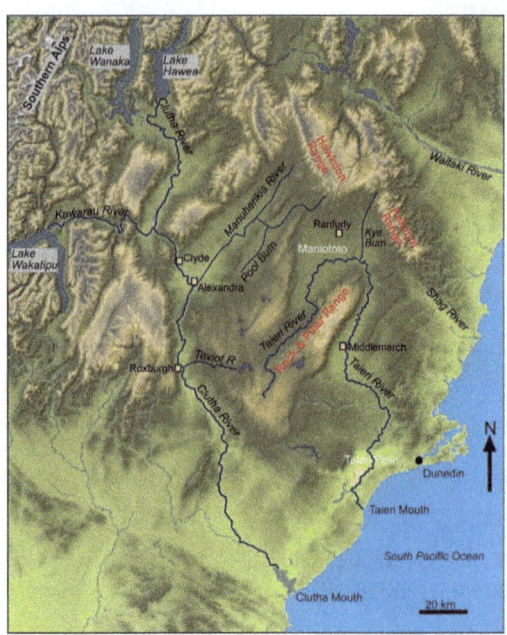

Topographical profile of Taeri River

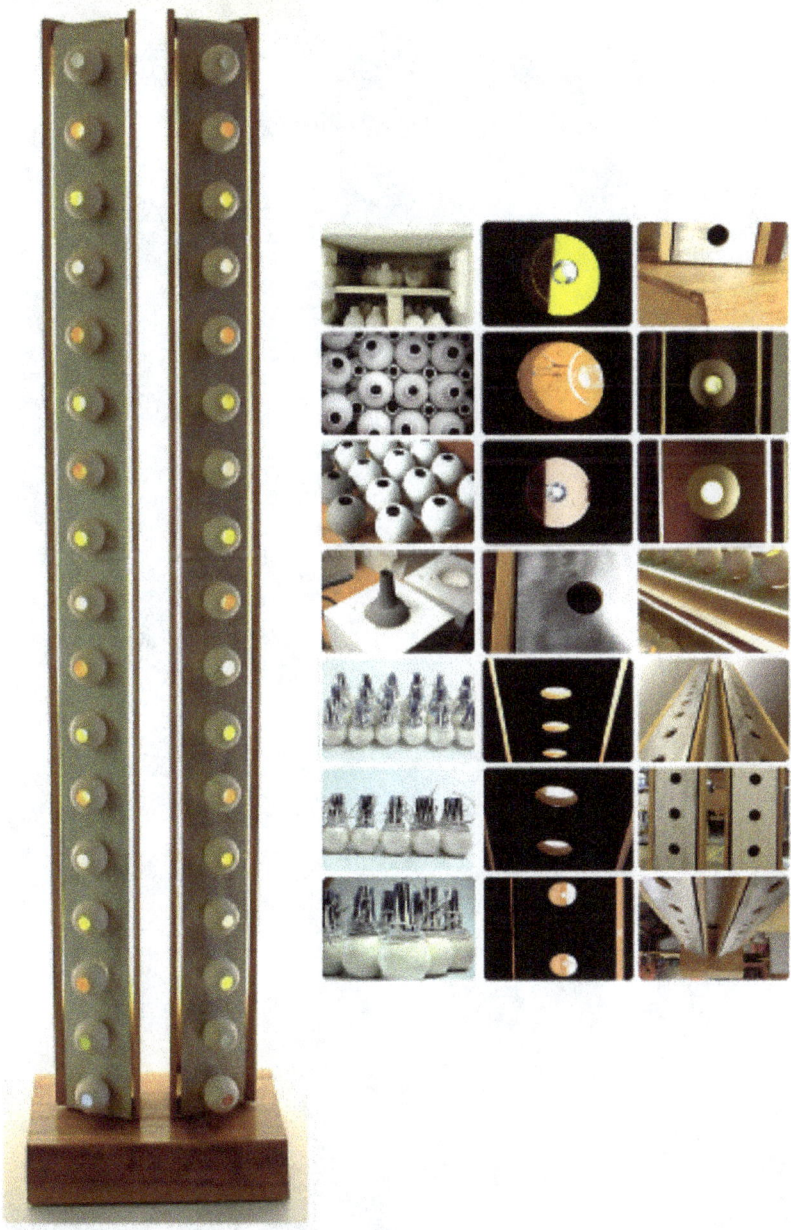

Enarah-1. Making process and the final working model. Rimu, New Zealand's native timber, ceramic slip casting, and LEDs, 300 × 400 × 1,800 millimetres, DLH.

Enarah-3. Acrylic transparency sheets, jarrah native timber and LEDs, 55 × 170 × 300 millimetres, DLH.

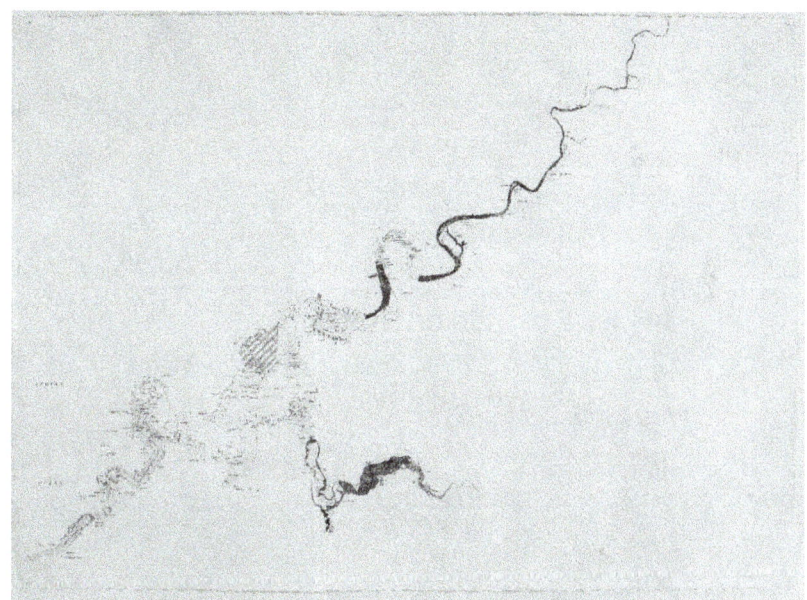

A Single Day's Riding. Gesso and screenprint on rag paper,
107 centimetres × 150 centimetres.
PHOTO BY ROBERT FRITH, 2021.

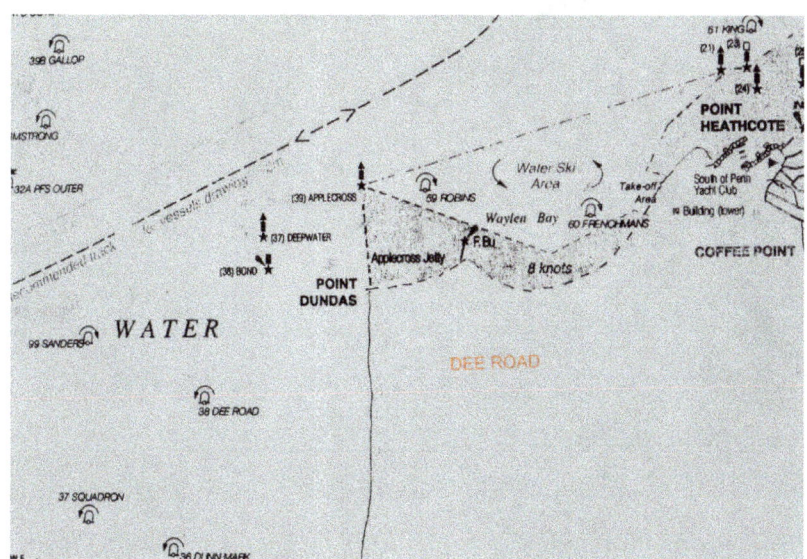

A Single Day's Riding. Detail.
PHOTO BY ROBERT FRITH, 2021.

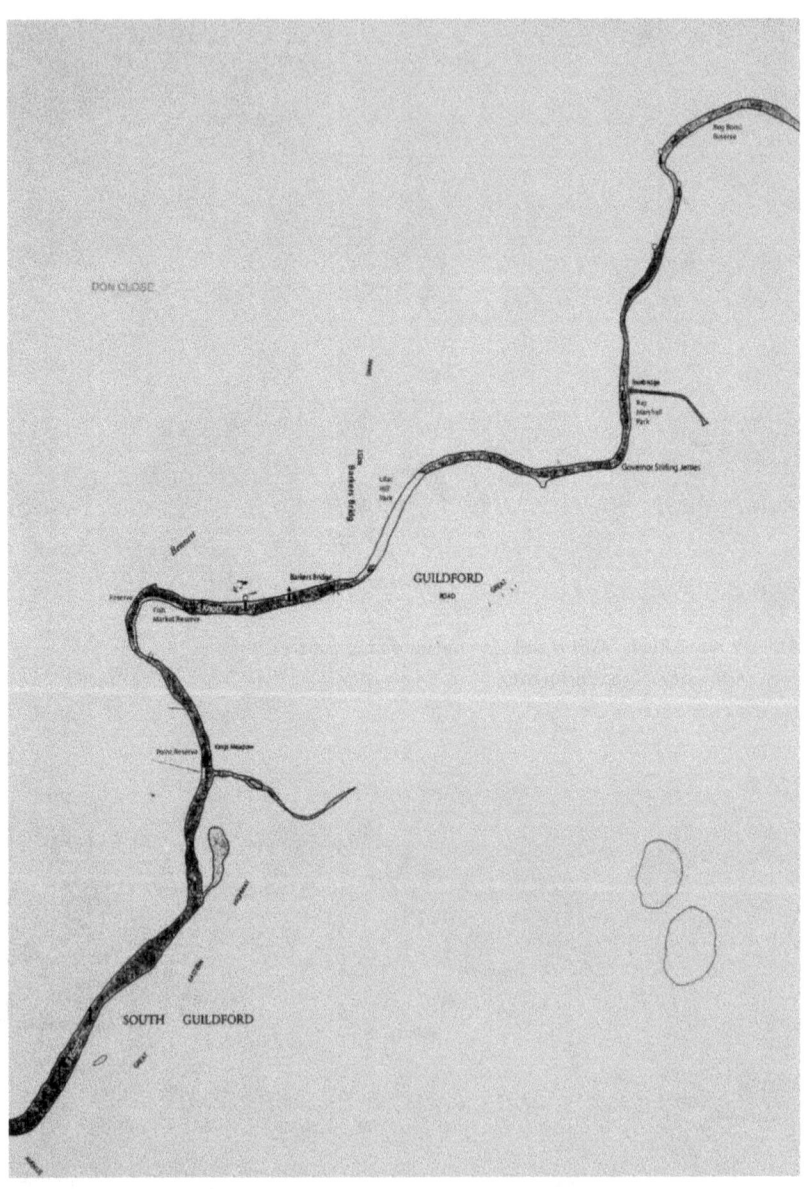

A Single Day's Riding. Detail.
PHOTO BY ROBERT FRITH, 2021.

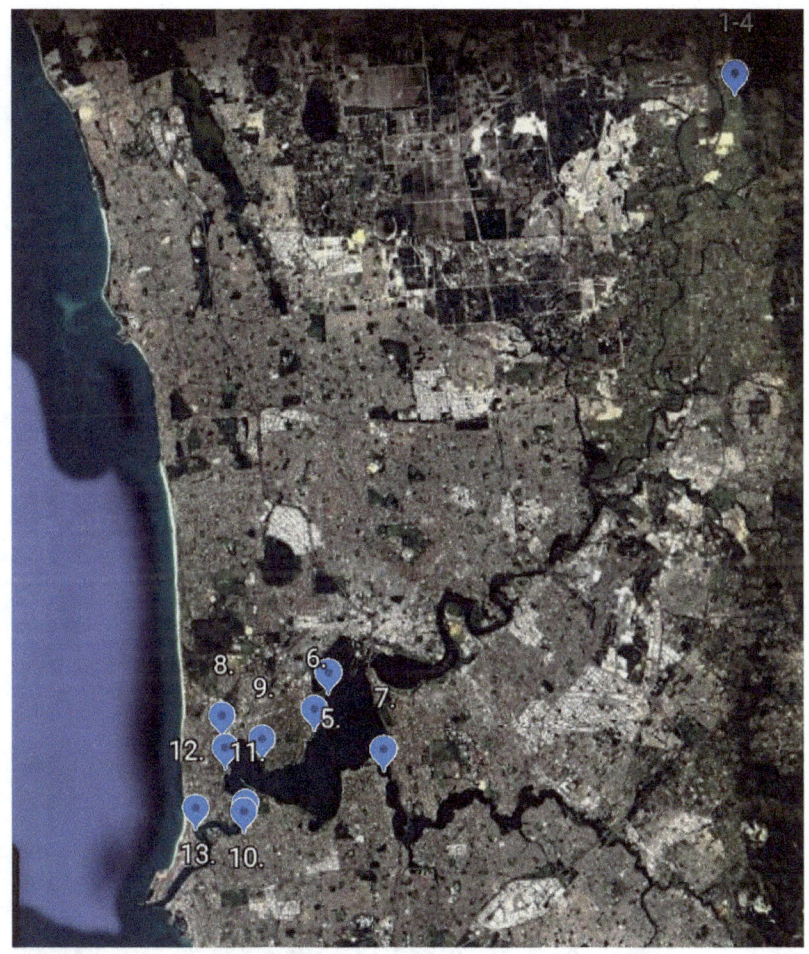

Stops on a decade-long journey down the Swan River. The numbers correspond with the sections of writing below.

IMAGE: GOOGLE DATA SIO, NOAA, U.S. NAVY, NGA, GEBCO CNES/AIRBUS.

Vanessa Corunna, *Eagle Warrior*.
WATERCOLOUR, 2013

www.ingramcontent.com/pod-product-compliance
Lightning Source LLC
Chambersburg PA
CBHW071735150426
43191CB00010B/1578